Italian Signs, American Politics

Current Affairs

Historical Perspectives

Empirical Analyses

EDITED BY
Ottorino Cappelli

JOHN D. CALANDRA ITALIAN AMERICAN INSTITUTE

QUEENS COLLEGE, CITY UNIVERSITY OF NEW YORK

STUDIES IN ITALIAN AMERICANA
VOLUME 4

John D. Calandra Italian American Institute
Queens College, CUNY
25 West 43rd Street, 17th floor
New York, NY 10036

ISBN 0-9703403-8-9
ISBN 978-0-9703403-8-2
Library of Congress Control Number: 2012943964

In memory of John J. Marchi.
Longest serving Italian-American
New York State Senator, 1956-2006

INTRODUCTION

TABLE OF CONTENTS

INTRODUCTION

The principal aim of this book is to analyze from different angles and disciplinary approaches the peculiar situation of *intra*-ethnic elections in the United States—in our case, American politicians of Italian descent who ran against each other in the State of New York.

What do we make of a situation in which the candidates of the two major parties belong to the same ethnic or ancestry group? To what extent is this significant, politically, for that group, for the general electorate, as well as for the political parties and the candidates themselves?

While an *intra*-ethnic race may signal the hegemonic presence of a social group among the general electorate, or at the very least its capacity to monopolize the party nomination process and election to public office, it also requires a fundamental shift in political strategy. By definition this kind of race, in fact, splits the vote of the ethnic group concerned and neutralizes the ethnic appeal of both contenders, for neither one can use ancestry as an argument to draw votes away from the opponent. Paradoxically, it creates a situation where ethnic themes are the least likely to be aired during the campaign, and the vote of the ethnic group that reflects both contenders is less statistically relevant than it would be in an *inter*-ethnic race. On the other hand, faced with a situation in which they are free from the possibility and the need to emphasize the ancestral aspect of their politics, the candidates will have to vie for the title of who can best represent the values and interests of the society at large.

For political observers, this is a unique opportunity to look at these politicians behind their ethnic mantle and gain better insight into their broader political resources and strategies. The authors of this book, all students of politics from different disciplines including history, sociology and political science, have set out to accomplish this task. But there is more. As we are interested in *ethnic* politics, we are also looking for the persistence, if any, of "ethnic signs" in these politicians and their politics. Our assumption is that, if there is any meaning to ethnic politics—that is, something less superficial than a generic appeal to vote on the basis of ancestral identification—this is where it should emerge, albeit with a lot of work. In other words, being the most difficult context in which to identify the ethnic factor, intra-ethnic races also represent a fascinating topic for students of politics, including ethnic politics.

This book contains revised versions of papers presented in November 2010 at the 43rd annual conference of the Italian American Studies Association (then known as the American Italian Historical Association). When, in the spring of that year, we decided to dedicate a session of our conference to this subject, we had in mind the upcoming gubernatorial election in New York. It promised to be the most important Italian-American intra-ethnic contest ever. Favorites for the nomination were, on the Democratic side, Attorney General Andrew Cuomo—formerly the secretary of the Housing and Urban Department in President Clinton's administration, and the son of former New York State Governor Mario Cuomo—and on the opposing side, Rick Lazio, a lobbyist for J.P. Morgan and a former Republican congressman who in 2000 had been the GOP candidate to challenge Hillary Clinton in the New York race for the U.S. Senate. Yet in a rapid, dramatic turn of the events, Lazio lost the Republican primary to conservative challenger Carl Pasquale Paladino, a businessman from Buffalo and a self-made, maverick politician who ran on an anti-establishment, Tea Party-style platform. So, incredible as it may seem—and it did seem incredible to us at the time—the New York gubernatorial election was still going to be an intra-ethnic, all-Italian race. As a consequence, we did not have to cancel our session nor change its title, which remained, "Italian Americans vs. Italian Americans: The Meaning of Intra-Ethnic Elections in New York."

The structure of the book mirrors that of our conference. It contains three sections: Current Affairs, Historical Perspectives, and Empirical Analyses.

The first section ("Current Affairs") opens with Jerome Krase's journalistic-sociological hybrid essay addressing the question, "Does Being Italian American Matter in New York City Politics?" The answer is a qualified "Yes." It matters in different ways that depend upon the arena in which political activities take place. To explain this point Krase contrasts the most Italian-American statewide contest in recent memory—the 2010 New York State gubernatorial race—with the past, present, and future of Italian-American politics in Staten Island, the most Italian-American borough of New York City.

He finds that Italian Americans win or lose statewide for reasons that are different from why they win or lose locally. Indeed in Staten Island's almost stereotypical Italian-American context, where intra-Italian elections are common, personal and local concerns are actually paramount. At the state level, on the other hand, being Italian American seems to matter more for those who write or talk about elections in the mass media where pundits need a comfortable handle to hold onto while writing. As has been true throughout American electoral history, race, ethnicity, and religion are some of the most comfortable of those handles—something that emerges in clear light when looking at major newspaper coverage of the Cuomo-Paladino battle, and paying special attention to how *italianità* was used as a subject and subtext in political discourse.

The author concludes that to win elections in the future, Italian-American politics of the past must change in the direction of broader ethnic and ideological appeal. Change is necessary because the demographic character of the borough, city, state, and nation as well as Italian America itself has changed. Although an above-average Italian-American electorate may still help Italian-American politicians to get elected, the latter must understand that being Italian American does not automatically transfer into a positive value for Italian-American voters. While activism in Italian-American affairs and organizations may result in official organizational support and endorsements, it does not necessarily earn the votes of organization members. The old days of classic ethnic politics (in which politicians engage "their own" ethnic electorate with ethnic appeals of one sort or another) are gone—for Italian Americans at least.

The following essay by Ottorino Cappelli takes a different look at the "ethnic content" of the 2010 gubernatorial race: one that is not centered on the relationship between the candidates, the media, and the voters, but rather on the internal composition and workings of a small group of "chosen influencers" who advised, organized, and directed the campaigns. Both Paladino and Cuomo's inner circles had an Italian-American component at their core, which mirrored the social, political, and cultural differences between the two candidates. Paladino's Italian-American men were mainly political outsiders from upstate New York who shared a conservative-populist attitude and an anti-establishment sentiment that made them a perfect fit for Paladino's underdog campaign. Andrew Cuomo's Italian-American men, conversely, were seasoned politicians, consummate government insiders, and top-level professionals—people with deep connections to elite circles at the state and federal levels who mainly came from the entourage of the candidate's father Mario, a former three-term governor of New York (1983–1994), an icon of the Democratic Party for close to three decades and its presidential candidate *in pectore* in the early 1990s.

Two very different (Italian) American political worlds thus confronted each other in 2010, which reminds us that once an immigrant community grows into a mature ethnic group, internal social differentiation, political divisions, and even harsh conflicts should not necessarily be seen as symptoms of weakness. They may as well reveal its richness and complexity and even signal its hegemonic capacity—enabling it to *incorporate* and *represent* the structure of the wider society within its own body politic.

Based on this framework, the essay engages in a detailed study of the political biographies of Paladino's and Cuomo's inner circle, and in doing so it revisits crucial moments in New York politics over the past three decades, revealing the quality and depth of the Italian *signs* that can be found in the most Italian of the American states. It is the story of a complex, multifaceted Italian-American political class that has penetrated and contributes to the major political dynamics of New York life. Its success depends upon not being an ethnic ghetto, but a microcosm of American society—indeed, upon its capacity to represent politically a wider range of values, interests, and opinions than ethnicity alone might allow

In the second section entitled "Historical Perspectives," we look at two illustrious precedents of Italian-American intra-ethnic races in New York.

Salvatore LaGumina considers one of the most paradigmatic examples of intra-Italian races: the 1950 New York City mayoral elections. It was a unique instance of intra-ethnic competition in that the three major candidates—Vincent Impellitteri, Ferdinand Pecora, and Edward Corsi—were all Italian-born and chosen because of their ethnic heritage—a phenomenon that had not occurred previously nor one that is likely to occur again.

While the ethnic saturation of the political tickets effectively split the Italian vote and diffused the electoral salience of all candidates' ethnic appeal, it also provided a striking illustration of Italian immigrants and their children coming of age in their adopted land, a positive account of American democracy at work, and an example of a nation where an immigrant could become hugely successful politically. The 1950 mayoral race in New York indeed showed that Italian Americans had grown to the point where they could monopolize an election that frequently had been regarded as second in importance only to that of the president of the United States.

In the second essay of this historical section, Stefano Luconi examines the legendary Congressional races between James Lanzetta and Vito Marcantonio in East Harlem in the 1930s. Italian Americans' monopoly over Congressional candidacies in East Harlem resulted from the fact that they were the largest ethnic group there. But it was also the legacy of the successful campaigns ran in this district by former Congressman and New York City Mayor Fiorello H. LaGuardia in the previous decade. It was LaGuardia's victories that persuaded the Irish-dominated Democratic machine to match his ethnic appeal by pitting an Italian-American candidate against him. Moreover, it was LaGuardia who designated Marcantonio as his heir on the GOP ticket after his own 1932 defeat to Lanzetta and 1933 election to City Hall.

Faced with a situation in which ethnic appeal was of little use, Lanzetta and Marcantonio ran much broader political campaigns. Lanzetta benefited from Franklin D. Roosevelt's coattails to get elected in 1932 and 1936. Conversely, Marcantonio relied on labor support, LaGuardia's patronage, and his own services to constituents to defeat Lanzetta in 1934 and 1938. *Italianità* was not foreign to these campaigns, however. Marcantonio, for instance, was also the 1940 winner because his call for U.S. neutrality in World War II secured him the votes of the pro-Fascist Italian Americans who had theretofore resented his opposition to Benito Mussolini's regime. Lanzetta's 1940 defeat, on the other hand, marked his retirement, but it did not mean the demise of Italian Americans' hegemony in the district. In 1942 Marcantonio was re-elected unopposed after securing the Republican, Democratic, and Labor Party nominations against other Italian-American contenders.

In an attempt to break the Italian-American political monopoly in East Harlem by gerrymandering Marcantonio out of office, in 1944 most of East Harlem was added to Yorkville in the reapportioned Eighteenth Congressional District. Such efforts were in vain, however. Thanks to his political machine, Marcantonio retained his seat until his opposition to the Korean War brought about his defeat in 1950. But the merger of East Harlem and Yorkville radically changed the demographics of his constituency. Italian Americans were no longer the most numerous cohort of voters in the district. Consequently, Marcantonio's challengers in the primaries and elections were no longer of Italian ancestry. Consequently, Harlem politics would no longer figure as an Italian-American matter.

Finally, in the third section entitled "Empirical Analyses," we investigate the relationship between social demographics and the political success of Italian-American politicians. Here Rodrigo Praino notes that, even though American political scientists have been engaged in the study of race as a fundamental political determinant, very little has been written about the political impact of ethnicity and ancestry and the behavior of specific ethnic groups. He undertakes this task by analyzing the electoral basis of Italian-American members of the U.S. House of Representatives from 1972 to the present. By stepping away from more traditional, class-centered approaches to the study of ethnic politics, he rediscovers the idea of status politics and provides a more accurate theoretical framework of analysis for the study of the political activities of ancestry groups. More specifically, with the help of a dataset designed for this study, and the use of sophisticated statistical analysis techniques, he tests the so-called "symbolic rewards hypothesis." He finds that, regardless of the lack of common socioeconomic conditions of the ethnic group as a whole, the presence of Italian-American voters in Congressional districts is the best predictor of the election of an Italian-American representative. This approach clearly transcends any policy-centered analysis. In essence, it reconfirms with quantitative data some of the qualitative considerations in other chapters of this book about the differences between inter-ethnic and intra-ethnic political conflict as concerns the policy dimension.

In the last essay, Ottorino Cappelli shows that this is also valid at the state level in New York. At the same time, by focusing on the "hegemonic districts"—i.e., where several intra-ethnic "monopolistic elections" occur over a decade or more—he finds that a key factor of success for Italian-American politicians rests in their ability to articulate a broader, multi-ethnic political strategy and to consolidate their power through consensus-building strategies of a different nature. These may include emphasizing party politics, both ideologically and organizationally, developing particular skills in constituency service and the representation of influential local interests, and stressing one's personal power through popularity, charisma, family connections, and direct control over local patronage networks.

Clearly, successful Italian-American politicians do not act, simplistically, as a cohesive "ethnic" political bloc, just as the Italian-American electorate does not behave as a deliverable voting bloc. In the main, they may benefit from, but do not aim in particular at the Italian vote, and do not necessarily run on ethnic issues; nor should we expect from them, while in government, more "Italian" policies in terms of ethnic interest representation. Paradoxically, even a preliminary study of intra-ethnic races suggests that it is precisely because they are not stereotypically ethnic, that American politicians of Italian origin can monopolize the party nomination process and elective office in districts where their fellow ethnics are a minority of the population, albeit a sizable one. Even though a comparatively larger Italian-American electorate clearly does help in producing an Italian-American political class, the latter's hegemonic capacity is to be measured on the basis of its ability to provide political representation to society as a whole—which is often happening, at least in the State of New York.

Ottorino Cappelli
(New York, July 2012)

I. Current Affairs

ITALIAN-AMERICAN POLITICS IN NEW YORK CITY
Bird's and Worm's Eye Views

Jerome Krase
BROOKLYN COLLEGE, CUNY

INTRODUCTION

Over several decades I have taken "bird's eye" and "worm's eye" views of Italian-American politics in New York City as a social scientist, a community activist, a political operative, and an alternative journalist. For example, I campaigned *for* Italian-American candidates such as New York State Governor Mario Cuomo and New York City Councilman Sal Albanese, and have campaigned *against* Mayor Rudy Giuliani and New York City Councilman Angelo Arculeo. I also provided "expert" advice to Italian-American political leaders on such partisan matters as post-census election redistricting, and lobbying tactics for advancing Italian-American cultural issues. Since the late 1980s I have also engaged in "alternative" and "citizen" journalism while writing about politics and urban issues for print and on-line publications such as the *Brooklyn Free Press* and *i-Italy.org*.

As to further disclosures of potential bias in this essay, I must confess that my wife and all three of my daughters have been active in one way or another with progressive politics at every level. My wife's Italian-American family, about which I have recently written (2010), was much more politically active than my own. I don't think my non- Italian-American father ever voted, and my Sicilian-American mother never said much about politics that was positive. My wife's relatives were for the most part what we called "Regular" Democrats, i.e. those who were entrenched in the Brooklyn Democratic political machine. My own initial ventures into the political arena were, as a U.S. Army veteran, in anti-Vietnam War activism, and then anti-Regular Democratic campaigning, in that order. My wife shared my left-leaning political biases and, so for my Regular Democratic Party stalwart in-laws, our marriage was not made in political heaven. Eventually I learned to get along with most of my in-laws when I discovered that some of the "regulars" were more progressive than those Democratic Party activists who called themselves "reformers;" but that's another, much longer story about which you can read in a book I co-authored with Charles LaCerra, *Ethnicity and Machine Politics* (1992).

As may have already been detected, this essay is intended to be a hybrid of journalism and sociology. The question addressed here is, "Does Being Italian

American Matter in New York City Politics?" In the two loosely interrelated sections that follow this introduction, the suggestion will be made that yes, being Italian American does matter, but it matters in several different, and occasionally conflicting, ways that depend upon the structure of the political arena in which political activities, such as election campaigns, take place. In the first section, the bird's eye view will give insight to the worm's eye view of the very special case of the past, present, and, perhaps, the future of Italian-American politics in New York State's Richmond County, or as it is better known—the New York City Borough of Staten Island. Here the bird's eye perspective is presented as historical and demographic overviews, and that of the worm as the result of some close-up experiences in the field.

The second section begins with brief descriptions and analyses of the most recent and the most "Italian American" of all contemporary elections—the New York State gubernatorial battle waged in 2010 between two Italian-American candidates Republican Carl Pasquale Paladino and Democrat Andrew Mark Cuomo. For this unusual instance of intra- Italian-American political competition in the statewide arena, we will look at how the battle was covered in the major newspapers, and especially how *italianità* was used as a subject and subtext in the mass media's political discourse. The statewide contest also allows for a contrast with more local Staten Island politics. The political activities there in Richmond County took place in an almost stereotypical Italian-American context where, as Ottorino Cappelli has shown in his work, personal and local concerns are most important for success. In other words, Italian Americans win or lose statewide for reasons that are different from why they win or lose locally. In the contemporary cases, as well as the historical, both perspectives support the argument that, in order to win in the future, Italian-American politics of the past, such as that still practiced on Staten Island, predicated on the assumed advantage of ethnic demographic dominance, has to change. It must change, I believe, in the direction of broader ethnic and ideological appeal as both the population of the borough, city, and state as well as the Italian-American electorate itself has changed.

In my practical political experience I have learned that being an Italian-American candidate does not automatically transfer into a positive value for Italian-American voters. For example, being active in notably Italian-American issues, affairs, and organizations such as Mafia stereotyping, Italian art and culture, the Sons of Italy, the National Italian American Foundation, or UNICO might result in official organizational support, such as an endorsement, but not necessarily the votes of the organizations' members. Being Italian American does, however, seem to matter for those who write or talk about elections in the mass media where pundits need a comfortable handle to hold onto while writing. As has been true throughout American electoral history, race, ethnicity, and religion are some of the most comfortable of those handles for political commentators.

In the 2010 gubernatorial race it seemed that Paladino was the "Italian" candidate—with many textual references to real and imagined Italian connections—while on the other hand, Cuomo was generally portrayed as what I would call the "un-Italian" candidate, with a great deal of subliminal attention to the absence of those qualities. Finally, being Italian American makes a difference to the candidates and their closest personal networks. A well-known Italian-American cultural quality is having relatively narrow small circles of advisers and friends. This, in turn, affects the way that campaigns take place, and then succeeds or fails. In other words Italian-American campaign strategies can be culturally constrained. Looking at the media coverage and the operation of the two gubernatorial campaigns, it seemed that Paladino operated as a "loner" and even though, in most informed opinions, Andrew Cuomo is also (like his father Mario) a loner, Andrew's inner circle of advisors had wider and ultimately better connections.

This is how David Halbfinger and Serge F. Kovaleski described Andrew Cuomo's personal political style shortly after his election in "Cuomo as Leader: Focused, Intense and at Times Alienating."[1] It was a story I have heard in many versions over the years from other operatives in the political business. While meeting with top aides Cuomo was losing his patience when he was informed of an unexpected half-year delay in his plan to crack down on college loan abuses.

> Someone suggested issuing an alert to consumers about important questions to ask before taking out student loans. But another lawyer worried that the office could get thousands of calls. Who would answer them?
> "You're going to" Mr. Cuomo replied, according to a participant. When the lawyer left the room, Mr. Cuomo complained, "He just doesn't get it." [...] Mr. Cuomo's record as a manager, though, shows that not everyone can thrive under his style: forceful, focused, insistent on results, and disinclined to entertain dissent....
> Mr. Cuomo, for sure, has attracted a loyal circle of advisers who have remained with him for decades. They feel exhilarated by his intensity. But he has also alienated subordinates, who call his demands unrealistic, his approach overbearing and his intolerance for disagreement dispiriting. [...]
> For all that, his loyalty is repaid among those he trusts.

---

[1] David Halbfinger and Serge F. Kovaleski, "Cuomo as Leader: Focused, Intense and at Times

"Once you're in, you're in, and it's hard to escape," said one person who has worked with him closely. "He demands that. But it does say something that the people who are in his inner circle—that they haven't left his orbit. He may be a very demanding boss, he may demand total loyalty, but he does not hypnotize them into staying."

Halbfinger and Kovaleski suggest that for Cuomo to succeed in the culture of Albany he will have to change his style and open himself to wider circles and the criticism of those who oppose him. I would add, "Good luck with that."

Another icon of political Italian Americana in New York City over the decades has been Mary Sansone. As demonstrated by excerpts from a recent *New York Times* article, it seems that her personal and political "Italian-American" style hasn't changed over the course of her active life. In the piece, the classic Italian-American style emphasizes the willingness to speak freely, perhaps too freely, about her political modus operandi. Mary's late husband Zachary was a dockworker and she was an accomplished social work professional. For decades she has used her connections inside and outside of the community to give aid to many people. Until they bought their own house in Borough Park, she, her husband, and their two children lived with her mother in "South Brooklyn." In "Need Any Help? Go Ask Mary," Constance Rosenblum wrote how her house was magically furnished.[2] The chandelier came from men she helped get into a union and the dining room set from someone whose son needed to get out of the army.

"I explained that he was the only child, and that he had medical problem." Turned out the father was in the furniture business and he said to her, 'Mary, when you get married, choose the furniture you like and I'll get it for you.' She ended up paying just $500—the discount price—for the dining room table, six matching chairs, two buffet tables and a breakfront.

She also got white lusterware pitchers, dinnerware, and silverware for helping people. The silverware came from someone who offered her money.

"I told him no, I couldn't accept money, but he could wait for a holiday and give me something then. That's the way it worked with all of them. I really never took a penny from anyone." [...]
A color photograph of Mrs. Sansone being hugged by President Obama at an event in Lower Manhattan is taped to the fridge. [...] The civil rights leader Bayard

---

[2] Constance Rosenblum, "Need Any Help? Go Ask Mary," *The New York Times*, January 30, 2011.

Rustin was a dear friend and a frequent visitor. Former Mayor Rudolph W. Giuliani ate meatballs and rigatoni at her dinner table. Mayor Michael R. Bloomberg gave her a key to the city.

"Politicians and community leaders were in and out day and night,' she said. 'The house was never empty."

In Rosenblum's article there was no mention of the fact that the organization that Mary created, CIAO, was forced to close in 1978. To save the programs that Sansone had worked so hard to develop for Italian-American families, they were transferred to an organization that I helped to create in 1979. The American Italian Coalition of Organizations (AMICO) was led by a board of directors who were a who's who of Italian-American leaders at the time. Part of the story was related in another, even more "ethnically" titled article about her: "A Godmother of Politics For Giuliani," by Elizabeth Bumiller[3]:

> [...] [I]n 1964 [Mary Sansone and her husband Zachary] started the Congress of Italian-American Organizations, known as CIAO, which at its height in the mid-1970's ran 23 social programs with an annual budget of $1.6 million, mostly from government funds. During the 1977 mayoral race, she supported Mr. Cuomo while Mr. Esposito, the powerful Brooklyn Democratic leader, supported Mr. Koch.
>
> "Meade got hold of me one day and said, 'You forget I'm county leader,'" Mrs. Sansone recalled. And I said, "You forget I don't give a damn."

Koch won and her problems started. The State Comptroller found irregularities and indications of nepotism in an audit of CIAO. Board members also accused her of forging the CIAO president's signature, but she said it was authorized.

> "I like working with my relatives," she said at the time. "I feel secure with them. During the early days, when some undesirable Italian-American organizations wanted to take us over, they were the only ones I knew I could trust."
>
> Last week, Mr. Koch responded to Mrs. Sansone's explanation. "While it's not a bad answer," he said, "it's not what the real world permits."
>
> Mrs. Sansone sat out the 1985 mayoral race between Mr. Koch and David N. Dinkins.

---

[3] Elisabeth Bumiller, "A Godmother of Politics for Giuliani," *The New York Times*, January 17, 1996.

ITALIAN-AMERICAN POLITICIANS: THE CITY AND THE ISLAND

The recent prominence of New York City-based Italian-American politicians such as father and son New York State Governors Mario (1983-94) and Andrew Cuomo (2011-), Democratic Party Vice Presidential Candidate Geraldine Ferraro (1984) and former Congresswoman from Queens (1978-84), and New York City Mayor Rudolph Giuliani (1994-2001), has given the false impression that in the Big Apple Italian Americans have always been an ethnic political powerhouse. However, prior to World War II and during the Great Depression, Italians in New York City were not nearly as politically influential as they might have been considering that at those times they were a much larger proportion of the total population. There were several important reasons for this historical anomaly, not the least of which was anti-Italian discrimination. The negative impact of ethnic bias against Italians as relatively new (post-1900) immigrants was compounded by the intensive inter-ethnic struggle in the New York City political arena to climb what urban ecologists, sociologists, and political scientists referred to as the "ladder of succession" in urban machine politics.

Another related reason for the lack of political success on the part of Italian Americans in New York City was their attitude toward political involvement. The earliest Italian immigrants, having come to the United States from mostly southern Italian semi-feudal societies, had little understanding of democratic, electoral politics and those who came later had little regard for the way that "democracy" operated against heir interests in Italy. It must also be noted that the most active, and visible, of Italian political figures in the United States tended to be involved in radical, even anarchistic, political movements. The more conventional of the Italian-American activists, although still on the left of the political spectrum, were deeply involved in labor and union activities. Italians also tended to move at a slower rate than other contemporaneous immigrant cohorts toward the politically empowering statuses of naturalization, and subsequent voter registration.

Although some cite Fiorello LaGuardia as an icon of specifically Italian-American ethnic politics, it must be noted that his broad appeal and persona for the period as an Anglican Episcopalian with a Roman Catholic father and a Jewish mother was quite multicultural. In a sense, his success was as "out of character" for Italian Americans as was that of Peter Vincent Cacchione who was elected by Brooklyn voters to the New York City Council 1941-45 as a member of the Communist Party. Congressman Vito Marcantonio is another unusual example in that he was elected to Congress in 1934 for the American Labor Party and served there until 1950. The anti-Tammany, but eminently practical, radical politician was considered by some as a protégé of La Guardia.

In New York City and New York State politics, it wasn't until the end of World War II that a new, more recognizable, active breed of Italian-American voters and politicians came on the scene and began to make serious inroads in the rough and tumble of the electoral political arena. After the war, Italians continued to play important intermediary roles in politics and also worked on generating public and private relief to Italians abroad who had suffered during the war. Although some continued to rail against machine politics, the "political coming of age" came in the form of Carmine DeSapio who was the first Italian American to be recognized as the leader of the Democratic Party's all-powerful Tammany Hall in 1949. Not coincidently, the next year there were three Italian-American candidates for running for election as mayor of New York City: Democrat Ferdinand Pecora, Republican Edward Corsi, and Independent Vincent Impellitteri. Each of the candidates was Italian-born; Impellitteri in 1900 and Pecora in 1882 both in Sicily, and Corsi in Abbruzzo in 1895 (LaGumina, 1992).

The stage for the unusual contest was set in 1950 when Mayor William O'Dwyer resigned to be ambassador to Mexico and as a result City Council President Vincent Impellitteri became acting Mayor. In an unexpected move, Tammany managed the designation of Pecora who was a New York State Supreme Court judge for the Democratic mayoral candidate. The Republicans responded with the endorsement of Corsi. In response, Impellitteri ran on his own Experience Party ticket and surprisingly won, becoming the first and only Italian-born mayor of New York City. Although there have been many as candidates for the office, the next Italian American to win the mayoralty was Rudolph Giuliani in 1993.

Despite the success of many, the persistence of anti-Italian bias in city politics was clearly demonstrated in the mayoral election of 1969. In the following excerpt from Nathan Glazer and Daniel P. Moynihan's near classic study of New York City ethnic politics, they expound upon such prejudice at an incredibly high, academic, level: "Significantly, by the way of illustration, he (Michael Lerner) cited a world-famous Yale professor of government who, at dinner, on the day an Italian American announced his candidacy for Mayor of New York," remarked that "If Italians aren't actually an inferior race, they do the best imitation of one I've seen." It was also said of Mario Procaccino that he was so sure of being elected that he had ordered new linoleum for Gracie Mansion. No one said much of anything about John Marchi, the Republican and Conservative candidate whose Tuscan aristocratic style was surely the equal of Lindsay's WASP patrician manner, and who conducted perhaps the most thoughtful campaign of the three. Procaccino was made out the clod, and was beaten (1970, lxxiii-xiv).

In the same text, Glazer and Moynihan's, few, yet prescient comments about stable Italian neighborhoods and politics clearly established Staten Island as the future for Italian-American New Yorkers. "The North Bronx Italian sections developed (as did similar areas in Queens) when Italians went to the end of the subway lines and beyond, seeking cheap land on which to build houses and raise vegetables and goats. The sections are still heavily Italian, and helped elect Representative Paul Fino from the Bronx. Staten Island, which was also attractive to Italians forty years ago because it offered a semi rural life, remains heavily Italian. It was the first borough to have an Italian borough president" (187). What Glazer and Moynihan had no inkling of was that between 1934 and 2006 Italian Americans would hold onto the position of Staten Island Borough President for more than three-quarters of the time while representing the Conservative, Democrat, and Republican Parties. The following list of Italian-American holders of that office is impressive: Joseph A. Palma, 1934–45; Albert V. Maniscalco, 1955–65; Anthony R. Gaeta, 1977–84; Ralph J. Lamberti, 1984–89; Guy V. Molinari, 1990–2001; and James P. Molinaro, 2002–present.

It is obvious that Italian Americans from New York City in the second half of the twentieth century have been successful at many levels of politics. In addition to those already mentioned, the short list of notables would include New York City Comptroller Mario Procaccino, New York State Senator John Calandra, New York State Supreme Court Justices Anthony Travia, Michael Pesci, and even county leaders such as one-time Brooklyn "Boss" Meade Esposito. It is in Staten Island, however, that Italian Americans have shown overwhelming political muscle. For example in 2008, Italian Americans were still holding the majority of the available elective positions for the borough, again representing all major parties: U.S. Congressional Representative Republican Vito Fossella; Staten Island Borough President Conservative/Republican James Molinaro; two of three members of the New York State Assembly Democrat Matthew Titone and Republican Louis Tobacco; both New York State Senate Senators Republican Andrew Lanza and Democrat Diane Savino; and two of three New York City Councilmen Republicans James Oddo and Vincent M. Ignizio. Other Staten Island Italian Americans also served in the elective and appointive judicial systems such as Justice of the New York State Supreme Court Thomas P. Aliotta and U.S. District Judge for the Eastern District of New York Eric Vitaliano.

For some, like the Molinaris, politics was, like for the Cuomos, almost "the family business." It began with Italian-born Democratic Party Assemblyman S. Robert Molinari of the New Dorp section who served briefly in the New York State Assembly (1943–44). His son Guy Victor Molinari also served in the New

York State Assembly as a Republican from 1975 to 1980. He then ran for and won the post of U.S. representative and served in that office until 1990. At that point he became Borough President of Staten Island and remained in that capacity until 2001. His position in Congress was assumed in 1990 by his daughter Susan Molinari, also a Republican, who was re-elected for four consecutive terms before retiring from office in 1997 to pursue a career as a television journalist.

Because of their almost legendary status, some of Staten Island's political icons such as John Marchi (1921–2009) and Vito J. Titone require more than passing notice. Senator John J. Marchi before his retirement in 2008 at the age of 87 had served in the New York State Senate since 1957 and was then recognized as the longest serving legislator—at all levels—in America. Marchi was born in Staten Island and attended local grade and high schools. In addition to his undergraduate and law degrees he was awarded the degree of Doctor of Laws from Staten Island's Wagner College. He has been a leader in Italian and Italian-American affairs for which, in 1968, he received the highest award Italy bestows on a non-resident: Commander of the Order of Merit of the Republic of Italy. Then in 1992 he was given the Filippo Mazzei Award for public service and strengthening relations between the United States and Italy. In 1969 and 1973, he was the candidate of the Republican Party for the Office of Mayor of the City of New York. When the New York City Charter revisions reduced both the executive and legislative powers of the five boroughs, Marchi led the unsuccessful movement for Staten Island's secession from New York City.

It is this activity that has enshrined him in New York's political pantheon. As Bill Kaufman[4] wrote:

> Staten Island's 400,000 citizens had one last, best hope: independence. In 1993, led by the "George Washington of Staten Island," the scholarly Republican-Conservative State Senator John Marchi, islanders voted two-to-one for freedom. (The Times editorial page rebuked the secessionists for their "passions.") State Assembly Democrats, however, insisted that the secession request had to come from the entire city, not just Staten Island. Meanwhile, Republicans, having just elected Rudy Giuliani thanks to the votes of Staten Islanders, were not all that eager to cut loose the island and its GOP voters, either. The free Staten Island movement drifted into limbo.

---

[4] Bill Kauffman, "Big City in Little Pieces", The City That Won't Die, *American Enterprise On-Line*, June 2002. <www.taemag.com/issues/issueID.143/toc.asp.>

In many ways New York State Court of Appeals Judge Vito J. Titone was the obverse of John Marchi. As chronicled by *Staten Island Advance* columnist Mike Azzara[5], upon the death of the well-respected jurist, almost everyone who eulogized him mentioned his sense of humor. In contrast Marchi's deadpan delivery has consistently obscured his sharp sense of humor. In the 1960s, left-leaning Titone had tried to unseat right-leaning Marchi twice and lost by large margins. A few more of Azzara's recollections are worth repeating to capture Titone's essence. When, in 1985, he appeared before the State Senate for confirmation for his judicial appointment by Governor Mario Cuomo to the Court of Appeals, Titone began his presentation: "I am particularly happy to be here on the 25th anniversary of Senator Marchi's 39th birthday." Characteristically, Cuomo enjoyed telling people that he and Titone graduated at opposite ends of their St. John's University law school class; Cuomo the top and Titone the bottom. After Cuomo appointed him to the State's highest court, "he had a response the next time the governor made the statement. Now I'm number one in the law and that's what counts."

The light-hearted contrast between Marchi and Titone also underscores the contemporary partisan political scene in Richmond County. The Marchi-Titone personal rivalry continued to add spice to the Republican-Democrat inter- as well as intra-party struggles in Staten Island.

When Senator Marchi announced that he would not run for re-election after five decades of incumbency in 2006, three candidates, representing Conservatives, Democrats, and Republicans vied for the seat. In an attempt to conserve the position for the Republican Party that held a majority in the New York State Senate, the Conservative Party candidate, Robert J. Helbock was persuaded by Marchi and Senate majority leader Joseph L. Bruno to drop out of the race according to *New York Times* journalist Jonathan P. Hicks. Hicks also noted that "[t]he Democratic candidate was Matthew J. Titone, a lawyer and the son of the late Vito J. Titone, a justice on the New York State Court of Appeals, who twice lost to Mr. Marchi and was a well-known figure in Democratic politics on Staten Island. The Senate district, which includes most of Staten Island, has slightly more registered Democratic voters than Republicans. The Democrats have been heartened by the possibility that Mr. Titone might squeak through in an election in which a strong Democratic candidate for governor could convince Republicans to stay home on Election

---

[5] Mike Azzara, "A respected judge ... and a funny guy. The late Vito J. Titone was known as much for his sense of humor as he was for his legal expertise," *Staten Island Advance*, July 17, 2005.

Day."[6] Lanza won the 2006 election but in 2007 Titone was elected to the New York State Assembly in a special election to fill the seat created by the death of John Lavelle. It should be noted that Assemblyman Titone is openly gay and was re-elected in 2010.

ITALIAN AMERICANS: THE CITY AND THE ISLAND

Staten Island politics is clearly linked to the growth and the demographic characteristics of the Italian-American population in the county. The number of people living in New York City who identify themselves as Italian American has been steadily declining. Italian Americans, however, continue to be a large part of the white, European American minority that remains in the Big Apple. For example, the 1990 Census found that only 857,700 New Yorkers identified themselves as being of Italian ancestry or only 11.5 percent of the city's total population. In 2000, the number had declined by almost a fifth (17%) to 692,733 since 1990. During the same time, as the city as a whole became proportionally less Italian, Staten became more so. In 2000, 152,422 Staten Islanders identified themselves as Italian for their first ancestry and another 14,750 indicated Italian as their second ancestry for a total of 167,172. Almost a quarter of all New York City's Italian Americans were living in Staten Island. More importantly, in 2000 the total population of Staten Island residents was 443,728. Therefore Italian Americans comprised almost forty percent (38%) of the island's residents. However, as the population of Richmond County has been steadily growing, that proportion of the population which is Italian American has declined even though in terms of actual numbers it has grown. Ancestry numbers are very different from those pertaining to nativity or country of origin. In 2000, according to the Census there were only 8,245 Staten Islanders who were born in Italy. As to other indicators of ethnicity and culture such as language, the Census also reported that 16,482 Staten Islanders who were eighteen years of age or older speak Italian in the home. As to the younger population (5–17 years of age), there were only 1,709. If we look at figures on Italian immigration between 1988 and 2002 we find that there were 5,019 who came to New York City and of these 244, or slightly less than 5 percent, decided to settle in Staten Island.

The general profile of the Italian-American population in New York continues to age. In 1990 for example, 18.6 percent of all those who identified themselves as Italian American were 65 years and over. This was in contrast to only 13 percent of

---

[6] Jonathan P. Hicks, "Staten Island Candidate Drops Out of Senate Race," *The New York Times*, September 26, 2006.

all New Yorkers. On average Italian Americans were three and one-half years older than their fellow New Yorkers. In 2000, the proportion over 65 has remained the same. The Staten Island Italian-American population is significantly younger than their co-ethnics in the rest of the city. At the end of the twentieth century there were more than 21,000 Italian Americans who were sixty-five or older or 13 percent of the total in Richmond County. The median age of all of New York's Italian Americans in 2000 was 40.2, which is higher than New Yorkers in general (34.4). In contrast, Staten Island Italians are much younger with a median age of only 36.3. In many ways we might say that the Staten Island Italian-American population is more vigorous and vital than in the rest of the city.

According to William Egelman, "[t]he percent of Italian Americans never married has risen significantly between 1980 and 2000 for both males and females. In 1980 one out of five females (20.6 percent) had never been married. In 2000 the figure had increased to almost one out of three (30.6 percent)." In other words singlehood for Italian Americans was approaching the norm for the rest of the city. Egelman also reported that "Italian-American New Yorkers have shown a rather consistent pattern with respect to divorce. There does not appear to be any significant changes in patterns of divorce for males or females. In 2000, both males and females have a slightly lower, though not significant, percentage of divorced persons than in the general population." In 1990, it appeared that fewer Italian Americans were getting married, but they still registered higher in the "married, spouse present" category as compared to the general population. This situation was still true in 2000 when in only 62 percent of all New York families was the spouse present, while among Staten Island Italians it was 82 percent and for all Italian-American families in the city it was 76 percent.

Even though a growing proportion of Italian-American men and women earned college degrees in 1990, unfortunately a large number continued to be at the lower end of the educational spectrum. Italian-American males increased their level of educational attainment and the percent of those who were "college graduates," was 28 percent in 2000. Fifty percent of all Italian-American males had attained at least "some college." Compared to all persons in New York City, Italian-American males have smaller proportions at the lower levels of educational attainment, and higher percentages of high school graduates but the percent of college graduates is equal according to Egelman (2002).

Over the last two decades of the twentieth century, the educational attainment of Italian-American females paralleled that of their male counterparts. At the lowest level of educational attainment the proportion of Italian-American females decreased by half. In 2000 only 23 percent did not have a high school education, while the proportion of Italian-American female college graduates in 2000 city-wide was 23.7 percent. Egelman also noted that compared to all females in New York City, Italian-American females had a lower percent at the lowest level of educational attainment, have a higher percent of high school graduates, but were slightly less likely to be found in the "college graduate" category. In Staten Island the situation was much better for Italian Americans. Thirty-four percent of Italian-American females and forty-two percent of males graduated from college in 2000 as opposed to only 28.9 percent and 26 percent for all male and female New Yorkers respectively.

In 2002, Egelman reported that among Italian-American New Yorkers from 1990 to 2000 there was a 39.7 percent increase in household income, as compared to "all New Yorkers," whose percentage increase was only 30.4 percent. Considering data on median family income in the population, the difference between the increases was even more striking. For Italian Americans, there was a 41.1 percent increase in as compared to only 22.9 percent for all New Yorkers. Egelman argues that to some degree, family income has also increased because of the increased employment of Italian-American females in higher status and better compensated occupational categories. According to Egelman, "[a]nother way to illustrate income differences is to examine the percentage differences in income. In 1990, household income for Italian Americans was 19 percent *more* than for all New Yorkers. In 2000, there was a 25.8 percent difference. The same pattern emerges for median family income. In 1990 Italian Americans earned 25.7 percent more than all New Yorkers, while in 2000 the difference grew to 44 percent" (2002 9).

Finally as to income, New York's Italian families are more likely to earn $75,000, and have higher median incomes than others. In 2000, the percent of Staten Island families with annual incomes greater than $75,000 was 28%. This was slightly less than for all Italian New York families. On the other hand, there were fewer lower income Italian Americans on the island as indicated by the fact that only 2 percent of the total were earning less than $10,000 annually. In the year 2000, the median household income for Staten Island Italians was $59,691 and the median family income was $69,309. Both were higher than the averages for all New York City Italian Americans.

In 1999, this writer reported:

> While one-third of males remain in blue-collar occupations, there has been an increase in the number in the two highest occupational categories: "Executive and Managerial," and "Professional Specialty." In fact, for the "Executive and Managerial" category, the number of Italian-ancestry males exceeded that for all male New Yorkers. Almost one out of five Italian-American male New Yorkers earned their

living in "Precision Production" fields that includes the highly skilled crafts such as electrical work, carpentry, and masonry.

For Italian-American women in the labor force the change in the occupational profile is even greater. In 1980, almost twelve percent of Italian-American women were in blue-collar occupations. In 1990, this was cut in half. In the highest occupational category, "Executive and Managerial," the percent almost doubled, to 16.1 percent in 1990 which is higher than for all female New Yorkers. Italian-American women are also better represented in the "Executive and Managerial" and in the "Professional Specialty" occupations.

In 1990 it seemed that there were two different Italian-American communities in New York City. One was educationally under-achieving with too many males trapped in declining traditional blue-collar fields. On the other hand Italian-American New Yorkers were increasingly completing high educational levels and going into upper level occupational niches. Italian Americans, and their neighborhoods, have been especially impacted by "de-industrialization" which has reduced the traditional sources of employment and advancement for working class and blue-collar communities (1999, 163).

Egelman explored this situation and noted that by 2000 the proportion of Italian-American males in blue-collar work (Census categories: Construction, Extraction, and Maintenance, and, Production, Transportation, and Material Moving) was the same as for all male New Yorkers or approximately one out of four. In higher status occupations such as management, business and financial operations, professional, and related occupational categories the proportion of Italian Americans increased to the point that they do not differ significantly from that of all male workers in New York City. For Italian-American females patterns are similar to that of the males. "The most significant change appears to be in the 'professional and related field' category with Italian-American females almost tripling their representation in this category (from 10.7 percent to 30.0 percent). Italian-American females now have higher percentages than 'all females' in the two top occupational categories" (7). He cautioned, however, that despite improvements over many decades in education, income, and occupation, Italian Americans have not done as well as other comparable European ethnic groups in New York City of Greek, Irish, Polish, and Russian ancestry.

In 2000, Staten Island's Italian-American women seemed to be doing better occupationally than both the city as a whole as well as other New York City Italian Americans. For example, 26.8 percent were in the professional and related occupational group and an additional 38.6 percent in management, business, and financial operations. For Staten Island males, there are more in the blue-collar (32.2 percent) and less in the top-level occupational categories management, business, and financial operations, and professional and related (16.2 and 12.9 percent respectively). This brief profile may be deceptive in that many of the blue-collar workers are in the higher income and skilled occupations in the blue-collar category. It should be noted, for example, that many are uniformed civil service workers as well as those in employed in the skilled trades.

The stereotype of Italian Americans as being homeowners is not erroneous but based on facts. The 2000 United States Census showed that in New York City 33.7 percent of the total population lived in their own homes, or 2,700,864 individuals. For all New York Italian Americans the figures were 61.2 percent and 387,519 respectively. On Staten, Island Italians are the most likely to live in their own homes. The number of such persons was 121,977 or 80 percent of all Staten Island Italian Americans live in residences that they themselves own.

As the New York Department of City Planning map of Italian Ancestry below shows that historical Italian-American neighborhoods have significantly shrunk in size while newer ones, away from the center of the city, are growing. It is clear that Staten Island is an especially important new location of Italian-American life.

The Italian-American population in New York City in the year 2000 (first ancestry reported) was numerically distributed in the five boroughs in the following descending order: Brooklyn (171,753); Queens (171,594); Staten Island (152,422); Manhattan (73,185); and The Bronx (63,979) for a total of 632,933 persons. If, however, we arrange the order by the percentage of the total population that reported Italian as their first ancestry, the result is Staten Island (22.9%); Queens (7.7%); Brooklyn (7%); The Bronx (4.8%); and finally Manhattan (4.7%).[7]

According to the 2009 American Community Survey, the borough's population was 75.7% White (65.8% non-Hispanic White alone); 10.2% Black or African American (9.6% non-Hispanic Black or African American alone); 0.2% American Indian and Alaska Native; 7.4% Asian; 0.0% Native Hawaiian and Other Pacific Islander; 4.6% from some other race; and 1.9% from two or more races. Hispanics or Latinos of any race made up 15.9% of the population. The survey also showed that the top European ancestry was Italian at 35.7%, with the Irish as distant second at 13.2%. Staten Island continues to be a county with one of the highest percentages of Italian Americans in the United States.

The demographic data and historical discussion of Staten Island's Italian-American political history has become embedded in Wikipedia which is, in my

---

[7] Unless otherwise indicated all 2000 data is obtained from Census 2000 Summary File 4 (SF 4)-Sample Data via *American Factfinder Online* <http://factfinder.census.gov/home/saff/main.html?_lang=en.>

opinion, the modern equivalent of what we refer to as "common knowledge." According to the Wikipedia entry, Staten Island is a "suburban and white Catholic borough" whose politics is very different from the rest of New York City.

Figure 1. Italian Ancestiy Population in New York City, 2000

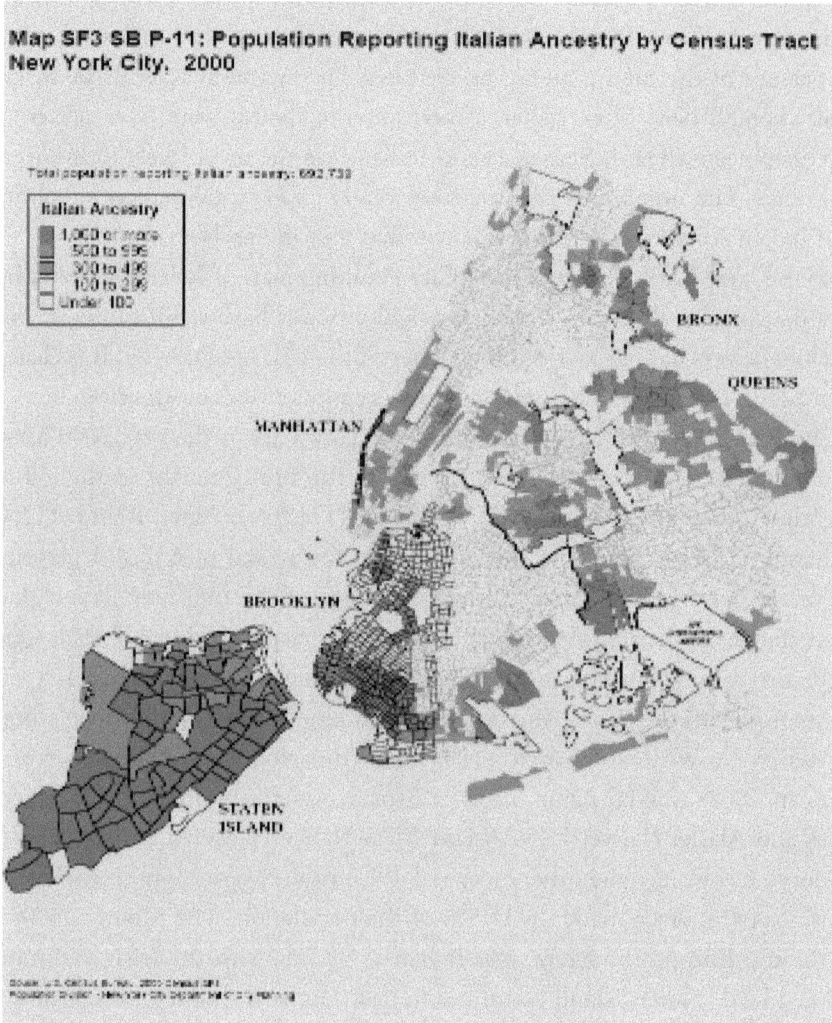

Despite the predominance of registered Democratic Party voters (119,601 versus 82,193 in 2005), as in the rest of the city, Republicans are more likely to be elected. According to local political experts, "law and order" was the issue that resonated most strongly with voters there. In national elections, Staten Islanders have been less conservative voters than in local ones and the island has become more

Democratic in recent years as have other New York City metropolitan area suburbs.

Democratic Presidential standard-bearers have received the majority of Staten Island only three times since 1952, and to emphasize the ideological difference, in 2004 "George W. Bush received 57% of the island's votes to 42% for John Kerry; by contrast, Kerry outpolled Bush in the city's other four boroughs cumulatively by a margin of 77% to 22%." In 2008, Staten Island was the only county in New York City where Democratic President, Barack Obama, did not win. Staten Islanders voted 51.7% for McCain and only 47.6% for Obama. As we shall see in later paragraphs, this conservative voting has continued as a trend for many Italian Americans.

Most importantly for the purposes of the discussion at hand, Wikipedia[8] argues that "[t]he difference between the clear domination of the Democratic Party in registration and the slight domination of the Republican Party at the polls can be attributed to the massive incoming of mostly middle-class Italian-American families from the overwhelmingly Democratic inner boroughs, mainly Brooklyn. Those people, although mainly registered Democrats, tend to vote mainly Republican when they settle in the borough, as they become the archetype of the Republican voter: suburban, white and middle-income, quite religious and married with children. However, given the near-total Democratic domination of city politics, they do not bother to change their registration, becoming Democrats in Name Only (DINOs)."

THE FUTURE OF I-A POLITICS ON STATEN ISLAND AND ELSEWHERE

From a bird's eye view, it is obvious that the conduct and prospects of Italian-American politics in New York City and on Staten Island has changed and will continue to change. Since about 1960, Staten Island rapidly became an Italian-American political oasis, perhaps even a political utopia based primarily on ethnic demographic dominance. It is also became a place where, with few exceptions, the youngest, most educated, and wealthiest Italian Americans have come to live, buy homes, and raise families. The future of Italian-American politics in the borough is therefore dependent on how such people participate in politics. They are not what we often refer to as the "typical" Italian-American voter, a figment that exists mostly in the imagination of political pundits. The future is equally dependent on Italian-American politicians themselves—who they are and how they act in an increas-

---

[8] "Staten Island," *Wikepedia* (last accessed, June, 2006) <en.wikipedia.org/wiki/Staten_Island.>

ingly more ethnically diverse borough. In this regard, my worm's eye view might be helpful.

I have had the distinct pleasure, and occasionally the honor, of working with, for, and as often against many of New York City's most distinguished Italian-American elected officials who have been members of the Republican, Democrat, Conservative, Liberal, Right to Life, Working Families, as well as various versions of "Independent" Parties. What this experience has taught me is that the most successful of these elected officials have been firmly rooted in a solid Italian-American ethnic base, but all of them have used that comfortable base to reach out to other ethnic, class, and interest groups. As Staten Island inevitably changes, and becomes less dominated by the many generations of Italian Americans, their success will be predicated on creating wider political bases.

In Staten Island, my collection of honored political experiences includes interactions with John Marchi who is at the top of my list for the promotion of Italian culture and language, from kindergarten to doctoral programs. Every Italian-American organization in which I have been active, and that sought support for cultural activities, found a sympathetic in Albany because of John Marchi. He was not a one-dimensional conservative Republican in the most conservative borough. On principle, he opposed the death penalty, and, despite his opposition to abortion, he went against party leaders by supporting public funds for abortions for poor women.

Many know of the many accomplishments of current Federal Judge Eric Vitaliano. Few, however, know that as a Democrat Party Assemblyman he vigorously led an effort to identify and correct the educational problems of Italian-American youth. For a time I was a member of the Steering Committee of the Italian American Educational Achievement Task Force of the New York State Assembly which he chaired. This was a woefully neglected issue, as historically the Italian-American community tended to treat negative issues, such as low educational attainment, organized crime, and family violence as personal concerns, or those which simply brought shame on the community. Vitaliano understood that ignoring problems allowed them to fester.

Republican Party stalwart Guy V. Molinari is known for many important contributions to Italian America and to Staten Island. When he was Borough President, he was also extremely helpful to a community group with which I worked on racial segregation and low-income housing issues in the 1980s in a Staten Island neighborhood referred to as "Jersey Street." While most allegedly "liberal" New York City officials ignored the pleas of local African American homeowners and renters to prevent the further concentration of low-income housing in their community the Borough President did what he could to assist them.

Other Italian-American elected officials with whom I have worked in reference to Staten Island include an old friend, Salvatore Albanese, often described as a Bay Ridge Liberal who ran for Congress against Susan Molinari in 1992 in a district which stretched across the Verrazano Bridge. Albanese also sought the Democratic Party nomination for mayor in 1997 as the candidate of the Working Families Party. As to a much shorter relationship, most recently I had the pleasure of working with one-time Staten Island Borough President Ralph Lamberti on an Italian-American history project for the Leonardo Da Vinci Society of Wagner College.

In 2008, the political reign of Italian Americans in Staten Island was challenged because of a number of factors. At the macro-sociological level it is the increasing size and diversity of the borough's population and, potentially, their more liberal political leanings. At the micro-sociological level it was the personal problems of Congressman Vito Fossella that led him to resign from his once "safe" seat. This created a wide opening for a Democratic, non- Italian-American candidate in the fall 2008 election. This would be the first time since 1981 (John M. Murphy, D.) that a non-Italian American, and non-Republican Party member, held the seat. The likelihood that the first African-American Presidential candidate, Barack Obama, would appear on the ballot increased the likelihood of minority and liberal voters coming to the polls in November. The retirement of John Marchi had also created a huge leadership vacuum and further undermined the Conservative Party and Republican Party electoral hegemony. With the recent re-elections of Italian-American Democrats Diane Savino and Matthew Titone it appeared that the future of Italian-American politics in Richmond County might not be as dim as first appeared. Both Savino and Titone appeal to a broader spectrum of Italian and non- Italian-American voters, and add even more diversity to the Italian-American political spectrum.

In 2011, the roster of elected officials in Staten Island, based on outcomes from the 2009 and 2008 elections was as follows: New York State Assembly: Nicole Malliotakis (Republican-Conservative), elected in 2010 to represent the 60th District which includes a part of Brooklyn; Matthew Titone (Democrat) re-elected in 2006 to represent the 61st; Lou Tobacco (Republican) elected in 2007 to represent the 62nd; Michael Cusick (Democrat) re-elected in 2006 to represent the 63rd; New York State Senate: Diane Savino (Democrat) re-elected in 2006 to represent the 23rd Senatorial District; Andrew J. Lanza (Republican) re-elected in 2006 to represent the 24th; District Attorney Daniel M. Donovan, Jr. (Republican) re-elected in 2010; Staten Island Borough President James Molinaro (Conservative) re-elected in 2009; New York City Councilmembers: James Oddo (Republican) re-elected in 2009 to represent the 51st Council District; Vincent Ignizio elected in 2007 to represent the 50th Council District; Deborah Rose (Democrat) elected in 2009 to represent the 49th Council District; U.S. House of Representatives: Michael Grimm (Republican) elected in 2010 to represent the 13th Congressional District.

As this essay concerns the "Italian-American" aspect of nominally Italian-American candidates, it might be expected that their biographies posted on their official websites might mention their families' national origins. However, a search for the word "Italian" in online biographies of all seven Staten Island Italian-American elected officials showed that only the Staten Island Borough President included an Italian ethnic reference: "[...] The son of Italian immigrants, Molinaro was born on March 11, 1931 on the Lower East Side of Manhattan. Prior to becoming a public servant, Molinaro operated a successful recycling business..." [9]

The politics of Staten Island are also noteworthy in regard to American *italianità* as useful political currency, in that Andrew Cuomo barely garnered a majority of voters there. It also came to my attention from reliable but unnamed sources that Richmond County Republican Party political leaders were unable to agree on an Italian-American Congressional candidate to run against the non- Italian-American incumbent Democrat Michael McMahon. As a result, a relative political novice, Michael Grimm, won in a race where, in my opinion, just about any politically conservative congressional candidate would have won. The Congressional district includes a conservative-leaning part of Brooklyn, and Italian-American voters have increasingly been trending to the right in elections.

In an article by Tom Wrobleski, "House GOP race leads primary ballot,"[10] he noted that, on the Island, the GOP was split. Former Representative Vito Fossella and the Staten Island as well as the Brooklyn Republican Party organizations backed Michael Allegretti. "Allegretti, whose family owns the Bayside Fuel Company in Brooklyn, also received endorsement from former GOP Assemblyman Matthew Mirones and the National Italian-American PAC." One the other hand, former Republican Party Borough President Guy Molinari, Fossella's onetime mentor supported Michael Grimm, who also had the backing of the Conservative Party. Wrobleski wrote that "Grimm, a Gulf War Marine vet and former F.B.I.

[9] "Biography. Borough President James P. Molinaro," *Staten Island USA* (last accessed June 2012) <http://www. statenislandusa.com/molinaro.html>.

[10] Tom Wrobleski, "House GOP race leads primary ballot," *Staten Island Advance*, September 13, 2010.

agent, visited a number of churches in Brooklyn yesterday and also attended the Greek Festival on the Island." It is important to note in this regard that the nominally Greek candidate Nicole Malliotakis (Republican-Conservative) was elected in the same general election to represent the 60th New York City Council District, which covers parts of Staten Island and Brooklyn.

Additional insights about the campaign were provided by David W. Chen[11] in the *New York Times* where he reported that there were only three Congressional districts in New York State in which the ultra-conservative Tea Party were particularly successful. One was located:

> [...] on Staten Island, in the 13th Congressional District, two Republicans vied for the opportunity to take on Representative Michael E. McMahon. It was an odd race, marked as much by party disarray as Tea Party momentum: at first, Republican leaders wanted former Representative Vito Fossella to return to politics despite drunken driving charges and his admission in 2008 that he had fathered a child during an extramarital affair. Mr. Fossella declined and backed Mr. Allegretti, a small-business man.
> But Mr. Grimm, a former F.B.I. agent, had the support of Mr. Giuliani, Ms. Palin and the Tea Party.

As to a worm's eye view of the race, ex-Congressman McMahon's brother is a friend and a fellow board member on a Brooklyn community development corporation and another (half-Italian American) friend was the treasurer for Michael Grimm's campaign. In an effort to increase the attention of both campaigns to the Italian voters in Staten Island, I contributed a copy of my book, *The Staten Island Italian American Experience* (2006), to their respective campaigns, obviously to no or little effect. As to Michael Allegretti, the loser in the Republican primary for Congres, I served with his uncle Victor many years ago on a project to raise funds in order to send American oncology doctors to Italy and Italian doctors to come to New York City. Although I cannot claim any extensive inside information about this not unusual failure of Italian-American political activists to give greater weight to ethnic solidarity, I can assert that, other than my own injections of Italian-American concern, it seemed hardly an issue.

---

[11] David W. Chen, "Results are mixed for tea party in New York," *The New York Times*, September 15, 2010.

THE NEW YORK STATE GUBERNATORIAL ELECTION

In the summer of 2010, based on the content of public attention, it appeared as though the top two Italian-American candidates for governor in New York State were Andrew Cuomo and Rick Lazio. To test the mass media association of the two with *italianità*, I conducted Boolean searches on Google. Boolean searches allow you to combine words and phrases using the words "and," "or," "not," and "near" (otherwise known as Boolean operators) to limit, widen, or define your search. They are statements that mimic Venn diagrams (Venn diagrams indicate the hypothetically possible logical relations between a finite collection of sets).

First I combined the name "Rick Lazio" *and* "Italian." The result was: "About 3,730 results (0.24 seconds)." When I discovered that "Rick" was really an Americanized "Enrico," I entered "Enrico Anthony Lazio" *and* "Italian" and got "About 24 results (0.57 seconds)." I then gave "Andy Cuomo" the same treatment producing "About 535 results (0.34 seconds)" and "Andrew Cuomo" for "About 42,700 results (0.29 seconds)." As a control variable I entered "Jerry Krase" as well as "Jerome Krase" which produced "About 12,200 results (0.35 seconds)" and "About 6,400 results (0.37 seconds)" respectively. I am sure that the results for "Andy" and "Andrew" Cuomo were skewed in a positive direction because of web references to his well-known mother and father, Mario and Matilda Cuomo. In fact, Matilda Cuomo has been a leading figure in Italian and Italian-American cultural affairs for several decades.

Considering there is a semiotic difference between "Italian" and " Italian American," I repeated the process with the hyphenated version of *italianità* with similar results. If the Cuomo family factor is taken into account, it is clear that my own non-Italian name produced greater results, implying that neither of them would be deserving of an Italian-American voting bloc, if there was one.

It's not unusual for Italian-American politicians seeking higher (as opposed to local) office to keep their *italianità* somewhat hidden, unless they are playing an especially local ethnic role on a larger stage such as did U.S. Senator "Pot Hole" Al (Alfonse Marcello) D'Amato, or showing the expected oratory excellence and passion as did Mario Cuomo when he delivered the keynote address at the Democratic National Convention in 1984, an ethnic piece of which is excerpted:

> That struggle to live with dignity is the real story of the shining city. And it's a story, ladies and gentlemen that I didn't read in a book, or learn in a classroom. I saw it and lived it, like many of you. I watched a small man with thick calluses on both his hands work 15 and 16 hours a day. I saw him once literally bleed from the bottoms of his feet, a man who came here uneducated, alone, unable to speak the language, who taught me all I needed to know about faith and hard work by

the simple eloquence of his example. I learned about our kind of democracy from my father. And I learned about our obligation to each other from him and from my mother. They asked only for a chance to work and to make the world better for their children, and they – they asked to be protected in those moments when they would not be able to protect themselves. This nation and this nation's government did that for them. [12]

Italianità doesn't play well on the national political stage despite the numerous Italian Americans one can find thereupon from Samuel Alito to Nancy Pelosi, even though they are regularly called upon to meet with various Italian government dignitaries who visit our shores upon occasion. Both deracinated Rick Lazio and Andrew Cuomo presented themselves not as Italian-ethnics but as tough-minded, prosecutorial, levelheaded, almost White Anglo Saxon Protestant (WASP) budget cutters.[13] They also seemed to be emulating the campaign of Abraham Beame whose ethnically provocative campaign slogan, "He Knows the Buck," got him elected mayor, and ironically where he led the Big Apple into near-bankruptcy. Running for a second term in the 1977, Democratic Party mayoral primary candidate Beame came in third to Edward I. Koch and Mario Cuomo, respectively. According to Corky Siemaszko in "The Bronx is Burning,"[14] Cuomo had a reputation as a "take no prisoners" campaigner where he was credited with some divisive strategies. Governor Hugh Carey, who had convinced Cuomo to run for mayor in the first place, threw his support to Koch and urged Cuomo to stand down for the sake of party unity.

Once again, Cuomo refused. And on the streets, his supporters took the campaign to a new low by posting "Vote for Cuomo, Not the Homo" signs. A number of commentators have intimated that Andrew Cuomo might have had a hand in the mutual mudslinging.[15]

With the 2010 victories of Cuomo and State Comptroller-elect Thomas DiNapoli, in an ethnic sense, the Executive Branch of the New York State government had almost been taken over by Italian Americans, both of whom also ran

---

[12] Mario Matthew Cuomo, "1984 Democratic National Convention Keynote Address delivered 16 July 1984 in San Francisco," American Rhetoric (last accessed June 2012) <www. americanrhetoric. com/speeches/mariocuomo1984dnc.htm.>

[13] See Rick Lazio's and Andrew Cuomo's official websites <http://lazio.com> and <http://www. andrewcuomo.com.>

[14] Corky Siezmaszko, "The Bronx is Burning," *The New York Daily News*, 2007. <www.nydailynews. com/features/bronxisburning/battle-for-the-city.>

[15] See: Fredric U. Dicker, "Andy's getting a 2nd cuom-ing," *The New York Post*, September 22, 2009; "Mario Cuomo Patched Things Up With Ed Koch For Andrew," *The Gothamist.* <http://gothamist. com/2010/05/03/andrew_cuomos_restoration_thanks_to.php.>

with the support of the left-leaning Working Families Party. As an aside it should be noted DiNapoli was the only statewide candidate who listed his membership in the Sons of Italy as part of his biography at Project Vote Smart: "Member, Sons of Italy, 1983–present."[16] After Cuomo's massive election victory over Paladino in November, in my online "Traces" column I considered, "What does this all mean for New York State's Italian Americans?"[17]

My informed guess was that, like his father Mario, Andy Cuomo knows that he owes little to the Italian-American voter for his election. Although there are few exit pollsters who thought to ask Italian-American voters for whom they voted, it is possible to extrapolate by a look at the County or Assembly District election returns. Given the conservative bent of Italian-American voters, it would be expected that Italian Americans (especially males) voted for Carl Paladino. This would be indicated by election districts with larger Italian-American populations having margins for Cuomo at lower rates than the 2:1 average vote for Cuomo in the state as a whole.

First one has to take into account the fact that New York State-wide elections are won and lost downstate. The combined population of the five boroughs of New York City and the Counties of Westchester, Nassau, and Suffolk that are part of the New York City metropolitan area in 2010 constituted about thirteen million of New York State's nineteen million residents, or almost two thirds of the total population. Since November's Election Day exit polls reported that 90% of Blacks and 85% of Latinos voted for Cuomo, we can make a pretty confident surmise that the anti-Cuomo-pro-Paladino vote was shared among the racial and ethnic "rest of the electorate." The Italian-American vote for Cuomo-Paladino can also be teased out of the voting returns for New York City and suburban counties which clearly show that the more these counties had Italian-American residents, the less the vote was recorded for Cuomo. The Richmond County (Staten Island) vote is most informative. As previously noted, Staten Island was the only place in New York City where the Republican Party won a congressional seat. There, Michael Grimm got 51% of the vote and the Democrat Michael McMahon got 48%, despite McMahon moving his campaign platform ideologically far to the right. The table below starkly presents the 2010 gubernatorial election returns by descending

[16] "Comptroller Thomas P. DiNapoli's Biography," *Project Vote Smart* <www. votesmart. org/bio.php? can_id=4303.> (last accessed, June 2012).
[17] Jerry Krase, "Eeny, meeny, miny, moe, vote for the guy whose name ends in 'O.'" *i-Italy*, June 16, 2010 <www.i-italy.org/14641/eeny-meeny-miny-moe-vote-guy-whose-name-ends-o,> Jerry Krase, "Andrew Cuomo: Coffee, Tea, or Cappuccino?" *i-Italy*, November 7, 2010 <www.i-italy. org/15953/ andrew-cuomo-coffee-tea-or-cappuccino.>

order of proportion of Italian-American residents and ascending order of increasing vote for Cuomo as well as descending order of the decreasing vote for Paladino.

Table 1. Percentage Vote for Cuomo versus Paladino
by County by Percentage Italian-American Residents (2010)

County	Percent I-A Residents	% Vote Cuomo	% Vote Paladino
Richmond	37.7	57	40
Suffolk	28.8	57	38
Nassau	23.9	60	36
Westchester	20.8	64	31
Queens	8.4	76	19
Kings	7.5	78	16
New York	5.5	83	10
Bronx	5.2	86	9

Our last task in this essay is to show examples of how *italianità* was handled in the major press coverage of the two Italian-American candidates for governor. In general, journalists seek easy formulas for communicating with the public. In that regard, the New York City press corps tried to present Cuomo and Paladino as contrasts. To simplify things here, this discussion is limited to selected excerpts from what most media experts would agree is the least partisan of daily newspapers, the *New York Times*, where for example, it seemed that the figure of Carl Paladino was "forged in Italy" whereas Andrew Cuomo's avatar was "forged in America." Semiotically speaking, obviously "ethnic" terms like "Italy" or "Italian" or "immigrant" were not frequently used when their central issues and political platforms were covered in the press, but many more personal or characterological narratives had emotional references such as "passion." Perhaps to make up for the lack of "color" in many media missives, one particular article comparing Cuomo and Paladino was crammed with the ethnic, even though, as discussed earlier in this essay, neither candidate was especially active in Italian or highly identified with Italian-American causes such as anti-Mafia stereotyping.

Michael Barbaro, in almost double entendre, wrote in "In New York Governor Race, Two Italian Identities,"[18] that "[s]trategy sessions have been held at a restaurant called Sinatra's. 'Sopranos'-style gold chains have shown up in campaign advertisements. Ethnic-tinged terms, like 'goumada,' and wisecracks about Sicilian grudges have been bandied about. And television news crews from Italy have descended on the candidates.... In the raucous race for governor of New York this year between Andrew M. Cuomo and Carl P. Paladino, an unexpected debate is mesmerizing the Italian-American community and increasingly spilling out into public view: Is the contest shattering long-held ethnic stereotypes or reinforcing them?"

More nuanced comparisons come from two other contrasting articles. *The New York Times Magazine* article "The Making of Andrew Cuomo" by Jonathan Mahler starts by talking about Andrew Cuomo renting an R.V. to go upstate with his daughters on a combined campaign/family vacation:

> The trip infelicitously coincided with what turned out to be a historic heat wave across New York, and he couldn't get the R.V.'s air-conditioning to work. At his first stop, a community college in Rockland County, Cuomo emerged from the Gulf Stream, his blazer slung uncharacteristically over his shoulder and a bead or two of sweat on his forehead, calling his new vehicle 'a toaster oven on wheels.'

And ends with:

> Spitzer, ever the prosecutor, relished the role of combative crusader. Cuomo is casting himself as a very different sort of character. During our conversations about the Legislature, he repeatedly quoted a homespun homily — "You get more flies with honey than with vinegar" — from his grandfather Andrea, a grocer who came to America by boat from Southern Italy. 'Everybody is bracing for a confrontation,' Cuomo told me. 'I don't believe there's going to be a confrontation. The Legislature doesn't want trouble. They want good news from a P.R. point of view. They need redemption. They need a friend. Eliot could have been their best friend. I think I can be their best friend'.[19]

On the other hand, Gaia Pianigiani's "A Village in Italy Embraces Paladino" article starts with:

---

[18] Michael Barbaro, "In New York Governor Race, Two Italian Identities," *The New York Times*, October 10, 2010.

[19] Jonathan Mahler, "The Making of Andrew Cuomo," *The New York Times Magazine*, August 11, 2010.

SANTA CROCE DI MAGLIANO, Italy — To many in this hilltop village in southern Italy, Carl P. Paladino is simply known as 'O'Mericano,' or the American. Most of the town's 4,876 residents do not spend much time on the Internet and know little about United States politics. But word of mouth travels fast, and when the news hit that Mr. Paladino, whose family left here in 1926, was running to be governor of New York, residents were excited.

And ends with:

Mr. Paladino's Democratic opponent, Andrew M. Cuomo, also has roots in Italy, in a town not far from Naples. But in rural areas of Italy, the connection to the local soil is more important than bonds of nationality.
As Teodoro Colombo, 75, a retired construction worker from Santa Croce, put it, 'We always like our *paesani* better' [20].

One of the most semiotically interesting Italian-American ethnic references was made by Michael Barbaro in *The New York Times* when he exclaimed, "Out With the Lamb Chops and In With the Lasagna"[21], and explained that the former Governor David A. Paterson's "favorite meal" was "lamb chops" and the new guy, Andrew M. Cuomo's "favorite meal" was "lasagna" with the parenthetic remark "(Just don't ask whose is better: his mother's or his girlfriend's.)"

There were some humorous Italian ethnic asides in the *New York Times* after the election. In "All That Time Serving the Public? Very Sexy," Michael Barbaro, one of the reporters who most often reported on Cuomo during the election, writes:

He is hailed as a paragon of timeless male beauty. His face is likened to the chiseled visages of Antonio Banderas, David Beckham and Ricky Martin. He is called, without irony, 'a sizzling stalwart.'
One of the sexiest men alive? According to People magazine, it is Andrew Cuomo. No, New York's governor-elect did not bare his chest, or appear clad in a T-shirt atop a motorcycle (though, truth be told, he does own a Harley). In fact, you can barely see the top of Mr. Cuomo's tie in the photograph in the magazine's current edition, an unabashed celebration of virility.
Mr. Cuomo, 52, snagged a coveted slot in the double issue of People, which surveys the international landscape of bulging pectorals and rippling abdominals. 'I was,' Mr. Cuomo said in an interview, 'slightly surprised initially.' [...]

---

[20] Gaia Pianigini, "A Village in Italy Embraces Paladino," *The New York Times*, October 24, 2010.
[21] Michael Barbaro, "Out With the Lamb Chops and In With the Lasagna," *The New York Times*, November 3, 2010.

Andrew Cuomo insisted it would not go to his head, though it already seemed to have gone to his vocal chords. At the end of an interview on Tuesday, Mr. Cuomo suddenly deepened his distinctive Italian-flecked accent.

'This,' he said, signing off after the interview, 'is my sexiest-man voice.'[22]

CONCLUSION

After reading this long, perhaps too long, essay asking whether being Italian American matters in New York City politics I think it would be safe to conclude that it does matter in several different, competing, and often contradictory ways. Firstly, being an Italian-American candidate does not automatically transfer into a positive value for Italian-American voters. Even being active in notably Italian-American issues, affairs, and being endorsed by organizations such as the prestigious National Italian American Foundation means little in the way of organizational support and the automatic vote of the organizations' members. Secondly, being Italian American does matter for those who write about or talk about the politicians and political campaigns in the mass media where writers and commentators need tropes of all sorts to make their work "connect" to the ethnic stereotypes of their audiences. Finally, being Italian American makes a difference in the behaviors of the candidates and the selections of their closest networks. As noted, an Italian-American cultural quality is to have relatively narrow and small circles of advisers and friends, and this in turn affects the way that campaigns are conducted and culturally bounded. This essay of course only scratches the surface of Italian-American ethnic politics phenomena. For future research I suggest a study of how Italian-American journalists gain or lose by the focus on Italian-American candidates. For example, I conducted a Boolean search at the *New York Times* online archive and found that two of its nominally Italian-American reporters, Michael Barbaro and Nicholas Confessore, accounted for 174 of the 631 matches of articles containing the words "Andrew Cuomo" in 2010.

---

[22] Michael Barbaro, "All That Time Serving the Public? Very Sexy," *The New York Times*, November 23, 2010.

WORKS CITED

Cappelli, Ottorino. "Re-interpreting Italian-American Politics: The Role of Ethnicity," in Jerome Krase, ed. *The Status of Interpretation in Italian American Studies*. Stony Brook, NY: Forum Italicum, 2011.

Egelman, William and Joseph Salvo. "Italian Americans in New York City, 1990: A Demographic Overview," in Jerome Krase and Judith N. DeSena, eds. *Italian Americans in a Multicultural Society*. Stony Brook, NY: Forum Italicum, 1994: 114-126.

Egelman, William. "Italian Americans in New York City: 1980 to 2000: A Demographic Summary," *Italian American Review*, 9. 2 (2002): 1-22.

Glazer, Nathan and Daniel P. Moynihan, *Beyond the Melting Pot.: The Negroes, Puerto Ricans, Jews, Italians, and Irish of New York City*. Second Edition. Cambridge, Mass.: The MIT Press, 1970.

Krase, Jerome and Charles LaCerra, *Ethnicity and Machine Politics: The Madison Club of Brooklyn*. Washington, D.C.: University Press of America, 1992.

Krase, Jerome. "New York City's Little Italies: Yesterday, Today- and Tomorrow?" in Philip V. Cannistraro, ed. *The Italians of New York: Five Centuries of Struggle and Achievement*. New York: New York Historical Society, 1999: 155-66.

_____. "The Missed Step: Italian Americans and Brooklyn Politics." In Francis X. Femminella, ed. *Italians and Irish in America*. Staten Island. New York: American Italian Historical Association, 1983: 187-198.

_____. "New Approaches to the Study of Italian Americans in Metropolitan New York," in Kenneth P. LaValle, ed. *Italian Americans on Long Island*. Stony Brook, New York: Forum Italicum, 1996: 32-51.

_____. "The Jordan Family as a Worm's Eye View of Machine Politics," in Dennis Barone and Stefano Luconi, eds. *Small Towns, Big Cities: The Urban Experience of Italian Americans*. New York: American Italian Historical Association, 2010: 35-51.

_____. *The Staten Island Italian American Experience*, Staten Island, NY: The DaVinci Society of Wagner College, 2007.

La Gumina, Salvatore J. *New York at Mid-Century: The Impellitteri Years*. Westport, Connecticut: Greenwoood Press, 1992.

THE INNER CIRCLERS

Andrew Cuomo, Carl Paladino, and Their Top Italian-American Aides

Ottorino Cappelli
UNIVERSITÀ DI NAPOLI L'ORIENTALE
JOHN D. CALANDRA ITALIAN AMERICAN INSTITUTE, QUEENS COLLEGE, CUNY

INTRODUCTION

The expression "ethnic politics" in the United States commonly refers to the political behavior of the "ethnic voter." Accordingly, the main research question is: Does the ethnicity of a candidate matter to voters of the same background? The common perception has long been that it does. In fact, American political parties have developed a practice of balancing their tickets according to the ethnic composition of the electorate (Glazer and Moynihan, 1963).

Through these lenses, however, the 2010 gubernatorial election in the State of New York would have little to reveal. Since the two contenders—maverick insurgent businessman Carl Paladino and Attorney General Andrew Cuomo—were both Italian American, their ethnicity could hardly be a factor at the polls, at least for Italian-American voters. Nor is there any plausible indication that the two major parties selected them on the basis of ethnic considerations.

But the study of politics need not be centered on voter behavior; besides, even electoral politics should not be seen as just a matter of the voter's individual choice among alternative candidates. The candidate-voter relationship is anything but direct and unmediated. Many things of great political relevance take place before such a relationship is activated, and in actuality several actors contribute to determining its outcome by mobilizing, manipulating, and steering the electorate—actors whose roles would not come into full light through a voter-centered study alone (Cappelli 2011). These include political parties, interest groups, social movements, and other organizations—but they also include informal networks of people who take part in organizing, directing, and advising a campaign.

The importance of these networks could hardly be underestimated, especially in situations where personal organizations prevail over weak political parties. Italian *ante litteram* political scientist Gaetano Mosca (1982 [1883]: 474-78), the 19th-century father of the "elitist school," described such clusters of people as the "organized minority" that determines the election of a candidate. Turning democratic rhetoric upside down, he affirmed that it is not the voters who choose their representative—but is indeed the representative "who has himself elected by the voters." And if this sounded too unpalatable, he added, "We could say indeed that it is his friends who have him elected." Well over a century later, throughout the democratic world, these coteries of "friends" are still of crucial importance. "The candidate's men," the inner circle of his campaign team, constitute a crucial group of people who often are the architects of his candidacy, the engineers of his success, and usually follow him throughout the ups and downs of his political career. These people are the subject of the present study.

When looking at the small elite groups around the two Italian-American gubernatorial candidates of 2010 in New York, it quickly becomes apparent that they comprise an inner circle of Italian-American men (an overwhelmingly male entourage indeed). And here an initial set of questions readily emerges: Is this a mere coincidence? Or does the ethnic factor play a role in building the web of informal relationships that revolves around a candidate? To what extent does being Italian American matter in order to be part of the "influential few" around an Italian-American candidate? Put in broader terms: Can the ethnic composition of these candidates' inner circles be accounted for in any meaningful way—*independently* of the eventual presence of ethnic themes in the campaign or of the presumed electoral relevance of the candidate's ethnic origin?

If these questions have any meaning, they suggest that there may be some significance to *ethnic politics* (and the study thereof) even when voters and voting behavior remain outside the framework. Besides, they imply a more nuanced approach to the relationship between ethnicity and politics than is usually the case. Indeed, we need not postulate that these Italian-American men aim for the Italian vote in particular, nor that they make the campaign (let alone the future policies of the winner) "more Italian" in terms of interest representation. Yet, their presence in the inner circle of their fellow-ethnic candidate does ring some bells that a researcher may want to heed.

These bells can be articulated as three interconnected sets of questions. The first has been outlined above and can be operationalized as follows: Who were the Italian Americans within the inner circles of Carl Paladino and Andrew Cuomo and how did they find themselves there? To what extent did common ancestry (i.e., shared ethnic experience) contribute to the formation of the top layers of the candidate's campaign teams?

Second: How did these people, individually and as a group, reflect the political, social, and cultural differences between their candidates? How did they contribute to defining the opposite styles of their campaigns as well as their ultimate success or failure? Additionally, what can this tell us about the internal differentiation within the Italian-American community as it grows and integrates into the fabric of American society and politics?

Third, and more generally: What can the political biographies of those in the inner circles, and the entire web of ethnic-political relations that revolves around them over time, tell us about the Italian-American presence and its role in New York politics? In other words, how can a study of this elite group help us to further measure the quantity and depth of the Italian *signs* that emerge from the political life of the most Italian of the American states?

These are the basic questions we shall address in this study, and in so doing, we hope that our findings will address a series of issues frequently articulated but not often studied among scholars of political science. Furthermore, we believe that this study and the ones that accompany it will lay the groundwork for further research on the Italian-American body politic and its varied constitution.

TWO ITALIAN-AMERICAN INNER CIRCLES: COMPARATIVE OVERVIEW

As shown in figures 1 and 2 below, the Italian-American presence was relevant in both candidates' inner circles.[1] Beginning with the Paladino campaign (figure 1), one can easily see how it was an all-Italian affair, with Tom Ognibene selected as Paladino's running mate, an Italian-American campaign manager (Michael Caputo), an Italian-American campaign chairwoman (Nancy Naples), an Italian-American pollster (Tony Fabrizio), and an Italian-American head of upstate operations (Nick Sinatra). The only non-Italian-American in the inner circle was the head of downstate campaign operations, John Haggerty from Queens. Haggerty, however, had strong ties to Italian-American conservative circles through Ognibene and his patron Serf Maltese—a former senator and head of the Queens Republican machine. Haggerty had also been a top aide to former State Attorney General Dennis Vacco, himself a conservative-leaning Republican. But there is more to be said about these people besides their common ancestry.

---

[1] The figures have been constructed on the basis of press accounts and are not necessarily complete: they reflect in part official positions held in the campaign structure (this is especially the case with the Paladino inner circlers), while in part they reflect the "news relevance" of the people involved in the campaign, including the media perception of the role some people play behind the scenes: this is evident in the case of the Cuomo inner circle, where most key Italian-American players were oldtime "Mario veterans" presented as informal advisers of the campaign.

Figure 1. Paladino's Italian Inner Circlers

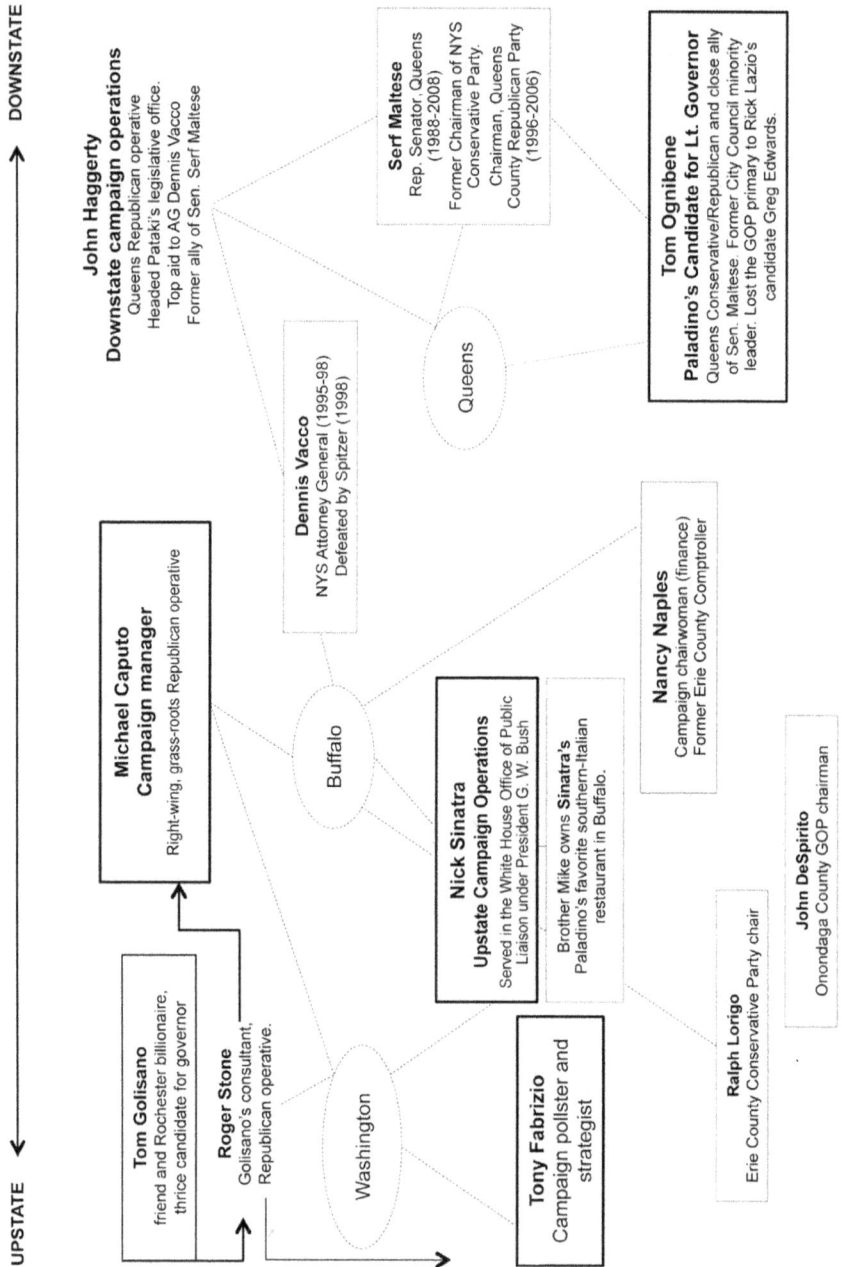

UPSTATE ← → **DOWNSTATE**

John Haggerty
Downstate campaign operations
Queens Republican operative
Headed Pataki's legislative office.
Top aid to AG Dennis Vacco
Former ally of Sen. Serf Maltese

Serf Maltese
Rep. Senator. Queens
(1988-2008)
Former Chairman of NYS
Conservative Party.
Chairman, Queens
County Republican Party
(1996-2006)

Tom Ognibene
Paladino's Candidate for Lt. Governor
Queens Conservative/Republican and close ally
of Sen. Maltese. Former City Council minority
leader. Lost the GOP primary to Rick Lazio's
candidate Greg Edwards.

Queens

Dennis Vacco
NYS Attorney General (1995-98)
Defeated by Spitzer (1998)

Michael Caputo
Campaign manager
Right-wing, grass-roots Republican operative

Buffalo

Nancy Naples
Campaign chairwoman (finance)
Former Erie County Comptroller

Tom Golisano
friend and Rochester billionaire,
thrice candidate for governor

Roger Stone
Golisano's consultant,
Republican operative.

Nick Sinatra
Upstate Campaign Operations
Served in the White House Office of Public
Liaison under President G. W. Bush

Brother Mike owns **Sinatra's**
Paladino's favorite southern-Italian
restaurant in Buffalo.

Washington

Tony Fabrizio
Campaign pollster and
strategist

Ralph Lorigo
Erie County Conservative Party chair

John DeSpirito
Onondaga County GOP chairman

Names in rectangles are Italian Americans

Figure 2. Cuomo's Italian Inner Circlers

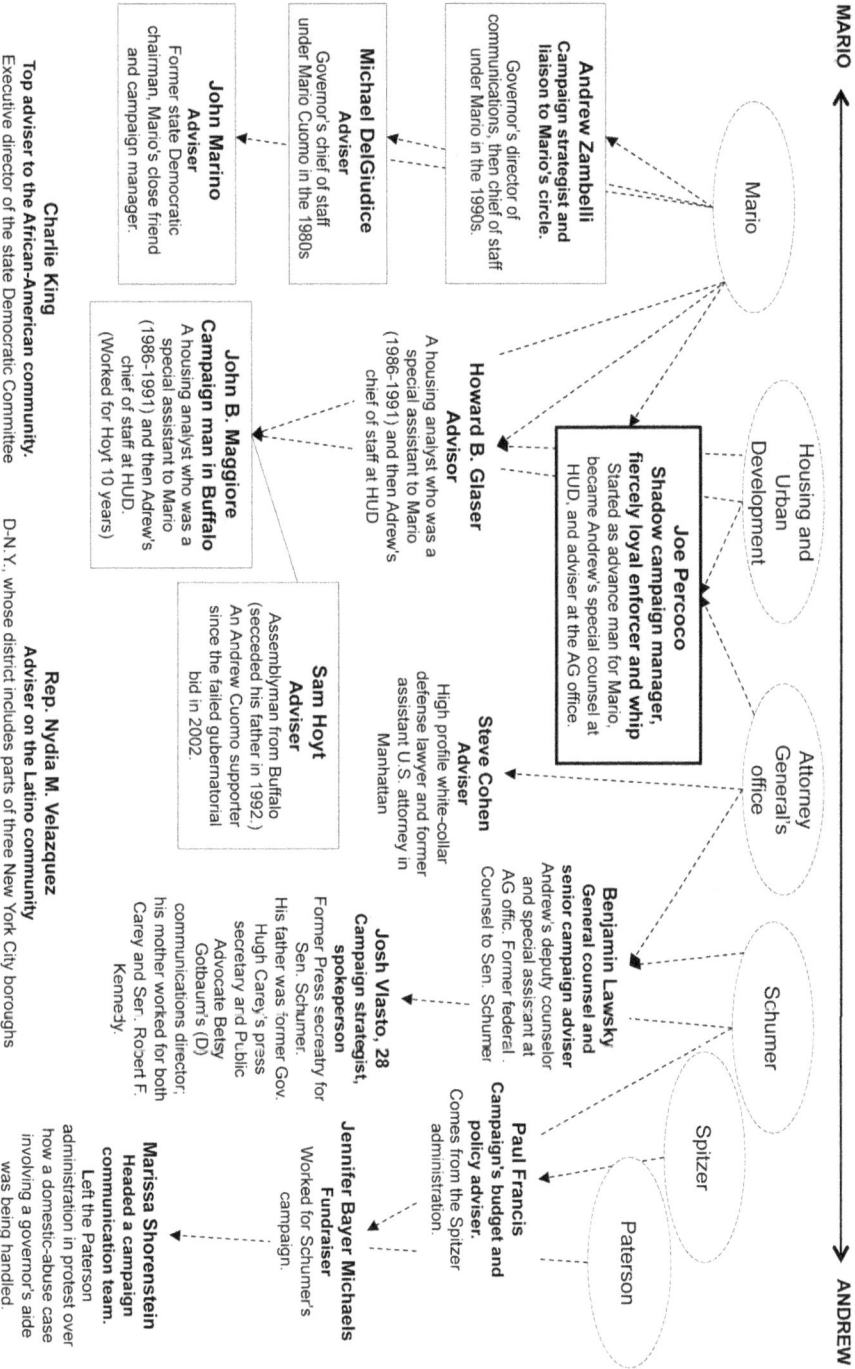

MARIO ←

Andrew Zambelli
Campaign strategist and liaison to Mario's circle.
Governor's director of communications, then chief of staff under Mario in the 1990s.

Michael DelGiudice
Adviser
Governor's chief of staff under Mario Cuomo in the 1980s

John Marino
Adviser
Former state Democratic chairman, Mario's close friend and campaign manager.

Charlie King
Top adviser to the African-American community.
Executive director of the state Democratic Committee

Mario

Housing and Urban Development

Joe Percoco
Shadow campaign manager, fiercely loyal enforcer and whip
Started as advance man for Mario, became Andrew's special counsel at HUD, and adviser at the AG office.

Howard B. Glaser
Advisor
A housing analyst who was a special assistant to Mario (1986-1991) and then Andrew's chief of staff at HUD

John B. Maggiore
Campaign man in Buffalo
A housing analyst who was a special assistant to Mario (1986-1991) and then Andrew's chief of staff at HUD.
(Worked for Hoyt 10 years)

Sam Hoyt
Adviser
Assemblyman from Buffalo (seceded his father in 1992.) An Andrew Cuomo supporter since the failed gubernatorial bid in 2002.

Steve Cohen
Adviser
High profile white-collar defense lawyer and former assistant U.S. attorney in Manhattan

Attorney General's office

Benjamin Lawsky
General counsel and senior campaign adviser
Andrew's deputy counselor and special assistant at AG office. Former federal Counsel to Sen. Schumer.

Rep. Nydia M. Velazquez
Adviser on the Latino community
D.-N.Y., whose district includes parts of three New York City boroughs

Schumer

Josh Vlasto, 28
Campaign strategist, spokeperson
Former Press secreatry for Sen. Schumer.
His father was former Gov. Hugh Carey's press secretary and Public Advocate Betsy Gotbaum's (D) communications director; his mother worked for both Carey and Ser. Rosert F. Kennedy.

Paul Francis
Campaign's budget and policy adviser.
Comes from the Spitzer administration.

Spitzer

Paterson

Jennifer Bayer Michaels
Fundraiser
Worked for Schumer's campaign.

Marissa Shorenstein
Headed a campaign communication team.
Left the Paterson administration in protest over how a domestic-abuse case involving a governor's aide was being handled.

ANDREW ↔

Names in rectangles are Italian Americans

Firstly, Paladino's inner circle was clearly dominated by an upstate clan. Caputo, Sinatra, Naples—like Paladino himself—are from Buffalo; the campaign's mentor, billionaire businessman Tom Golisano is from Rochester; lower level Italian-American field operatives upstate included, among others, the Conservative Party Chair of Erie County Ralph Lorigo and the Republican Party Chair of Onondaga County John DeSpirito. Furthermore, the upstate/downstate imbalance increased over time as Tom Ognibene, the sole political figure from New York City of some significance, lost the primary and did not run for lieutenant governor.

Secondarily, these individuals had no significant experience in governmental matters—with the partial exception of former Erie County Comptroller Naples, former New York City Councilman Ognibene, and the non-Italian Haggerty, who served in Governor Pataki's administration. Moreover, only Haggerty and Ognibene could vaunt some political connections at the state level, though mainly through people whose influence was by then nearly extinguished: former State Attorney General Vacco, former Governor Pataki, former State Senator Serf Maltese and, through the latter, former U.S. Senator Alfonse D'Amato. Some of them had had some Washington experience, but rarely first rate and generally of operative-professional rather than political nature: Tony Fabrizio had been a pollster and strategist for Bob Dole's unsuccessful presidential campaign in 1996,[2] and Nick Sinatra, a young man then in his late 20s, had served as a White House political director under Karl Rowe. Golisano's political consultant Roger Stone, who helped Paladino select the team, had worked for a few conservative politicians, including Jack Kemp and G. W. Bush, and Michael Caputo, Stone's protégé, also had some Washington experience during his adventurous career, though at a lower level.

No one in the Paladino crew, in sum, was a member of any significant social, political, or business circles nor had direct, meaningful contacts with the "powers that be." As we shall see, their biographies show a prevailing mix of upstate rural-suburban populism with a hint of downstate urban conservatism. They were mainly political outsiders: the perfect fit for the unconventional, anti-establishment style of Carl Paladino's underdog campaign.

---

[2] Tony Fabrizio also served as a key advisor to several U.S. Senators and Congressmen and numerous Governors and other statewide elected officials, as well as the Republican National Com-mittee, the National Republican Senatorial Committee, and the National Republican Congressional Committee. See Fabrizio's biography in: http://www.politico.com/arena/bio/ tony_fabrizio.html.

Let us now consider Cuomo's inner circle (figure 2). Here the "Italian connection" may seem less visible at first, which is due to two factors. On the one hand, the Cuomo circle was more crowded than Paladino's (e.g., more articles were published in the press about the Cuomo campaign, and a larger number of people was reported as being somehow involved in it); on the other hand, Andrew's Italian-American men were primarily from Mario Cuomo's inner circle, often playing informal advisory roles in the 2010 campaign.

The two top advisers were John Marino, former New York State Democratic chairman and one of the top campaign managers for Governor Mario Cuomo from 1986 to 1994; and Michael DelGiudice, a government insider and a top-level manager who was Secretary to the Governor during Mario Cuomo's first term in office (1983-85)—effectively second in command. DelGiudice had also been one the top-level New York State advisers during presidential primaries (he advised Dukakis vs. Gore in 1988 and Clinton vs. Obama in 2008) and election campaigns, including Michael Dukakis in 1988 and John Kerry in 2004. Both Marino and DelGiudice were in their 60s at the time of the 2010 campaign, as was Andrew Zambelli, chief campaign strategist for Andrew and former chief of staff under Mario in the early 1990s. These three men had all been close friends of the Cuomos for almost three decades and had known Andrew since he served as his father's closest political confidant in his 20s. The youngest member of the team was Joe Percoco, Andrew's "shadow campaign manager" and enforcer. Unlike the others, Percoco was just 22 when he joined Mario Cuomo's team, where he performed junior roles; his subsequent political career is entirely connected to Andrew, to whom he is tied by deep bonds of personal friendship and loyalty. The sole non-Italian-American in the inner core of Mario's veterans who became Andrew's men is Howard B. Glaser, a housing analyst and a senior adviser to Mario Cuomo in the late 1980s before following Andrew to Washington as his chief of staff at the State Department for Housing and Urban Development (HUD) under Bill Clinton's presidency. Even at a cursory glance, it is evident that we are speaking here of a very different political team than Paladino's. And this is without including the candidate's father himself, an icon of the Democratic Party for nearly three decades and once its presidential candidate *in pectore*.

Finally, and again in contrast to the opposing team, all of those in Cuomo's Italian-American inner circle were from New York City, although the campaign did have an Italian connection in Buffalo: the Irish-Italian Sam Hoyt, Andrew's longtime supporter and a member of a political dynasty, having succeeded his father in 1992 as an assemblyman from Buffalo. There was also John Maggiore, a personal assistant to Mario Cuomo until 1994, then Hoyt's chief of staff for about

10 years, and finally an adviser to Andrew both in the HUD and later in the attorney general's office.

Compared to Paladino's, Andrew Cuomo's Italian-American inner core was comprised of older people with much deeper political experience and much higher-level political connections at both the state and federal levels. They also had much closer ties to the candidate. While Paladino's men were selected with the help of Stone and Golisano, Andrew Cuomo's were basically former aides to his father Mario during his three-term governorship in the 1980s and early 1990s—family friends who had known Andrew for decades and had actively participated in passing the torch from father to son. True, as Andrew moved up in his political career, becoming HUD Secretary in Washington under Clinton and then New York State Attorney General, he picked new friends and collaborators whose ancestry was not Italian. He also drew his staff from top-level Democratic politicians like Senator Charles E. Schumer and former Governors Eliot Spitzer and David Paterson. But the old circle remained as close as ever to him and the family.

In other words, Andrew Cuomo's circle was the mirror-opposite of Paladino's: it was not comprised overwhelmingly of Italian Americans, although the Italian Americans in it are the closest, most experienced, and reliable old friends. It included seasoned politicians, consummate government insiders, and top-level professionals—people with deep connections to different elite circles in New York City, Albany, and Washington. It was the perfect fit for Andrew himself as the son of a former governor, a former member of President Clinton's administration, and now the New York State Attorney General.

In the end, these Italian-American inner circles mirrored the personal differences between the two candidates: both of Italian-American descent, but as different in terms of social standing, professional experience, and political vision as day and night. And this, in itself, is an indication of how deeply Italian Americans have penetrated the very fabric of American society, becoming a microcosm of its social, political, and cultural differences.

All this said, we shall now proceed by briefly examining three key Italian-American members of Paladino's inner circle—Michael Caputo, Nick Sinatra, and Tom Ognibene—and, in more detail, four of the most powerful Italian Americans within Andrew Cuomo's inner circle—John Marino, Michael DelGiudice, Andrew Zambelli, and Joe Percoco. Through their political careers we shall gain a better understanding of the different paths that led them to the core of New York politics in 2010, and the role, if any, their ethnic origin played in this journey. At the same time we shall see how, by connecting the Italian-American dots in their biographies, some crucial moments in the past three decades of New York politics will take shape—revealing the depth of the Italian mark left upon it.

PALADINO'S ITALIAN CONNECTION

In the spring of 2010, while Carl Paladino contemplated launching an overall challenge to the Republican establishment by breaking into the party's gubernatorial primary, he visited his friend and fellow western New York billionaire Tom Golisano for advice. In past years, the Italian-American businessman from Rochester had spent more than one hundred million dollars of his personal fortune staging three gubernatorial campaigns.[3] Golisano's advice as a self-financed political underdog reflected his quixotic personality: "He told me not to go around and kiss the rings," revealed Paladino. "And he told me to go out and hire the very best people. And that's what I did."[4]

MICHAEL CAPUTO: THE GLOBAL ADVENTURER

Golisano referred Paladino to his long-time political consultant Roger Stone—a self-described "dirty trickster" who has Richard Nixon's face tattooed on his back[5]—who in turn introduced Paladino to Italian-American Michael Caputo, a Buffalo insurance and PR man who proudly wore skull and crossbones cufflinks.

Caputo, then 48, began his career as a U.S. Army public affairs specialist based in Hawaii and had since had a rather intrepid life as a political agitator for conservative causes at home and abroad. According to news sources, he worked on several Republican presidential campaigns, from Jack Kemp's (where he met Stone) to George H. W. Bush's; managed to become a press aide for Oliver North and the Contras in Nicaragua; was kidnapped in El Salvador in a covert mission; and worked for the U.S. Agency for International Development, advising an aide to Boris Yeltsin and his duties included helping mobilize young voters for Yeltsin's re-election in 1996.[6] Back in the States, Caputo's and Stone's paths had crossed

---

[3] Tom Golisano created the Independence Party in 1994 "emulating the campaign approach at the presidential level of Ross Perot;" by 2002 he was able to gain 15 per cent of the vote in a gubernatorial race (Spitzer 2006: 73-74).
[4] Reid Pillifant, "Paladino's Boys," *The New York Observer*, September 7, 2010.
[5] Susan Schulman, Patrick Lakamp and James Heaney, "The Inner Circles. Paladino team has long history of bare-knuckle political tactics," *Buffalo News*, October 29, 2010.
[6] Javier C. Hernandez, "The Provocateur Loading Paladino's Slingshot," *The New York Times*, September 24, 2010.

again on different occasions. In the fall of 2000, when Stone organized rallies in Miami to protest the Florida recount in the Bush-Gore race—including one that ended in a riot at a county election office—Caputo accompanied young Republican troops from New York and Washington to participate to the protests.[7] Years later, when Stone served as an adviser to the Senate Republicans in Albany, Caputo was managing two angry anti-Eliot Spitzer websites.[8] Caputo thus had never met Paladino before—except for one episode that the latter does not seem to recall but was revealed to the press by Caputo himself. One day in Buffalo, when he was an adolescent and "a self-described juvenile delinquent," he was caught stealing a box of change in a building owned by Paladino. Within seconds, Caputo recalls, Paladino rushed downstairs, grabbed him by the ears, dragged him outside and kicked him in the legs six times, shouting, "Don't you ever come back!"[9] An Italian-American former juvenile delinquent turned a conservative global adventurer—Golisano and Stone, in short, had found the perfect match to run the campaign of the "Mad as Hell" candidate that Paladino was personifying.

Once he became Paladino's campaign manager, Caputo was part of a three-person team responsible for planning and executing the campaign. This included Nick Sinatra, a Buffalo resident and a former official in George W. Bush's administration who was responsible for upstate political operation, and John F. Haggerty, Jr., from Queens, who managed the campaign downstate and was the sole non-Italian-American in the group.

NICK SINATRA: THE TEA-PARTY ENTHUSIAST

Unlike Caputo, Nick Sinatra must have met Paladino before: if nowhere else, at a southern-Italian-style restaurant in Buffalo managed by Nick's brother Michael and called *Sinatra's*, where Paladino was said to dine often.[10] Furthermore, after founding *Sinatra & Company* in 2009, a corporation aimed at investing in distressed residential real estate projects,[11] Nick had shared business interests with real estate developer Paladino.

Not yet 30 years old at the time, Nick had studied at Yale and Wharton and had won a Silver Star while serving in the U.S. Army in Iraq. He then worked in

[7] Schulman et al., "The Inner Circles," cit.
[8] Pillifant, "Paladino's Boys," cit.
[9] Hernandez, "The Provocateur," cit.
[10] Javier C. Hernandez, "A Paladino Culinary Tour of Buffalo," *The New York Times*, September 29, 2010.
[11] See the Sinatra and Co. website at <http://chicago. sinatraandcompany.com/about-us> (last accessed, June 2012).

Governor George Pataki's economic development agency in Buffalo and was the field director for the Bush-Cheney '04 campaign in Pennsylvania. In 2005 he joined the Bush administration, serving in the White House Office of Public Liaison, where he acted as a link to the Catholic and Italian-American communities. The same year President Bush appointed him as deputy assistant director for U.S. intergovernmental affairs. In that capacity, Nick dealt with state legislators, secretaries of state, state treasurers, and tribal leaders across the country. In 2006, when the National Italian American Foundation brought a group of Italian-American students to a mentoring workshop in Washington, Nick Sinatra was mentioned in a press release as one of the "important political leaders" the students would meet, alongside U.S. Congressmen John Mica and Bill Pascrell, Jr., co-chairs of the Italian American Congressional Delegation.[12] Apparently building on these connections, Nick rose in the White House to become an associate political director, managing President Bush's political affairs in the northeastern United States under Karl "The Architect" Rove.[13]

When, at the end of Bush's second presidential mandate, Sinatra was asked by local GOP leaders to run for an elective position in Erie County, he declined, arguing that after his Washington experience he intended to go back to school and gain a master's in business administration. Instead, he ended up founding his real estate company. Paladino's call thus was his grand occasion to get back into politics, and he wholeheartedly embraced it.

For all of their ideological fervor, men like Caputo and Sinatra were able to see what others refused to see, namely that, two days into the Obama era, the Republican electorate—or at least those who vote in primary elections—were ready for a radical turn to the right couched in populist, anti-political overtones. In a private memorandum addressed to Carl Paladino but later disclosed by the *Daily News*, Nick Sinatra commented on the June 8 GOP primaries, focusing on several victories from Tea-Party-backed candidates and what that meant to his boss's campaign: "Yesterday was a great day across the country for outsider-type candidates like you. [...] The profile that voters flocked to on Election Day mirrors yours emphatically. Establishment, career politicians were the big losers." The message concluded that, contrary to common predictions, the raucous, idiosyncratic conduct of Paladino's campaign could indeed win him the Republican primary, even in New York:

---

[12] "Students to Leaders Program. High School Students to Attend Public Policy and Government Workshops in Washington, D.C." *National Italian American Foundation*, July 14, 2006 <http://www.niaf.org/news/index.asp?print=1&id=467> (last accessed, June 2012).
[13] Sinatra and Co. Website, cit.

Carl, the message that won yesterday all across the country is one of reform and change. [...] Unconventional is trumping conventional. Party darlings and legacy candidates waiting in the wings for their chance to run for office went down to defeat. You should be emboldened by the results. Your candidacy is exactly what voters are craving. Your message—I'm going to take Albany by storm and clean it up with a baseball bat—is what is what New York voters will respond to overwhelmingly.[14]

On that Sinatra was right, to his credit. But his mistake was not seeing that what was right for the exasperated electorate of the Republican primary was not equally right for the general voter.

TOM OGNIBENE: THE ITALIAN STALLION

An imposing six-footer often portrayed "as part henchman and part statesman," (or, in a less politically correct fashion, the "Italian Stallion from Ridgewood"), Ognibene is known as a power-hungry figure whose style "has earned him a reputation among opponents as self-serving, mean, and vindictive." A native of Queens, he entered politics in the 1980s as counsel to co-founder and chairman of the Conservative Party Serphin "Serf" Maltese.[15]

Maltese had emerged in the GOP in 1988, when an unusual coalition of conservatives and dissident Republicans in Queens made him their Republican candidate in a local senatorial race. After his victory, Senator Maltese switched parties and joined the GOP. The opportunity for him to become one of the party's most powerful leaders came in 1994, when New York City's liberal Republican Mayor Rudolph Giuliani made the headlines by endorsing liberal Democratic Governor Mario Cuomo against conservative Republican challenger George Pataki. After the Giuliani-Cuomo "Italian deal" failed at the polls, a conservative upsurge stirred the GOP. A few months later, Maltese's men staged a party coup and seized the Republican organization of Queens County, until then headed by a Giuliani ally.

The insurgents comprised a visible Italian-American inner core led by Thomas Ognibene, who meanwhile had won a City Council seat.[16] Back in March 1994,

---

[14] Celeste Katz, "New Paladino Advisor Sees Good News In Primary Outcomes," *Daily News*, June 9, 2010. The memorandum can be seen integrally at <http://www.scribd.com/doc/ 32790604/Memo-to-CPP-on-Primary-Election-Results-June-9-2010.>

[15] On the New York Conservative Party and the role of Serf Maltese, see Sullivan (2009).

[16] The takeover of the Queens organization by the Maltese men took place in October 1995, when Tom Ognibene succeeded in installing his candidate, the Italian wine importer Joseph M. DeFronzo, as county committee chairman. The incumbent county leader, Frances M. Werner, was supported by

Rudolph Giuliani had used his influence in the Republican Party to block Ognibene's election as the Council Minority Leader. By November of the same year,
however, the winds had changed: with the "Giuliani-Cuomo deal" defeated in the
polls, Ognibene capitalized on the anti-Giuliani sentiment in the GOP and got the
post. Seeing himself as the anti-Giuliani champion, he issued the mayor a certifi-
cate from "Dupe University" for having shown "a unique ability to abandon his
principles."[17]

The Maltese-Ognibene Queens coup thus was part of a major political development in the Republican Party, stirred by the alliance between a liberal-
Democratic governor and a liberal-Republican mayor–both Italian American. And
it is significant to notice that conservative insurgents rallied behind still another
Italian-American: Senator Alfonse D'Amato–then the most powerful Republican
in the state, a most vocal critic of the Giuliani-Cuomo deal, and the architect of
Pataki's gubernatorial victory. Soon after, D'Amato and Pataki engineered a conservative takeover of the party, which involved among other things the demise of
moderate Republican Ralph Marino as State Senate Majority Leader and his replacement with their conservative protégé Joseph Bruno (again, both Italian American).[18] D'Amato, in turn, was Serf Maltese's patron and, by extension, Ognibene's. So, when the latter two seized the Queens organization, this could definitely
be seen as part of a conservative upsurge of the anti-Giuliani forces. Queens, on
the other hand, was crucial in this intra-Republican battle because its voters,
though nominally Democrat, were starting to show an increasingly conservative
attitude. By taking control of the county machine, Maltese and Ognibene were

Mayor Rudolph Giuliani. See David M. Herszenhorn, "Kingmaker Wannabe," *The New York Times*,
October 22, 1995. A year later DeFronzo resigned and was replaced by Maltese.

[17] As aptly summarized in *The New York Times*: "Putting his muscle behind his endorsement of Gov.
Mario M. Cuomo, Mayor Rudolph W. Giuliani has been campaigning the last two weeks as if he
were the candidate himself. But it is hard to distinguish whether he is running against State Senator
George E. Pataki or United States Senator Alfonse M. D'Amato." See Alison Mitchell, "Giuliani's
Two Battles: Pataki, Then D'Amato," *The New York Times*, November 6, 1994.

[18] Joseph Bruno, a conservative republican, became the Senate Majority Leader during the
"Thanksgiving coup" of November 1994, when governor-elect Pataki and U.S. Senator Al D'amato
ousted Ralph Marino from that post. Marino, who had ben majority leader during much of Mario
Cuomo's governorship, had often opposed the Governor, especially on budget issues. However, he
was considered, like Giuliani, a "Rockfeller Republican"–the moderate-liberal wing in the GOP that
D'Amato had tried to emarginate since 1981, when he defeated U.S. Senator Jacob Javits in a
legendary "underdog primary" and went on to win his Senate seat. Governor Pataki and Joseph
Bruno were considered "D'Amato men" and the ousting of Marino was a direct consequence of these
men's revolt spurred by the Giuliani-Cuomo deal. See: James Dao, "Ally of Pataki Replaces Marino
As State Senate Majority Leader," *The New York Times*, November 26, 1994. For an analysis of these
events in a broader context see Murtaugh, Pole, and Schneier (2009).

trying to launch a "conservative revolution," using Queens as their stepping stone, banking in part on a then large Italian-American presence.

Ten years later, the fight had not ended. In 2005, Ognibene was endorsed by the leaders of the Queens County Republican Committee, then still led by Maltese, to run for mayor against incumbent Michael Bloomberg—labeled RINO ("Republican-In-Name-Only").[19] With help from the Conservative Party, Ognibene first sought to do the "politically unthinkable" and challenged the mayor in the Republican primary. Having failed to gather enough valid petition signatures to get on the ballot, he ended up running only on the Conservative Party ticket and lost. Nor was he ever able to regain the Council seat he previously occupied.

As with Caputo and Sinatra, picking Ognibene as his running mate in 2010 seemed the right choice for Paladino, who was staging a bitter underdog campaign with the aim, first and foremost, to challenge the GOP establishment.[20] The fact that they did not seem to care about the ticket's ethnic imbalance can be explained by their apparent focus on the upstate/downstate balance: a core of (Italian-American) angry populists in the northwest, and a core of (Italian-American) staunch conservatives in New York City, based in Queens. And behind that, a decade-long conservative battle for the soul of the State Republican Party. This was the strategy, as it emerged from the makeup of the inner circle.

But things did not go as expected, even at the very beginning. While Paladino succeeded in overwhelmingly defeating the establishment's candidate Rick Lazio in the primary, Ognibene lost narrowly to Lazio's running mate Greg Edwards, the county executive in Chautauqua County. This gave Paladino an ethnically more balanced ticket, but left him with an upstate-only ticket—which obviously damaged his stance downstate and in the city. Left out in the cold by the Paladino campaign, Ognibene ended up running on the Taxpayer Party line for the Supreme Court in the Bronx against Rick Lazio himself—both were defeated by Democrat Edgar G. Walker.

---

[19] Bloomberg countered by trying to split the enemy's front and sought the endorsement of other powrful Queens Republicans among whom Senator Frank Padavan (himself an Italian American). Referring to the Queens County Republican Committee, he labelled it "that particular small Queens Republican group," and said they were unhappy with him because he was not interested in "turning City Hall into a patronage mill." See "4 Endorsements in Mayor's Race," *The New York Times*, February 12, 2005.

[20] See "Paladino To Meet With Ognibene, Maltese," *Daily News*, April 5, 2010; Tom Robbins, "Carl Paladino and Tom Ognibene: The All-Italian GOP Ticket," *The Daily News*, June 8, 2010.

Losing grip on the downstate campaign through Ognibene's defeat, of course, could not entirely explain Paladino's tremendous defeat. An (Italian-American) anti-establishment Buffalo clan led by a raucous businessman, a quixotic adventurer, and a young Tea-Party enthusiast, would not have seized the governorship even with the help of the Italian Stallion and his Queens troops. In 2010 these individuals lacked the leadership experience, the political machinery, and the elite connections to render them as powerful as the (Italian-American) politicians of the 1990s they seemed eager to emulate—men like Alfonse D'Amato, Serf Maltese, Joseph Bruno.

They were faced with the overwhelming superiority of the Cuomo clan and its Italian-American inner circle, which had all the qualities that the Paladino circle lacked. Two opposite strategies and two very different (Italian) American political worlds confronted each other.

CUOMO'S ITALIAN-AMERICAN INNER CIRCLE

JOHN MARINO: MAN OF STEEL

Commonly viewed since the mid-1980s as the "unofficial keeper of the [Mario] Cuomo flame," John A. Marino (now a crucial supporter of Andrew Cuomo) was born in 1948 to an immigrant working-class family in predominantly Italian East Harlem and raised in the equally Italian Bronx. There, the future chairman of the New York State Democratic Party developed an early and consuming passion for politics—he once recalled being only 12 years old when he nailed up his first political posters for John F. Kennedy.[21] After graduating from Fordham University, gaining two master's degrees, and beginning to work as a city public school teacher of English and social studies,[22] at 26 his life turned to politics when he volunteered for Hugh Carey's 1974 gubernatorial campaign in the Bronx. There, as he recounts, he "was discovered."[23] Co-opted into the first Carey administration, John Marino worked as assistant appointments officer, then as assistant state transportation commissioner, and briefly as the New York City regional director of the State Department of Transportation. Meanwhile, he grew up as a party operative under state Democratic Chairman and fellow Italian American Dominic Baranello.

---

[21] Kevin Sack, "Cuomo's Point Man Plays by Intuition," *The New York Times*, November 21, 1991.

[22] Frank Lynn, "In-House Team Heads Cuomo Campaign," *The New York Times*, July 6, 1986.

[23] Robert Borsellino, "Democrat John Marino A Tireless Cuomo Aide," *The Times Union*, May 18, 1989.

Entering the "Mario Cuomo School of Government"

A Carey man working for Baranello, Marino found himself at odds with Lt. Governor Mario Cuomo after the latter broke ties with both Carey and Baranello[24] and ran as an "outsider" in the 1982 gubernatorial primary. An apparently insignificant episode, long remembered by both Marino and the Cuomos, reveals the heated atmosphere of those days. It happened in Syracuse in the summer of 1982, when the State Democratic Convention met to choose between Cuomo and his old rival, New York City Mayor "Ed" Koch.[25] At one point during the convention, Baranello, who had endorsed Koch, ordered his men to fill the empty seats on the floor of the Syracuse Civic Center by clearing guests out of the balcony. Following his boss' directions, Marino policed the hall barking into his walkie-talkie that everybody should be pushed out of the balcony, including Cuomo's wife Matilda and her children. "Andrew thought and still thinks I did it just to throw his mother out of the balcony," Marino told a reporter 10 years later. "They were pretty upset." The same reporter commented, however, that "fortunately for Mr. Marino there was room in Mr. Cuomo's heart for redemption—particularly if it was earned with political toil." After his victory in fact, the new Governor, who had been impressed by the "political savvy" shown by Marino while working for Carey, "began to groom [him] as a political aide."[26]

---

[24] By 1981 Lt. Governor Mario Cuomo, who had never been able to become part of carey's inner circle, had decided to run for governor and even to challenge Carey if the latter decided to seek a third term. Cuomo's long-standing relationship with Dominic Baranello deteriorated in Summer 1982, when the State Democratic Chairman chose to endorse Koch against Cuomo in the gubernatorial primary. Cuomo (1984: 236, 364) noted in his diaries: "After all of this—and a dozen platform shared and a hundred embraces exchanged—Dominic, having told me he was neutral, ordered his delegation to vote with him for Koch at the Convention." Days after his november 1982 victory, governor-elect Cuomo "made an all-out effort to take hold of the party machinery" and had Baranello replaced by his associate Bill Hennessy.

[25] Koch was Cuomo's long-time archi-rival, having defeated him back in 1977 in the Democratic primary for Mayor. After that defeat, Mario Cuomo went on to run as Mayor on the Liberal platform. In the heated campaign which followed attempts were made to smear unmarried Koch as a homosexual with signs that read: "Vote for Cuomo, not the homo." The Koch camp blamend Cuomo's 19-year old son Andrew for the ad. Koch's version of that bitter fight and of his these relationship with Mario Cuomo is in Koch (2000, 12-13) and, in more detail, in Soffer (2010).

[26] Sack, "Cuomo's Point Man," cit. In 1984, after Cuomo endorsed the Mondale-Ferraro Democratic ticket of the presidential elections, John Marino reportedly worked 18 hours a day for the campaign in New York, together with Andrew Cuomo. Marino also used his position in the State Department of Transportation to "provide support services" to the campaign. See Jonathan Salant, "Cuomo's People Are Spectators in the Campaign," *The Post-Standard*, April 17, 1988.

An important step in Marino's political career under Governor Cuomo was his position as deputy secretary of the Department of State[27] with the duty of overseeing the Office of the Ombudsman. Started in the 1970s by Mario Cuomo when he served as Carey's secretary of state, this office was intended as a liaison to various communities, informing the public about state policy, and taking complaints about state agencies. The ombudsmen however—a little army of "citizens service representatives" placed in a dozen of regional offices—apparently acted as much as general informants as "partisan advocates."[28] The line was thin indeed and it was a general perception that with Cuomo at the helm and Marino as the office director, the ombudsmen acted "in many ways, as the governor's political arm throughout the state."[29] This was a pivotal opportunity for Marino, who could show all of his "political savvy".[30]

After that, Marino's ascent in the Cuomo circle was unstoppable. He quickly rose to become the chief executive officer of the governor's fund-raising committee Friends of Mario Cuomo, which gave him a key role in Cuomo's 1986 re-election campaign—a record victory. Also, on that occasion he consolidated his personal and working relationships with Andrew, then 27 years old, who had been given "total control" of the campaign. By the decade's end, with Mario Cuomo in his second term as governor, Marino was elevated to the highest ranks in the State Democratic Party, becoming first its executive director and then its chairman in 1989.[31]

Mario Cuomo's Party Leader

A press commentary from the day he won the party chairmanship illuminates the mix of personal and political resources that had brought Marino to that point:

> When people talk about J. Patrick Barrett, the incoming state Republican chairman, they talk about how much money he has. When they talk about Marino,

[27] Jeanie Kasindorf, "Mario's Man To Head State Dems?" New York Magazine, January 19, 1987 (Vol. 20, No. 3).
[28] Dan Janison, "Ombudsman Activity Blurs View of Office," The Times Union, October 30, 1988.
[29] Jon R. Sorensen, "Gordon To head State's Democratic Party," Buffalo News, May 20, 1993.
[30] Marino later married one of his employees, the Staten Island regional representative of the ombudsman office Donna DeBernardo. See "Donna A. DeBernardo Weds John Marino Jr.," The New York Times, October 8, 1989. A year earlier, an article in The Times Union noted that "'citizens service representatives' like DiBernardo often walk a thin line between carrying out their governmental duties and promoting political agendas." See Dan Janison, "Ombudsman Activity Blurs View of Office," The Times Union, October 30, 1988.
[31] See Sack, "Cuomo's Point Man," cit.; "Cuomo Son To Run the Show," The Associated Press, June 13, 1986; Lynn, "In-House Team Heads Cuomo Campaign," cit..

they talk about his allegiance to the Cuomos—Mario and son Andrew—and how hard he works.[32]

Marino's allegiance to the Cuomos was based as much on personal trust as on shared values and a common practical-political approach. He was, first and foremost, a true Cuomo believer, who looked at the governor "as the ideological and political heir of Thomas Jefferson, Franklin D. Roosevelt, and the Kennedys." His party office in Manhattan was even decorated with a framed poster of the text of Cuomo's famed keynote address at the 1984 Democratic National Convention.[33] On the practical-political side, Marino underscored two traditional elements of Democratic politics that were also typical of Mario Cuomo: grassroot, door-to-door campaigning and the mobilization of ethnic identity—or, more precisely, a special attention to the needs and sensibilities of immigrant communities.

In 1988, for instance, when Senator Al Gore and Massachusetts Governor Michael Dukakis battled for the Democratic presidential nomination, Marino—then the party executive director—was clear about why Gore was not doing well in the New York State primary. Money, political consultants, and the media "don't buy victory in state politics," he said implicitly referring to Gore. "You need field organization. You need to get your people out to vote. And you need a candidate who's able to travel this state from one side to the other."[34] One principal goal of that campaign, according to Marino, would be to secure the working-class, ethnic-Catholic vote that, especially upstate, had favored Mario Cuomo—"one of their own"—in 1982 and 1986, but had swung to Ronald Reagan in the 1980 and 1984 presidential elections. To this end, he reasoned, a son of Greek immigrants like Dukakis had better chances than a descendant of a Scott-Irish family that had settled in the United States two centuries earlier. As Dukakis's New York staff stated in public their intention to tap the "great connection between Irish, Italian, and Polish first-generation Americans whose parents came to Ellis Island like [Dukakis's] parents did," Marino echoed: "Whoever appeals to that vote comes out of this state, in my opinion, as a very strong candidate."[35] Although Dukakis ultimate-

[32] Borsellino, "Democrat John Marino A Tireless Cuomo Aide," cit.
[33] Sack, "Cuomo's Point Man," cit.
[34] Jonathan D. Salant, "4 Candidates in State Spent $2.7 Million plus Gore Shelled Out the Most in Fitile Campaign," The Post-Standard, May 29, 1988.
[35] Jonathan D. Salant and Erik Kriss, "Dukakis Makes Last Minute Swing Through City," The Post-Standard, April 18, 1988.

ly lost the White House, Marino's indefatigable campaigning in New York was largely credited for Dukakis's very good showing in the state.[36]

That campaign was not the last of the accomplishments that earned him Cuomo's nomination as party chairman a year later, when he was chosen by acclamation by the 352-member state committee.[37] His acceptance speech was aggressively partisan and inspired in typical Cuomo-style: he urged the Democrats to become "once again a party of ideas [...] designed with an eye toward the 21st century," and he promised to battle "until no Republican feels safe running in upstate New York."[38] Then, referring to his incoming Republican counterpart: "He has his money—and I have you!" he uttered, galvanizing the audience.[39]

Marino's record as the handpicked head of Cuomo's powerful organizational machine is mixed. In the years he ran the Party he did win a few important battles, including, first and foremost, the one to secure a third term for Cuomo in 1990.[40] On the other hand, he lost a few others: he sought unsuccessfully to bring down the Republican majority in the Senate led by Ralph Marino (no relation); he couldn't orchestrate the overthrow of Republican Senator Alfonse D'Amato and his replacement with fellow Italian-American Geraldine Ferraro; and—most importantly—he failed in the effort to win his boss a fourth term in 1994, when Marino had already resigned as party chief and was hired back to run the campaign just a few months later.

---

[36] According to Salant ("Cuomo's People Are Spectators in the Campaign," cit.) "[a]t the New York State Democratic Committee, Marino, now the party's executive director, spends the same 18 hours a day on the primary as he did in 1984. But instead of talking to county chairmen, literature distributors and labor leaders, Marino speaks with the candidates' top aides, national reporters and political offi-cials from around the nation."

[37] Gus Bliven, "State Parties Are Not Run as Democracies," *The Post-Standard*, May 31, 1989. As this commentator aptly noted, Marino was crowned party chairman by the Governor in a situation in which "by no stretch of the imagination did the state committee members exercise any decision-making powers in the selection. At the same time, added Bliven, the Republicans were "going through the same rubber-stamp process [as] a handful of state party leaders—Jonathan Bush, the president's brother; U.S. Sen. Alfonse M. D'Amato and Senate Majority Leader Ralph Marino—decided GOP State Chairman Anthony J. Colavita of Westchester County should be replaced." The choice was millioneer businessman J. Patrick Barrett of Fayetteville, the favorite choice of Al D'Amato. The overwhelming control exerted by an incumbent governor on his party was not unique to Cuomo (McCally Morehouse, 1998).

[38] Lillie Wilson, "Marino: GOP's Upstate Reign Has Ended," *The Post-Standard*, May 8, 1989.

[39] Erik Kriss, "Cuomo's Gripe: Barrett 'Can Snap His Fingers and Raise $15 Million'," *The Post-Standard*, May 18, 1989.

[40] Notwithstanding the low voter turnout and a general Democratic apathy about the race, Marino could proudly state that Cuomo had "broken Thomas E. Dewey's record for the largest proportion of the vote won by a governor seeking a third term." See Kevin Sack, "Voters Showed A Loss of Trust, Cuomo Asserts," *The New York Times*, November 9, 1990.

But what made Marino the best-known member of Cuomo's inner circle was his most hard-fought and bitterly lost battle: the one to persuade Mario Cuomo to run for the presidency in 1992.

Running the Presidential Campaign that Never Was

The process by which the governor, universally considered an almost certain presidential nominee, mused in public for months while allowing all sorts of speculations about his plans was unheard of in American political history[41] ("Mr. Cuomo says he has no plans to run, no plans to make plans, and no plans not to make plans," the *New York Times* colorfully summarized the process[42]). Cuomo's apparent indecision was certainly due to many factors—from the informal, underlying preoccupation that an Italian American could not win to the official explanation that the governor would not run until a budget agreement with the Senate Republican majority was reached. Be that as it may, it was John Marino, who, as the guardian of that long and twisted decision process, took much of the heat steering, maneuvering, threatening, and negotiating in order to keep Cuomo's options open until the end.

It all started in the summer of 1991 when, according to tradition, prospective candidates should start raising funds and setting up the organizational machinery in view of the late-December deadline to enter the New Hampshire primary. When the State Democratic chairman told the press that people like Cuomo, "who have recognition and some base [...] can wait longer than most people say is traditional,"[43] pundits started to look to him for signs of a decision. But while contradictory rumors about Cuomo's plans spread in the following weeks, the governor seemed to enjoy playing the "enigma."[44] "John Marino doesn't know what's on my mind,"[45] he once stated, hinting that his only real confidant on the question of running for president was his eldest son Andrew.[46] Marino, however, had long

[41] Mario Cuomo's 1992 "noncandidacy" is documented in some detail in Ceaser and Busch (1993), Loevy (1995).

[42] Sam Roberts, "Tick, Tick, Tick: Cuomo Can Afford To Wait on 1992," *The New York Times*, June 10, 1991.

[43] Robin Toner, "Democrats' Distress Grows As Presidential Field Shrinks," *The New York Times*, August 8, 1991.

[44] Sam Roberts, "An Eloquent Man And His Musings On the Presidency," *The New York Times*, October 14, 1991.

[45] Sack, "Cuomo's Point Man," cit.

[46] Kevin Sack, "Cuomo Advisers Discuss Possible Campaign Aides," *The New York Times*, December 5, 1991.

been seen as Andrew's personal friend,[47] which left the enigma unsolved and led reporters to investigate "the unconventional relationship between the governor and his small circle of advisers."[48] Marino himself had to admit that he relied on his own intuition to send signals he believed would benefit the governor: "I operate on the premise that he would say something to me if I was out of line," he once confessed, earning for himself the widely shared definition as an "occasionally reliable cryptanalyst of the governor's thinking."[49]

The closer the December 20 deadline for entering the New Hampshire Presidential primary drew, the harder Marino worked behind the scenes to create the best possible conditions for Cuomo—should he decide to run. On the one hand, he worked with New Hampshire's former Democratic chairman Joe Grandmaison to get firsthand information about the political situation of the state, its electoral demographics and economic situation, to enlist volunteers for the campaign, and to familiarize himself with essential technicalities of filing the declaration of candidacy with the New Hampshire secretary of state.[50] On the other hand, he joined Cuomo's former Chief of Staff Michael DelGiudice—another in Mario's inner circle who now advises Andrew—to lay the groundwork for a national campaign. Marino and DelGiudice started compiling a list of political professionals who could fill top staff jobs: campaign managers, media consultants, press secretaries, election lawyers, pollsters, and issue advisers. They also searched for office space to establish the campaign headquarters in New York City and Washington and, most importantly, they began to search for a team of fund-raisers in 20 states around the country. All this was to be conducted in a discreet manner and carefully leaked to the news media to let people know that Cuomo could still enter the game, but making clear at the same time that the project was his aides' initiative and did not reflect his own decision to run. "If he doesn't run because of the budget, I understand that [but] we're trying to minimize the disadvantage in the hope that he

---

[47] "I would definitely categorize myself as a friend of Andrew's, but the truth is, when I talk to him lately we don't even talk about politics," he had said years erlier, on the day he was selected the party chairman. See Borsellino, "Democrat John Marino A Tireless Cuomo Aide," cit.

[48] Sack, "Cuomo's Point Man," cit.

[49] Ibid.

[50] See Elizabeth Kolbert, "A Cage of Equivocation," *The New York Times*, December 21, 1991; "Getting Cuomo's Entry Form, Just in Case," *The New York Times*, December 17, 1991.

runs,"[51] Marino told the press. "I have come to the conclusion that I have to be prepared for any eventuality. We have to be ready just in case."[52]

The day before the deadline, while legislative negotiations on the budget bogged down in Albany, Cuomo told a press conference that he still had not made a decision. This heightened the suspense in a dramatic guessing game about the governor's plans. The *New York Times* reported: "Many of the governor's aides said they were feeling the anxiety in their guts, and John A. Marino [...] said the last two days had been 'good practice' for the coming birth of his first child."[53] On dead-line day, Marino had everything ready: a signed ballot application, a certified check for the filing fee, and two planes sitting on the runway in Albany waiting to fly the governor, his entourage, and reporters to New Hampshire in time to be at the sec-retary of state's office by 5:00 p.m.[54] But at 3:30 p.m., 90 minutes before the dead-line, Cuomo told a news conference that he was not going because his state did not yet have a budget. "It is my responsibility as governor to deal with this extraor-dinarily severe problem. Were it not, I would travel to New Hampshire today and file my name as a candidate in its Presidential primary."[55] Although Cuomo's mov-ing portrait of a man martyred by his sense of responsibility did not convince eve-ryone, Marino seemed deeply committed to it. He soon spoke of an alleged con-spiracy by the Republican-led Senate to sabotage a Cuomo presidential bid by de-liberately delaying negotiations on the state deficit. And, he promised the most bitter vengeance against the two top Republicans (who happened to be Italian Americans) whom he blamed for this–Al D'Amato and Ralph Marino.[56]

Over the next few months, Marino was left with the even more exhausting mission of supervising the most quixotic part of that famous non-campaign: a long, ambiguous period of maneuvers and speculations about how to "draft Cuomo" into campaigning for president. Spontaneously or not, supporters and activists tried all sorts of ways offered by the intricate system of presidential primaries: the

[51] Kevin Sack, "Albany Notebook: And Cuomo Chooses: (Budget? Duty? Ego? Gore?)," *The New York Times*, December 10, 1991. See also Kenin Sack, "Budget Showdown With Cuomo Set Up By G.O.P. in Albany," *The New York Time*, December 17, 1991.
[52] Kevin Sack, "Cuomo Advisers Discuss Possible Campaign Aides," *The New York Times*, December 5, 1991.
[53] Kevin Sack, "The Word From Cuomo Is: Stay Tuned," *The New York Times*, December 20, 1991.
[54] Kolbert, "A Cage of Equivocation," cit.
[55] Ibid.
[56] Luther F. Bliven, "How Final Curtain Fell on a 10-Week Melodrama," *The New York Times*, December 22, 1991. For Alfonse D'Amato's account of the episode see his *Power, Pasta and Politics*, op. cit., p. 265.

governor could run as a write-in candidate in New Hampshire in February,[57] or he could try to take over the California primary in March; in April, at the New York State primary, he could be entered as a "favorite son" candidate,[58] or county leaders around the state could run uncommitted delegates—the rationale being to allow the Cuomo camp to keep their options open in the event of a deadlock at the national convention in July.[59] Such initiatives were neither officially authorized nor necessarily discouraged by the Cuomo camp, and the party chairman was the pivot of such ambiguity: distancing the governor from those "dreamers" ("I think we're in the category of a dream here," Marino said in an interview), but adding at the same time that "[w]e all can dream."[60]

Meanwhile, Bill Clinton was doing increasingly well in primaries around the country. As Cuomo's presidential prospects faded away, it appeared that the governor nevertheless intended to remain neutral until after the New York primary. And John Marino, who had rarely had a word of appreciation for the Clinton campaign, made the headline in late March by noting that Clinton was still largely unknown in New York. His tone was personal and ironic: "Four years ago by this time, my mother was sold on Dukakis. She's not sold on Clinton."[61] This spurred new speculations in the press. As the *New York Times* put it:

> The reticence of Mrs. Marino, whose son is the Democratic State Chairman, [might represent] the latest twist in a plot by Gov. Mario M. Cuomo to undermine Mr. Clinton—all but guaranteeing that the nominee will be chosen in New York, if not in tomorrow's primary then at the national convention in July, and

---

[57] The *New York Times* reported that "A Chicago political consultant, Phil Krone, acting on a suggestion by Mike Royko, the columnist, has organized a Draft Cuomo drive, with a number, (800) 92C-UOMO), staffed by volunteers who instruct callers on how to complete a write-in ballot in whatever state they live." See Sam Howe Verhovek, "Political Talk," *The New York Times*, January 5, 1992.

[58] "Former Party Chief Tries to Toss Cuomo's Hat Into Primary Ring," *The New York Times*, December 26, 1991. A "favorite son" is a presidential candidate who gets to a national convention with the support of his own state delegates and is then able to negotiate his delegation's votes in the final nomination. It was a popular technique in 19th century uncommitted, brokered conventions, before the introduction of nationwide, binding primary elections. A recent review of the intricacies of the primary mechanism is in Barbara Norrande, *The Imperfect Primary: Oddities, Biases, and Strengths of U.S. Presidential Nomination Politics*, New York and London: Routledge, 2010.

[59] They were joined by a grass-roots movement in other states who intended to run as officially uncommitted but sentimentally pro-Cuomo delegates. See Verhovek, "Political Talk," cit.; and "Former Party Chief," cit.

[60] Bruce Weber, "State Democrats Consider Running Cuomo as Their 'Favorite Son,'" *The New York Times*, January 6, 1992.

[61] Sam Roberts, "Primary: Clinton, Facing Hurdles, Opens New York Drive," *The New York Times*, March 21, 1992.

that the host governor might emerge as a compromise candidate, which is what happened 40 years ago in Chicago.[62]

Conspiracy theorists, as it turned out, were to be disappointed. Clinton won New York State and then went on to be crowned the presidential candidate by the Democratic National Convention that opened in New York City's Madison Square Garden in July. John Marino helped negotiate Cuomo's presence as one of the convention's three keynote speakers (apparently, the governor had not been invited to speak) and then took charge of the New York Clinton-Gore campaign, which was chaired by Cuomo himself. The general election was a huge success—New York being second only to Arkansas in the proportion of votes for Clinton. After that *tour de force*, Marino left the party chairmanship for a job in the private sector and became the managing partner of Dan Klores Communications, a high-end public relations firm founded by a close friend of the Cuomo family.[63]

The Last Lost Battle and the "Cuomo-Giuliani Deal"

A year later, however, John Marino was called back as a chief political consultant to manage the 1994 campaign to win the governor a fourth term against challenger George Pataki. He joined a core of top campaign operatives, mostly family and friends, and Italian American. These included Cuomo's chief of staff and pollster Andrew Zambelli, the governor's youngest daughter Madeline Cuomo O'Donoghue, who handled fund-raising working closely with Lucille Falcone, the long-time head of Cuomo's political action committee. Andrew, who was then an assistant secretary at the Department of Housing and Urban Development in the Clinton administration, advised the Governor and his team "regularly by telephone from Washington."[64]

One aspect of that unfortunate campaign is particularly interesting from our perspective: the crucial role Marino played in engineering Mayor Rudolph Giuliani's endorsement of Cuomo. Giuliani crossing party lines was considered a seismic political event and a "major sea change" by Democratic leaders, not only in New

---

[62] Sam Roberts, "New York Primary's Multiple Choices," *The New York Times*, April 6, 1992.
[63] Presently Marino is still a managing partner at Dan Klores Communications, where he leads the Government, Not-for-Profit and Education Groups. See the DKC website <http://www.dkcnews.com/about-dkc/dkc-team/john-marino> (last accessed June 2012).
[64] Kevin Sack, "Cuomo Relies on the Loyal For Campaign's Inner Circle," *The New York Times*, October 28, 1994.

York, but in Washington as well. President Clinton himself telephoned Marino to offer his personal congratulations.[65]

To the broad public and the general media, the ethnic factor was not presented as crucial in the Giuliani-Cuomo alliance; their cross-party convergence on a shared platform of policy objectives was given more relevance.[66] But in practical political terms, given New York's demographics and John Marino's known sensitivity to the issue, it was clear that the governor's strategists were using Giuliani—in part at least—to appeal to ethnic groups "who might otherwise consider the Republican line." To the vast and politically divided Italian-American community, the implicit, symbolic suggestion was that common ancestry could help cross party lines—a strategy that is more common among Republicans than Democrats, at least in New York.[67] If there was a realistic possibility to unify and realign the Italian-American vote, that was it.

But the Giuliani strategy did not work, and in some cases even backfired. Cuomo did win an overwhelming, if largely expected majority in Democratic New York City, but he failed almost everywhere else. Partisanship, traditional ethnic alignments, and the upstate/downstate cleavage proved stronger than had been thought. The new, popular, Italian-American, Liberal-Republican mayor from "the City" could not arrest the decline of the incumbent, Italian-American and Liberal-Democratic governor seeking reelection for the fourth time. Interestingly, the impact on the Italian-American vote was very limited: Cuomo lost (albeit marginally) in heavily Italian-American *and* Republican-leaning districts in Staten Island and Westchester, and experienced the most burning defeats in Long Island's suburbia. But the real disaster happened upstate, where the Pataki campaign presented the Cuomo-Giuliani deal as an Albany-New York City "buyoff" that promised to divert upstate hard-earned taxpayer dollars to downstate areas. This, together with more

---

[65] Alison Mitchell, "Giuliani, Defying His Party, Backs Cuomo for 4th Term; Sees Pataki as Bad for City," *The New York Times*, October 25, 1994. For a political analysis that explores in some depth the relationship between Rudolph Giuliani and Mario Cuomo see Siegel (2005).

[66] See for instance Todd S. Purdum, "Who Can Do the Most? Mayor's Endorsement of Cuomo Reflects Political Interests and Financial Realities," *The New York Times*, October 25, 1994; Eric Pooley, "An Affair to Remember. Charging in to Save Cuomo, Giuliani Gets the Role of a Lifetime," *New York Magazine*, November 7, 1994.

[67] See Cappelli (2011: 223-24). Perhaps not suprisingly, the Cuomo-Giuliani team included a small Italian-American inner core. The Governor's top strategists working directly with the Giuliani camp were, of course, John Marino and Andrew Zambelli. Their Italian counterparts on the other side included Giuliani's chief of staff Randy M. Mastro, the appointments officer Tony Carbonetti, and press secretary Cristyne F. Lategano. Carl F. Grillo, the Liberal Party official who ran Giuliani's campaign field operation, worked with Cuomo's street coordinators. See Alison Mitchell, "Giuliani's Two Battles: Pataki, Then D'Amato," *The New York Times*, November 6, 1994.

partisan accusations of Giuliani as a "turncoat," ultimately defused whatever potential the ethnic factor could produce and sealed the fate of the Cuomo-Giuliani strategy. While not commenting on the ethnic failure of his strategy, John Marino recognized that Giuliani "cost us upstate," although he maintained that "if I had to do it over again, I would take the mayor's endorsement wholeheartedly."[68]

Engineering Andrew's Future

By 1998 Marino's name resurfaced in the press as "a Cuomo confidant"—but this time referring to Andrew rather than Mario. At that time Andrew Cuomo, who had risen in Washington to become HUD Secretary, was considering the Democratic nomination for the New York Senate seat that was to be vacated in 2000 by Daniel Patrick Moynihan. "I think he has an excellent shot at the nomination," the family confidant John Marino stated to the press, "and I think he can beat whoever the Republicans throw at him, Giuliani or whomever." The former manager of Mario Cuomo's campaigns also urged New York's first son "to make a decision very, very early in 1999" and start raising funds.[69] But when in January 1999, speculations emerged that Hillary Clinton might enter the senatorial contest,[70] it was Marino again who came forward to announce that "Andrew is not running for the U.S. Senate. [...] His commitment is to HUD and to the vice president and to the president."[71] If Marino's diplomatic words concealed the inner circle's disappointment, former Governor Mario expressed the feelings of the family more bitterly: "He'd make a great candidate, a great candidate," he said of his son. "Listen, his education is the best you could have, watching me make mistakes for twelve years. If he is not the best-prepared candidate in America, I don't know who is."[72]

The "clan," however, still had plans for Andrew. The HUD Secretary wouldn't rule out a run for governor in 2002, Marino said. "Certainly that's the next logical goal."[73] And, balancing the roles of the family friend and the political strategist, he advised: "The more logical path for Andrew is to complete the commitment with HUD and then make a decision about coming back to New York to run for office

---

[68] James Dao, "The Endgame: For Pataki, Fighting Giuliani Became the Way to Fight Cuomo," *The New York Times*, November 10, 1994.

[69] Marc Humbert, "Cuomo to decide on Senate race as McCall bows out; Rudy eyes run," *The Associated Press*, December 30, 1998.

[70] Ron Fournier, "Senator Hillary? Stay Tuned," *The Associated Press*, January 7, 1999.

[71] Marc Humbert, "Andrew Cuomo decides against Senate run; Sharpton looking at it," *The Associated Press State*, January 8, 1999.

[72] Idem.

[73] Idem.

here. He has always focused on running for the Senate or for governor, and I happen to believe that remains in his mind."[74] It is no wonder that at this point the
news media perceived Marino as a permanent participant in the "kitchen cabinet"
meetings where Andrew's political future was mapped out, and the unofficial
spokesman of "the first family of New York Democratic politics."[75] He now appeared to be as close to Andrew as he was to Mario, to the point where he would
accept being renounced in public when politically necessary. For example, when
Marino first disclosed Andrew's intention to run for governor in 2002, revealing
to the press that he had had several conversations with him "and it's really my be-
lief that he's thinking about the governorship in 2002," Andrew publicly denied
it.[76] But a few months later, Marino was among the top fund-raisers for Andrew's
2002 campaign, even accommodating the campaign's temporary headquarters at
the Manhattan offices of Dan Klores Communications—just as he had done ten
years earlier when running the "covert" presidential operation for Mario Cuomo.[77]

Andrew's first attempt at running for governor was a disaster.[78] He fought in
the Democratic primary against State Comptroller Carl McCall, the favorite candidate of the Party establishment and an older and much respected black leader
who, among other things, had been Mario Cuomo's running mate in the 1982
primary. The campaign ended badly in September 2002, with Andrew finally
bending to pressure to not split the party and resigning a week before the vote.
[...][79] As for Marino, he was at Andrew's side to the end, eventually meeting with
the McCall team in an attempt to negotiate a dignified withdrawal. (He reportedly
proposed that Andrew be given a high-profile role in McCall's campaign in return,
as well as McCall's blessing in any future campaigns—but team McCall refused).[80]

---

[74] Lara Jakes, "HUD chief says no to Senate bid," *The Times Union*, January 9, 1999.
[75] The *Observer* reported a Democratic operative as saying: "Everybody knows John Marino doesn't
take a piss without consulting Andrew first." "That's not the way I operate," Marino fumed in
responde. "Anyone suggesting otherwise doesn't know me." See Devin Leonard, "Can Dollar Bill
Bradley Dunk Al Gore?" *New York Observer*, September 27, 1999.
[76] Marc Humbert, "Confidant: Andrew Cuomo interested in running for governor," *The Associated
Press*, September 13, 1999.
[77] Fredric U. Dicker, "Unemployed Andy Revs Up Gov Bid," *The New York Post*, January 22, 2001.
[78] Andrew Cuomo later reflected on that experience in his *Crossroads: The Future of American Politics*
(2003).
[79] Nicholas Confessore, "In Cuomo Corner, a Burly, Pugnacious Enforcer," *The New York Times*,
April 8, 2010.
[80] Marino, who was accompanied by Brooklyn Councilman Bill DeBlasio, former campaign manager
for Senator Hillary Clinton, also reportedly asked McCall to state that Andrew's withdrawal had been
brokered by Mr. Clinton. "All terms were rebuffed by the McCall camp, who found them
presumptuous, according to the McCall advisers." See Confessore, "In Cuomo Corner," cit.

On that occasion press reports also hinted at a personal, even emotional dimension of Marino's relationship with the Cuomos. When Attorney General (and future Governor) Eliot Spitzer endorsed comptroller McCall against Andrew Cuomo, Marino—who had worked as a consultant for Spitzer few years earlier—was heard to say that he was "never speaking to Spitzer again."[81]

What followed was a time of crisis and regeneration for Andrew Cuomo, who also had to face the divorce from his wife Kerry Kennedy. As would have been common in pre-modern European dynastic politics, this personal loss could have had vast political implications as the first (Italian-American) family of New York Democratic politics struggled to find its place alongside more established (and perhaps ethnically more acceptable) American dynasties. This is why the core members of the loyal team of "Mario veterans," including John Marino and others, appeared in public at Andrew's side, carefully acting to minimize the public-relations damage and engineer his political comeback.

And within a few years, Andrew was back indeed, winning the primary and the general election as New York State Attorney General in 2006 with full Democratic endorsement. Not surprisingly, Marino could emphatically state: "When you get knocked to the ground, you've got to be like the Greek god and get up stronger. [...] In 2003 at some point I said to him, or I said to myself, that Andrew Cuomo could be a great comeback story and that's exactly what happened."[82]

The comeback story of course continued throughout the years, until the 2010 gubernatorial election—clearly the inner circle's ultimate goal. Although Marino was now seen as an outside advisor to the campaign, he was still perceived by pundits as "the ultimate guy in Cuomoland."[83] Despite his public statements that he would only provide some political consulting from time to time, media sources reported the widespread opinion that "[i]t's inconceivable that he wouldn't play a role" in the campaign.[84]

Marino indeed played a crucial if subtle role in 2010. Besides issuing public statements of encouragement[85] and providing precious if informal advice, he

---

[81] Tish Durkin, "Shall I Run for Governor? Mario-Like Musings From Andrew Cuomo," *New York Observer*, March 20, 2000.

[82] Rick Karlin, "Political winds shift back to Cuomo; Attorney general has found redemption in Albany after an accomplished first year," *The Times Union*, December 23, 2007.

[83] "Team Cuomo," *New York Observer*, February 18, 2009.

[84] "Cuomo's plans," *Crain's New York Business*, May 3, 2010.

[85] "He has this ability, a proven ability, to get things done, and people want things done. They want action in Albany and on the local level," Marino added. "This is actually a good moment for someone like Andrew Cuomo." See Tom Precious, "Coronation for Cuomo? But as candidacy for

worked behind the scenes building political support within the New York business community. He did so in his capacity as managing partner at Dan Klores Communication (DKC)—whose Manhattan offices had already been used as temporary headquarters for one or the other Cuomo in the past. So in late 2009, as Andrew prepared for the campaign, Marino oversaw the creation of the government affairs group at DKC, a "political unit" aimed at providing "government relations strategy and political counsel" to major corporations. As stated on DKC's website, "John brings over two decades of experience in public administration and politics, including five years as New York State Democratic Party Chairman and a three-time posting as campaign manager and advisor to Governor Mario Cuomo."[86] Most importantly, he "remains engaged in political strategy at the state and federal level."[87] This is not to say, of course, that DKC or its government affairs unit had as their primary goal to lobby for the election of Andrew Cuomo. Nonetheless, the role played in this regard became evident soon after the election, when a group of business leaders came together as the Committee to Save New York to raise $10 million "in support of Governor-elect Andrew M. Cuomo's looming showdown with government employees' unions over wages and pensions."[88] The Committee was run by Bill Cunningham, himself a managing director at DKC, and Marino had been reportedly "active in the effort" to create it. Moreover, it was mainly through Marino's connection that the Committee even found a surprising ally in one of the most powerful union officials in the state, Gary LaBarbera—the same person who Andrew Cuomo had just named as a member of his transition team.[89] In other words, informal ties of policy affinity and personal connections would easily draw the conclusion that Marino's major contribution to Andrew's 2010

governor becomes official, inner circle shuns all talk of inevitable victory," *Buffalo News*, May 23, 2010.

[86] See the biography of John Marino in the DKC website <www.dkcnews.com/about-dkc/dkc-team/john-marino.>

[87] See the descritption of the government affairs group in the DKC website <www.dkcnews.com/why-dkc/government-affairs.> See also "Klores Opens a Lobbying Shop," *New York Observer*, September 10, 2009. According to the DKC website veteran lobbyist Allison Lee is the director of Government Affairs at DKC. However John Marino—who is the sole managing director to be also a managing partner—is the most senior member of the group. In addition, his DKC biography states that "John leads the Government, Not-for-Profit and Education Groups at DKC."

[88] Charles V. Bagli, "Cuomo Gains an Ally for a Looming Fight With the Public-Employee Unions," *The New York Times*, December 10, 2010.

[89] Idem. La Barbera was the president of the Building and Construction Trades Council of Greater New York, a 100,000-member federation of electricians, iron workers and operating engineers who work on large building sites around the region. His role in the Committee was seen to provide it with some insulation from criticism that the elite is looking to solve the fiscal problems of the state on the backs of working people.

campaign and subsequent government experience came through such channels. John Marino—Mario Cuomo's loyal party soldier turned Andrew's "mover and shaker" at the elite level—remained a pivotal member of the (Italian-American) inner circle that is at the heart of Andrew Cuomos' success. As the *New York Times* aptly summarized:

> As in many rising dynasties, the torch was effectively passed years ago. Former aides explained that today, "[Mario] Cuomo people" are by definition "Andrew people." Yet for older hands, there is an almost familial satisfaction in seeing Mr. Cuomo, who joined the family business in his early 20's, rise to the top job. "It's the staffer going to the chamber to be the boss," said John A. Marino, who was a state party chairman under the elder Mr. Cuomo and is a close adviser to the new governor."[90]

MICHAEL DELGIUDICE: THE *ÉMINENCE GRISE*

Nicknamed in the press as "Andrew's political rabbi,"[91] Michael DelGiudice has been the *éminence grise* of the Cuomos' political machine for decades—as much the man in the shadows as John Marino is the frontman. His vast experience in Albany and his far-reaching connections in both the business community and the Democratic elite make him someone the governor trusts implicitly. His long-standing, personal relationship with the family, dating back to the era of Mario Cuomo's administration, adds to this trust.

Like Mario, DelGiudice was born in Astoria, Queens in 1943 and demonstrated an early passion for public office and an equally passionate faith in the Italian Americans as a potential voting bloc. He lost both early on in his career. In 1968, when he was a 25-year-old graduate of City College working in the Nassau County executive's office, young DelGiudice persuaded the Democrats to let him run for Congress. His argument was based on the heavy Italian-American presence on Long Island: "I used to have a theory that there was an Italian base [...]. And I lost. It ruined my theory," he declared to the *New York Times* years later.[92] Indeed in those years Nassau County's Italian Americans were busy aligning with the other side: they comprised the backbone of the county Republican machine headed by

---

[90] Nicholas Confessore, "Back in Albany, 16 Years Later, To Serve Another Gov. Cuomo," *The New York Times*, January 1, 2011.

[91] "The Main Players on Team Cuomo," *Crain's New York Business*, February 28, 2011 (Vol. 27, p. 12).

[92] Maurice Carroll, "The Enigmatic Italian-American Voter," *The New York Times*, October 3, 1980.

legendary boss Joseph Margiotta, and later formed the base for the conservative upsurge of the 1980s, which elevated Alfonse D'Amato to the U.S. Senate.[93]

That episode also determined DelGiudice's choice to stay out the spotlight: "I got the public stuff out of my system early," he said explaining why he had since functioned as a governmental insider and never ran again for elective office.[94] He went on to work for State Assembly Democratic Minority Leader Stanley Steingut, and became his secretary after the Democrats recaptured the Assembly in 1974. Four years later, when Steingut was defeated, DelGiudice—who by then had also become an established professional in the private sector—was co-opted into the highest ranks of Governor Carey's administration. There he served as Director of State Operations and Policy Management, the third highest executive staff position in the state.[95] Given Governor Carey's habit of delegating day-to-day decision-making to his inner circle, DelGiudice had extensive responsibility in the administration, sharing it with the governor's secretary and second in command Robert Morgado.

From Inner Circle to Inner Circle

In those days, dealings between Carey's inner circle and Lt. Governor Mario Cuomo were at times "irritating," according to Cuomo's own memoirs. He blamed them for jealously guarding access to the governor, frustrating his attempts to get closer to him. By the end of Carey's second term, Cuomo had decided not to let them "dispose casually of whatever my usefulness is" and warned Morgado and DelGiudice that he might be unavailable to run on Carey's ticket in 1982 (Cuomo 1984: 61, 66). This notwithstanding, Cuomo had enormous consideration for DelGiudice. When, in the summer of 1981, DelGiudice announced that he was leaving the Carey administration, Cuomo invited him to a meeting to investigate the possibility of having him aboard his own gubernatorial campaign even if that could mean challenging Carey himself, should the latter decide to seek a third term. Here is how Cuomo (1984: 87-88) recounts the episode in his memoirs, giving a sense of their relationship:

---

[93] For Alfonse D'Amato's legendary capacity to mobilize the Italian-American vote in Long Island and elsewhere in the New York State see his *memoires* (D'Amato 1995) as well as my interview with State Senator Serfin Maltese, who was one of D'Amato's top political aides (Cappelli 2011).

[94] Maurice Carroll, "As Cuomo's Chief Adviser, DelGiudice Wields Power From Outside the Spotlights," *The New York Times*, May 15, 1985.

[95] DelGiudice was also the first vice president for public finance at Shearson/American Express. Michael Oreskes, "Cuomo Fills 3 More High Posts in Administration," *The New York Times*, December 3, 1982.

I met with DelGiudice for lunch at the Palm Court. I think he is a big loss to the government and would try to have him if I were governor. He assumes Carey is running. Although he didn't take any firm position vis-à-vis my running against him, his questions indicated a negative view of it. [...] I told him that if I chose to run against the governor I could sharpen my rationale to the point of saying the following: "The polls, my feedback from editorial writers, and everything else tell me Carey cannot win against the Republicans and I can. I think the Democrats must win." [...] If Michael's failure to dispute the rationale could be fairly read as meaning he thought it was a good one, then he did.

Cuomo courted DelGiudice for months, noting in his diary that "he is a person I would want close to me in any campaign," but DelGiudice continued to be "helpful with suggestions without making any commitment." As soon as Carey announced that he would not run, Cuomo called DelGiudice, hoping to be able to "use his name as soon as possible." DelGiudice replied that he "would be helpful, down the road," but for the time being he "didn't know how the pieces would fit." (Cuomo 1984: 110, 119). He actually helped the Cuomo campaign from behind the scenes, but it was only after the election that the two men met to discuss his possible involvement in the administration. DelGiudice told the governor-elect that he would be interested in serving as secretary—the top position on the executive staff—and he got what he wanted. Cuomo was overjoyed to be able to announce the news, noting that DelGiudice "will be considered part of the old guard, and some will call this a continuation of the old ways. [...] But so what?" DelGiudice was also happy: "Having had senior positions, you always thought about how you'd operate as number one." (Cuomo 1984: 358, 361).

The Governor's Second in Command

As Cuomo had anticipated, having DelGiudice on board proved a smart move, judging at least from a very positive comment that appeared in the *New York Times*: "So far, so good," wrote the paper in an unsigned editorial dedicated to the first Cuomo appointments. "Mr. DelGiudice mastered the intricacies of New York State government and won support for many legislative initiatives. He begins with a head start: significant respect throughout Albany."[96] As a Republican lobbyist told *The Wall Street Journal* years later, DelGiudice, with his unrivaled understanding of the machinery of state government, was "one of the rare people who understood policy and politics equally. That's one of the things you always look for."[97]

---

[96] "A New-Old Cuomo Team," *The New York Times*, December 4, 1982. See also Carroll (1994).
[97] Jacob Gershman, "A Main Cuomo Adviser Runs A Low Profile. Del Giudice Was Mario Cuomo's Chief," *The Wall Street Journal*, November 27, 2010.

The inner circle par excellence, DelGiudice thus became part of the "big five" people in the governor's executive chamber—actually six, since the governor's son Andrew, then 25, joined them with the title of "special assistant" to the governor (a position for which he was paid a symbolic salary of $1).[98] Half of these were Italian American, and among them the secretary to the governor was "the principal point of focus for all major decisions," effectively serving as "chief of staff, chief political strategist, and chief crisis manager."[99]

During the two and a half years DelGiudice worked with Mario Cuomo, they developed a strong, almost symbiotic personal relationship to the point that the governor once said that "[i]t would be very unlikely Mike's opinion and mine would be very different about a human being."[100] He was also one of the few people whose criticism Cuomo would accept and even appreciate: "Mike from the beginning had a legitimate concern that my style of inclusion would mean we'd lose coordination and cause chaos. And sometimes he's been right."[101] But most of all, Cuomo appreciated his secretary's political loyalty. Along with the honor and power of being the governor's top adviser, in fact, DelGiudice took it upon himself to shield Cuomo from anything that went wrong. "The team sound of our chamber is the *splash*," Cuomo once recalled, "the sound created when someone is thrown into the tank." And "one of the loudest splashes" came when DelGiudice took the blame for the administration's proposal to do away with the State Investigation Commission—a proposal that outraged the State Senate and had to be abandoned: "What a splash DelGiudice's body made when it hit the tank!"[102]

Besides being Cuomo's shadow in formal policy making, DelGiudice was his most trusted aide in all kinds of delicate matters, from overseeing the use of state planes by the staff's family members[103] to fixing the toughest backroom controver-

[98] The group originally referred to as the "big five" included the Secretary Michael J. DelGiudice, the Budget Director Michael Finnerty, Counsel Alice G. Daniel, Special Counsel Fabian Palomino, and Timothy J. Russert, Counselor to the Governor in charge of press relations. With the passing of time the press begun to note that "Mr. Cuomo runs his administration through an inner circle of six people"—i.e. the "big five" plus Andrew. See by Michael Oreskes: "Cuomo Fills 3 more High Posts...," cit., "Cuomo Chooses Moynihan Aide for a Major Post," *The New York Times*, December 9, 1982, and "Cuomo As Executive: Thight Rein Criticized," *The New York Times*, August 23, 1983.

[99] Carroll, "As Cuomo's Chief Adviser," cit.

[100] Sam Roberts, "Is Cuomo Backing Koch? 'No.' Dinkins? 'No.' Anyone? 'No.'" *The New York Times*, August 16, 1989.

[101] Carroll, "As Cuomo's Chief Adviser," cit.

[102] "The Governor's New Right-Hand Man; Gerald Christopher Crotty," *The New York Times*, July 31, 1985.

[103] In June 1983 the Governor issued new rules on who could fly on state planes. According to press reports, the rules stated that "Family members of top state officials may use the planes at state

sies. In 1985, for instance, a position for special prosecutor in New York City became vacant; Governor Cuomo wanted his old friend Charles J. Hynes for the job,
while Attorney General Robert Abrams wanted one of his assistants. It was Del-
Giudice who telephoned Abrams and delivered the threat without bluster: "Back
off, he warned, or the administration might ask the United States Attorney for the
Southern District [Rudolph Giuliani, who aimed at Abrams's job] to conduct a
full-scale investigation of the Attorney General's dealings with the special prosecutors. Mr. Abrams backed off."[104]

DelGiudice, on the other hand, deeply admired Cuomo's political mind, although he was apt to translate the governor's emphatic slogans into more sober
policy-oriented terminology. They both intended the administration as a chance to
"make the fullest possible mark on the government"—with Cuomo pushing for
what he solemnly called his "democracy agenda," which in his secretary's subdued
terminology became "a broader plan to get more private citizens involved in government."[105] In the early 1980s, like many others, DelGiudice marveled at how
rapidly the new governor was imposing himself on the national scene through his
oratorical skills.[106] A crucial aspect of this success was Cuomo's ability to coordi-
nate his vision of government as a tool for helping people in need with themes
often adopted by conservatives such as family, religion, and immigrant roots. Del-
Giudice recognized Cuomo's enormous potential in this area and began considering him "much more a man of communication and dialogue than most other public officials."[107] And, being an eminently practical person, he also appreciated the
impact of all this on the administration's daily activity. After the speech at the

---

expense only in conjunction with an official function of state and with the advance approval of Mr.
Cuomo's secretary, Michael J. Del Giudice." See "Cuomo Sets Rules on Use of Planes," *The New York
Times*, June 5, 1983.

[104] Carroll, "As Cuomo's Chief Adviser," cit.

[105] Josh Barbanel, "Cuomo Proposes a Broad Agenda in Annual Speech," *The New York Times*,
January 5, 1984. In a book published after the end of his governorship, Cuomo (1994) himself
presented his experience as "An Experiment in Democracy."

[106] It took only a few months for the Governor to capture the imagery of Democrats well beyond the
borders of the New York State: from his widely hailed inauguration speech in January 1983 (*The
Family of New York*,) to his tremendously successful keynote address at the San Francisco National
Democratic Convention in 1984 (*A Tale of Two Cities*). See by Michael Oreskes, "As Governor,
Cuomo Now Begins to Get Some Respect," *The New York Times*, March 27, 1983; "Cuomo Is Proving
a Tough Beat to Cover," *The New York Times*, May 29, 1983; and "San Francisco Speech Leaves
Cuomo a Superstar of Politics," *The New York Times*, July 26, 1984. See the speeches in Cuomo
(1994).

[107] "He is much more a man of communication and dialogue than most other public officials,"
DelGiudice once stated to the press. "The best part of our communciation process is our
communicator." See Oreskes, "Cuomo Is Proving a Tough Beat to Cover," cit.

1984 San Francisco National Democratic Convention (the famous "Tale of Two Cities" address), DelGiudice predicted a "reinforcing effect" as legislators and constituent groups would now be "more eager than in the past to appear at bill-signing ceremonies with Mr. Cuomo."[108]

But beyond all this it was Cuomo's "populist" disposition which, according to DelGiudice, represented his main political strength: "Mario will always be a very popular governor because his instincts are very pro-people and anti-institutional government," he once said.[109] Just as DelGiudice was the quintessential government insider, Cuomo was the quintessential public figure, a first-class politician: "What I came to know about the governor is that his sense of the body politic, if you will, is very keen. He reads constantly, he talks to people, he samples the mail. He is able to see patterns as they're developing—before others see them—and to make a judgment and move on them."[110]

King Maker by Avocation

Cuomo's instinctive capacity for sensing the public's mind, and his ability to present himself as an outsider while working within the system, was what made this great liberal communicator look like a feasible alternative to the great conservative communicator—then President Ronald Reagan. Just one year or so into his first mandate, Cuomo had emerged as a national political figure and pundits and politicians alike begun to talk of him as a candidate for higher office, a man of presidential stature. DelGiudice was one of the staunchest supporters of the idea that Mario Cuomo should run for president, and remained convinced of this through the years. Although he left the administration in 1985 to work in the private sector, he made clear that he would return to Cuomo's side should he decide to run for president in 1988.[111] In early 1987, he even headed a select group to explore the possibility[112] and drafted a few memos for him to that effect.[113] When Cuomo announced that he would not run—apparently yielding to the opinion that

[108] Oreskes, "San Francisco Speech Leaves Cuomo a Superstar of Politics," cit.
[109] Oreskes, "Cuomo's Personal Touch," *The New York Times*, January 29, 1984.
[110] As reported in Jefferey Schmalz, "Behind Cuomo's Actions: Instinct and Calculation," *The New York Times*, January 23, 1986.
[111] Jefferey Schmalz, "Del Giudice, Top Aide to Cuomo, leaving Job," *The New York Times*, July 31, 1985.
[112] "It's Lobbying Time in State Capital," *The Post-Standard*, February 1, 1987.
[113] Jonathan D. Salant, "Cuomo Sets ' Decision Deadline for 1988," *The Post-Standard*, February 6, 1987.

"an Italian-American cannot win"[114]–DelGiudice voiced his disappointment in public: "I'm surprised. I think he would have made a terrific candidate and think he would have been elected president." [115]

This notwithstanding, DelGiudice continued to support the idea that Cuomo should play a larger role in the national political arena. He formed and chaired a federal political action committee to finance Cuomo's political activities outside New York State, which included sponsoring local forums for presidential contenders and supporting candidates around the country.[116] And when he became the chairman of the New York State committee for the presidential campaign of Michael Dukakis, then governor of Massachusetts, DelGiudice worked as the main link between the two governors, actively involving Cuomo in the campaign.[117]

DelGiudice and others in the inner circle, as we have seen, never abandoned the dream that Mario Cuomo would run for president. So in the winter of 1991, it was DelGiudice who, along with Democratic State Chairman John Marino, engineered the famous "unofficial campaign" that made the headlines for months. As we have seen before, faced with the governor's apparent indecision, his two closest aides began to lay the groundwork for a possible campaign, gathering names of prospective campaign staff, consultants, lawyers, and pollsters. They also carefully leaked the news to the press in a way that exerted definite pressure on Governor Cuomo, who up to that point had distanced himself from their initiative and told the press that his only real confidant on the matter was his son Andrew. DelGiudice and Marino had to back off and declare, admittedly with little credibility, that the governor did not even know about the search process they had initiated on his behalf.[118]

Since Cuomo ultimately declined to run, DelGiudice–a kingmaker by avocation–turned to other causes. Mainly lost causes, it must be said: he co-chaired the committee for Senator Bradley against Al Gore in the 2000 presidential primaries;

---

[114] In early 1986 Cuomo reportedly stated he might be willing to run for President "if only to prove wrong those who say an Italian-American cannot win." See Jefferey Schmalz, "Behind Cuomo's Actions," cit.

[115] Jonathan D. Salant, "Cuomo Won't Run in '88. Governor Declines Presidential Race," *The Post-Standard*, February 20, 1987.

[116] Frank Lynn, "Cuomo Forms Action Committee To Pay for His National Agenda," *The New York Times*, April 15, 1987; Richard L. Berke, "Political Committee For Cuomo Reports Raising of $18,000," *The New York Times*, July 28, 1987.

[117] Frank Lynn, "Cuomo Shares Optimism of His Area's Democrats," *The New York Times*, July 25, 1988.

[118] See by Kevin Sack, "Cuomo Advisers Discuss Possible Campaign Aides," *The New York Times*, December 5, 1991; "The Word From Cuomo Is: Stay Tuned," *The New York Times*, December 20, 1991.

he was a big supporter of John Kerry in 2004 and Hillary Clinton in her 2008 primary bid against Barack Obama. Meanwhile, his personal and political relationships with the Cuomos remained rock-solid, giving him a definite role on the team of family political architects who, in those years, were planning the future career of another Cuomo.

On Andrew's Side

DelGiudice's relationship with Andrew dates back to their days in Mario's administration. That young man in his 20s who served as his father's special counsel even before passing the bar exam was not looked upon favorably, and his influence in the administration was resented by many. The tone of a 1984 article in the *New York Times* is very telling in this regard, as it tried to pit DelGiudice and other senior aides against Andrew:

> The governor's political accomplishments may be all the more surprising since he apparently relies as much on his 26-year-old son Andrew as on two older and presumably wiser hands, Mr. Russert, who has considerable Washington experience, and Mr. Cuomo's secretary, Michael DelGiudice, an Albany veteran. There has been talk of late that the younger Cuomo, having recently passed the bar, would soon strike out on a legal career of his own. Judging by the past year, Mr. Cuomo may already be able to get along without him.[119]

DelGiudice always defended Andrew from such criticisms, which he attributed to the fact that "many of [Andrew's] detractors were simply jealous of his influence on the governor." He once even lamented in public that Andrew had been "sometimes blamed for actions that were initiated by the governor"—thus implying that, if anyone, it was the father that should take the blame.[120]

This is not to mean that the two always shared the same political stance. In 2000, for instance, while DelGiudice supported Bradley in the Presidential primary, Andrew Cuomo supported Al Gore.[121] But this notwithstanding, it certainly should not come as a surprise that DelGiudice was on Andrew's side at the time of his failed attempt to challenge Carl McCall for the democratic nomination to governor in 2002. It is true that some news media outlets did insinuate that DelGiu-

---

[119] Frank Lynn, "A Clubhouse Outsider With Surprising Political Savvy," *The New York Times*, January 1, 1984.

[120] Jeffrey Schmalz, "Younger Cuomo Steps From father's Shadow," *The New York Times*, March 14, 1986.

[121] Katharine Q. Seelye, "Gore Unites Most New York Democrats and Pulls Even With Bradley in Poll," *The New York Times*, December 19, 1999.

dice might be supporting McCall instead: one paper even rejoiced that "whatever love and affection" Mario Cuomo's former aides might hold for him "it isn't being transferred to Mario's son." But that allegation proved untrue.[122] On the contrary, some form of "emotional" or "familial" factor should probably be evoked to explain why DelGiudice supported that untimely, ill-planned campaign, which eventually found the Cuomo family isolated from all Democratic leadership circles that counted. In the end, Andrew was persuaded to withdraw from the race at the last minute by his "closest supporters"–DelGiudice being among them.[123]

It is, therefore, no wonder that DelGiudice's name resurfaced in the press in the late 2000s, when Attorney General Andrew Cuomo was preparing for his next step. In 2009, DelGiudice organized an upscale breakfast at the exclusive University Club in midtown Manhattan to allow Andrew to meet influential Democrats and political donors, and discuss ways to cure the "total dysfunctionality of the state government."[124] The press labeled that meeting the start of a "charm offensive"–the first of a series of moves intended to transform Andrew's image from abrasive outsider to broad-based Democratic champion. At that time it wasn't even clear whether Andrew would seek re-election as attorney general or felt ready to fight for the governorship. What was clear, though, was that he was about "building the most effective, intimidating, and well-funded campaign machine possible."[125]

By the spring of 2010, political analysts would bet that the "machine" was preparing for the gubernatorial race, and everyone began to notice that at the helm was a small crew of Italian-American veterans from Mario Cuomo's circle, in which DelGiudice was always mentioned, usually followed by John Marino, Joe Percoco, and Andrew Zambelli.[126] True to his role as the machine's éminence grise, DelGiudice mostly escaped public exposure during the campaign, but pundits never disregarded rumors that he was behind the scenes all the way–up until the immediate aftermath of the vote, when Andrew's administration-in-waiting began preparations for the transition phase. As had occurred decades earlier in

---

[122] "Off the Record; Putting the Racial in Race," *The New York Post*, June 6, 2000. The "increasing role" of Del Giudice in Andrew's primary campaign was only later acknowledged by the *Post*. See Robert Hardt, Jr., "Lineup Change for Team Cuomo," *The New York Post*, July 11, 2002.

[123] Shaila K. Dewan, "Cuomo Quits Race and Backs McCall for Governorship," *The New York Times*, September 4, 2002.

[124] "Andrew Cuomo Grinds Toward 2010, Nicely," *New York Observer*, April 7, 2009.

[125] Ibid.

[126] "Campaign Update; Cuomo's plans," *Crain's New York Business*, May 3, 2010.

Mario Cuomo's time, DelGiudice's name still continued to be surrounded by an air of mystery and respect, if not deference:

> While Mr. Cuomo has not yet announced a leader of his formal transition committees—wrote the *New York Times* on November 4—he was said to be relying heavily on Michael J. DelGiudice, an Albany veteran who served as chief of staff to his father, Gov. Mario M. Cuomo, in the 1980s. Few members of Mr. Cuomo's senior staff in the attorney general's office have extensive Albany experience, but Mr. DelGiudice does.[127]

If, as insiders say, Andrew Cuomo's ultimate goal is "to fulfill his father's ambition of becoming the first Italian-American president,"[128] it would be hard to imagine that his "political rabbi" and kingmaker *in pectore* would not be at his side with the rest of the inner circle.

ANDREW ZAMBELLI: THE CONCEPTUAL ARCHITECT

"In many ways typical of Andrew Cuomo's inner circle," reads one of the rare portraits of him published in the press, Andrew J. 'Drew' Zambelli, born in 1948, is "a Mario man who has known the governor-elect for decades; smart, savvy, Italian-American [with] very little name recognition, and no apparent appetite for it."[129] As Andrew Cuomo's chief pollster and media strategy consultant, the 2010 campaign represented for Zambelli a sort personal revenge: 16 years earlier, in fact, he had supervised Mario Cuomo's last and unsuccessful re-election campaign, ending up as the head of the transition team that handed power over to Governor-elect George Pataki.[130] Now he found himself again in a gubernatorial transition team, but this time taking power back for a Cuomo.

In Mario's Circle–Through Andrew

Like other members of the Cuomo inner circle, Zambelli came from the opposite side. In 1982, in fact, when Mario Cuomo defeated New York City Mayor Ed Koch[131] in the Democratic primary for governor, Zambelli—in his early 30s with a

---

[127] Nicholas Confessore, "Voting Just Ended, but the Shift to Governing Is Well Under Way," *The New York Times*, November 4, 2010.

[128] "Campaign Update; Cuomo's plans," *Crain's New York Business*, May 3, 2010.

[129] Dana Rubinstein, "Andrew Cuomo's 'conceptual architect' works quietly," *Capital New York*, December 14, 2010. See also: "Governor Hopeful Andrew Cuomo's Team on the Road to Albany," *Daily News*, Monday, May 24, 2010.

[130] Jon R. Sorenson, "Pataki Claims Cuomo Kept Deficit Secret; Vows To Push tax Cut Despite $4 Billion Gap," *Buffalo News*, November 11, 1994.

[131] On the long-standing Cuomo-Koch rivalry see footnote 25 above.

PhD in psychology—was the campaign manager for Koch's running mate Alfred DelBello. The latter, in turn, defeated Cuomo's running mate Carl McCall and ended up on the Cuomo ticket as his lieutenant governor. And so as DelBello's campaign manager, Zambelli entered the administration as the chief of staff for a former Cuomo opponent. But the governor and his lieutenant never got along well.[132] DelBello finally resigned in 1985, and Zambelli, who according to his former boss had gotten "very close to Andrew in the meanwhile,"[133] switched to the Cuomo camp. In a few years he became a central figure in the administration, serving as director of communications, chief of staff and secretary to the governor—the post held by Michael DelGiudice in the first Mario Cuomo administration.[134] Then in 1994 he oversaw Mario Cuomo's unsuccessful re-election bid—sharing with chief consultant John Marino the responsibility for the campaign strategy, including the "Cuomo-Giuliani deal."[135] This was surely his most bitter defeat—personally, professionally, and politically—as he had the unenviable duty of heading the governor's outgoing transition team.

Once outside Albany, Zambelli went on to work as a pollster and a college instructor. By the fall of 1995, when Cuomo's former aides met in New York City for a social gathering ("The alumni of the Mario Cuomo School of Government," the press dubbed them),[136] he had become a partner at Strategic Frameworking, Inc., an innovative marketing firm of self-defined "conceptual architects" and "identity experts"—"psychologists specializing in brand marketing."[137] He also headed a polling center at Manhattanville College.[138]

Andrew's Conceptual Architect

In this professional position, Andrew Zambelli continued to stay close to the Cuomos and assisted Andrew in his long-planned comeback to New York politics at the end of his Washington tenure in the Clinton administration. He has been

[132] See Sydney H. Schanberg, "Me and My Shadow," *The New York Times*, March 19, 1983; Lena Williams, "A Look Back at al DlBello's 20 years in Politics," *The New York Times*, January 13, 1985; Edward A. Gargan, "Day of Reflection and Farewell for DelBello," *The New York Times*, February 1, 1985.
[133] Reported in Dana Rubinstein, "Andrew Cuomo's 'conceptual architect' works quietly," cit.
[134] See Zambelli's biographical outline on the website of his company Strategic Frameworking, Inc. <www.strategicframeworking.com/team.htm>.
[135] James Dao, "The Endgame: For Pataki, Fighting Giuliani Became the Way to Fight Cuomo," *The New York Times*, November 10, 1994.
[136] Harvy Lipman, "And where are they now? Cuomo alumni touch base," *The Times Union*, September 27, 1995.
[137] As reported in the Strategic Frameworking website, cit.
[138] Steve Malanga, "New York, New York," *Crain's New York Business*, March 9, 1998.

Andrew's pollster since the early 2000s, working for him both in the 2002 attempt to challenge McCall in the Democratic gubernatorial primary, and later in the successful race for attorney general in 2006.[139]

As one might expect, in May 2010 when Andrew announced his intention to run for governor, Zambelli was mentioned in the press as his "campaign adviser and liaison to the ex-governor's circle."[140] Like other veterans from Mario's administration, he was seen as operating exclusively behind the scenes, the big-picture guy focusing on how the message was communicated. After the elections, however, Zambelli's role became more public, as he, along with Michael DelGiudice, were members of Mario's old inner circle who took power back for Andrew, handling the day-to-day transition[141] and tackling the delicate task of staff selection and recruitment.[142] Moreover, unlike other Mario veterans, after the election Zambelli remained actively involved in the administration, playing both an informal and a formal role. Informally, he was "someone with vast institutional knowledge of the governor's office, and who can act as liaison between the new executive and other old-timers." Formally, he was appointed "senior advisor to the governor," the person responsible for the oversight and "strategic integration of the communications, inter-governmental, legislative, and constituency efforts of the Office of the Governor."[143] Insiders read this title as something like "handler in chief." In the words of Fred Siegel: "That's an extraordinarily important position. It's someone with continuous access to the governor, someone who's at the governor's side."[144]

It does not come as a surprise, thus, that in the spring of 2011, Zambelli emerged as the mastermind behind the shrewd "outside of Albany" tactics that the governor used to push through his new budget—by bringing the message more to the people than to politicians and the media. In Zambelli's own words: "You're not going to get the people involved unless you talk to them directly. [...] You've

---

[139] Ben Smith, "Parties' Pols Vie To Catch Bloomy Aye," *Daily News*, May 8, 2006.

[140] "His Team On Road To Albany," *Daily News*, May 24, 2010.

[141] Kenneth Lowett, "Now Comes the Tricky Bit for Cuomo & Team," *Daily News*, November 4, 2010.

[142] As noted by Jimmy Vielkind "people familiar with the Democrat's rise to power say aides to [Andrew Cuomo's] father, Gov. Mario Cuomo, are playing a major role, and their presence in the advisory group shows an appreciation for the seasoned even as Cuomo has spoken of the need to attract 'talent' back to government as he seeks to 'recalibrate' state agencies and programs." See by Vielkind "Cuomo Talks Budget Personnel," *The Times-Union*, November 10, 2010, and "Transition Taking Shape," *The Times-Union*, November 12, 2010.

[143] According to the official description provided by the governor-elect's office, as reported in Rubinstein, "Andrew Cuomo's 'conceptual architect'," cit.

[144] Idem.

got to get out of the Capitol."[145] This "go to the hustings and bypass the Capitol" strategy—which involved fewer press conferences and media appearances as well as an elaborate mix of endless tours of districts and behind-the-scenes negotiation and co-optation—gave Andrew Cuomo better control of the political agenda and the ability to define the political discourse behind it. Whatever the content of his policies and their ultimate fate, in fact, the tactic's success was evident. In the spring of 2011, polls showed Cuomo's approval rating at 77 percent—better than any governor in recent memory at that point in his term—and general support for his budget. Siena College pollster Steven Greenberg, who described Cuomo's efforts in such basketball terms as "a full-court press, orchestrated within government and outside of government," commented: "That is something I've not seen in my lifetime from any governor of New York."[146] And Douglas Muzzio, a Baruch College political scientist and frequent political commentator, marveled at this shrewd use of "permanent political campaign" tactics to solve such a big legislative issue as the state budget.[147]

In this, the hand of the conceptual architect was clearly visible indeed—the practical application of an adage found on Strategic Frameworking, Inc.'s website: "Powerful brands succeed by establishing a relationship, a connection, with their customers."[148]

JOSEPH PERCOCO: THE ENFORCER

The other member of the inner circle who, like Zambelli, also got a job in Andrew Cuomo's administration, is the youngest of the group—the only one younger than Andrew himself. Joseph "Joe" Percoco, born in 1969, joined Mario Cuomo's team right out of college in 1991, at the time when the governor was rumored to be considering a presidential run, and would serve as "body man" and a scheduler. There he met Andrew, and that encounter changed his life.

What Percoco did for Andrew over two decades has been defined in countless ways, including right-hand man, henchman, political fixer, and troubleshooter. More elaborate definitions portray him as "a stealth adviser who shuns the media spotlight day,"[149] a "point man for monitoring the political winds,"[150] and the

---

[145] Yancey Roy,"Guv taking budget to the people; Making his case directly to voters since February; Preferring statewide tours than events at Capitol," *Newsday*, March 21, 2011.

[146] Idem.

[147] Idem.

[148] See the Strategic Frameworking Inc. website, cit.

[149] Judy L. Randall, "Cuomo names Islander his executive deputy secretary Governor selects longtime ally Joseph Percoco of Huguenot for the position," *Staten Island Advance*, January 5, 2011.

"most pugnacious Cuomo enforcer"[151]—actually "an extension of Mr. Cuomo's will."[152] He is also considered someone particularly adept at behind-the-scenes deal-making,[153] a common characteristic of those in both Mario's and Andrew's inner circles, as we have seen. In short, the duties of the man who, after the 2010 elections, became the governor's executive deputy secretary escape formal, clear-cut definitions. This is due in part to his remarkable discipline in never talking to reporters about himself, and in part to the fact that his goals and *modus operandi* are opaque: "[Percoco] doesn't appear to have formal responsibilities but does whatever is needed,"[154] is the common wisdom about him. On the other hand, all accounts emphasize his intense devotion to the Cuomo family as well as his tendency "to hold grudges against those who get in [Andrew's] way."[155] Percoco is known to be "quick to respond to slights, real or perceived,"[156] and obsessively vigilant against any "threats,"[157] especially when coming from the media. And, to those familiar with their relationship, he is "the most trusted, most loyal friend that Andrew ever had. He's been with [him] through thick and thin."[158]

This combination of characteristics makes Joe Percoco an invaluable aide. "Everyone should have someone like him working for them," a union official once told the *New York Times*. "He has no other interest or agenda except in being *the man behind the man*."[159] And this, in turn, accounts for the common perception that he wields considerable, if informal, power: "No matter what his title, the person who spends the most time with a candidate or elected official is the person with the most influence," says Assemblyman Sam Hoyt, a state legislator of mixed Italian and Irish descent and a Cuomo supporter.[160]

Perhaps the best way to characterize Joe Percoco in relation to Andrew Cuomo is to compare his role with that played by others in the inner circle like Michael DelGiudice and John Marino in preparation of the 2010 campaign. While Del-Giudice and Marino pulled strings with top politicians, businessmen, and poten-

---

[150] Niicholas Confessore, "On Governor's Race, Cuomo Plays a Game of Wait and See," *The New York Times*, August 3, 2009.
[151] Nicholas Confessore, "In Cuomo Corner," cit.
[152] Jimmy Vielkind, "Cuomo Welcomed," *The Times-Union*, July 18, 2010.
[153] According to a Cuomo aide quoted in "The Main Players on Team Cuomo," *Crain's New York Business*, February 28, 2011.
[154] Idem.
[155] Idem.
[156] Confessore, "In Cuomo Corner," cit.
[157] Vielkind, "Cuomo Welcomed," cit.
[158] Susan Schulman, "The Inner Circle," *Buffalo News*, October 29, 2010.
[159] Confessore, "In Cuomo Corner," cit.
[160] Schulman, "The Inner Circle," cit.

tial donors, Joe Percoco laid the groundwork at the grassroots level. He met count-less party officials and tried to stay in touch with them "as much as he possibly could," offering help from the attorney general, negotiating his presence at their fund-raising events, and building relationships to understand what their needs might be. "He was very gracious," the party chairwoman of an upstate county re-called: "I'm a brand-new county chair and he gave me his personal number and he said don't hesitate to call at any time." Percoco seldom discussed Andrew's politi-cal ambitions during those meetings, leaving unclear whether his boss was up for re-election as attorney general or aimed at other state offices: "It's more just, 'how've you been, how's your family, is there anything we can do for you' sort of stuff," said another county leader.[161]

The different levels at which these men operated reflects an interesting diversi-ty within the inner circle. Unlike DelGiudice and Marino (and Andrew himself), Percoco is not a member of Manhattan's elite, playing the big game of policy plan-ning and grand political strategy. He is, rather, the man on the ground: an Italian-American middle-class guy from Staten Island with "'a real-world understanding' of the politics and policies that grease the wheels of government."[162]

The Personal and the Political

A native of Rockland County, in his younger years Percoco moved with his parents to Staten Island—New York City's most Italian borough.[163] He went to high school there and worked as a landscaper and snow remover to pay his tuition at Wagner College, where he went on partial scholarship. A big man and a base-ball and football player, he was also an officer of his college's political science club, and graduated with a major in political science in 1991. He had, according to one of his professors, "a keen interest in the practical application of the theory he was learning in class."[164] This old definition of young Percoco is remarkably similar to another recently offered by Steven M. Cohen—Andrew Cuomo's chief of staff at the attorney general's office and later the governor's secretary—who worked along-side Percoco for many years: "Joe is the guy who takes the big legal theories and

---

[161] Based on testimonies from three Democratic County Party chair: Sean Hennessey, of Jefferson County, Lorie Longhany, of Genesee County, and Daniel McCoy, of Albany County, as reported in "Andrew Cuomo Grinds Toward 2010, Nicely," *New York Observer*, April 7, 2009.

[162] According to a Cuomo aide quoted in "The Main Players on Team Cuomo," cit.

[163] A third-generation Italian American, Joe Percoco married his college sweetheart, Italian American Lisa Toscano, now a foreign language teacher. The Percocos and their two daughters belong to Our Lady Star of the Sea Roman Chatolic Church in their home community in Staten Island. See Judy L. Randall, "The Islander Behind the Scenes in Albany," *Staten Island Advance*, December 5, 2010.

[164] Idem.

translates it into a practical reality. How do you actually accomplish these initiatives? Who has a stake? What are the effects going to be? And how do you move them forward?"[165]

Given these descriptions, it does not come as a surprise that Percoco started to work for the Cuomo administration when he was only 22 years old, nor that he was particularly fascinated by Andrew, with whom he developed a tight bond of personal friendship. When the *Staten Island Advance* found out that an Islander had become "one of the most powerful men in New York State"–and Percoco, as usual, declined to be interviewed–Andrew himself phoned in to heap praise on his friend and long-time right-hand man. The *Advance* proudly reported the governor-elect's words:

> A great friend, a superior talent, a great public servant, a great guy, a great husband. I can't say enough good things about him. [...] He volunteered with my father. He was with me at HUD. He cares about his community. He is giving. He is competent. [...] He will work for me directly, he will report directly to me.[166]

Similar remarks were reiterated a few months later, when the governor went to talk about the state budget at Wagner College, Percoco's alma mater. "I owe you a debt of gratitude for giving me Joe Percoco," Andrew told an audience filled with school administrators and students.[167]

After Mario Cuomo's defeat in 1994, Percoco enrolled at St. John's University, where he earned a law degree, and worked briefly for Mayor Rudolph Giuliani and Public Advocate Mark Green. He then joined Andrew again in Washington at the Department of Housing and Urban Development,[168] serving as his special assistant and later assistant general counsel.[169] Percoco was Andrew's right-hand man i the first and unsuccessful shot at the governorship in 2002, helping John Marino set up temporary campaign headquarters at Dan Klores Communications in Man-

---

[165] Confessore, "In Cuomo Corner, a Burly, Pugnacious Enforcer," cit. Note that Cohen too interned with Mario Cuomo, worked with Andrew at the Attorney General office as chief of staff, and then led Andrew's gubernatorial administration as Secretary to the Governor, while Percoco was Executive deputy secretary. He left the administration in September 2011. See: Thomas Kaplan, "Governor's Right-Hand Man Returns to Private Sector," *The New York Times*, September 21, 2011.

[166] Randall, "The Islander Behind the Scenes in Albany," cit.

[167] Tom Wrobelski, "Cuomo lavishes praise on Molinaro, Titone," *Staten Island Advance*, March 13, 2011.

[168] Confessore, "In Cuomo Corner, a Burly, Pugnacious Enforcer," cit.

[169] Judy L. Randall, "Cuomo names Islander his executive deputy secretary. Governor selects longtime ally Joseph Percoco of Huguenot for the position," *Staten Island Advance*, January 5, 2011.

hattan.[170] During that short-lived primary campaign, Percoco used to "[drive] his own car to Buffalo and back to save money on plane tickets."[171] After the ensuing burning defeat put Andrew in political limbo for a time, Percoco remained close, performing different functions as usual, including handling media relations in connection with the Cuomo-Kennedy divorce.[172] He then briefly took a job at a consulting firm, but left in 2006 to become the "political director" of Andrew's campaign for attorney general.[173]

It was at that time that the news media began to take notice of what later became known as Percoco's peculiar ability to be "everything from Cuomo's chief political messenger to a 'body man' whispering a name or moving through a crowd."[174] One gains a distinct sense of this from a well-informed Cuomo portrait written by *New York Magazine*'s Jennifer Senior. One day during the campaign, Andrew Cuomo drove to a meeting with the pipe-fitters union in Sunnyside, with Senior at his side. Upon arriving at the destination, they found Percoco waiting and he soon began to brief the candidate on the scene:

> He [Percoco] sticks his head in the car window.
> "Okay. Jack Torpey is gonna introduce you. And Ed Malloy from the building trades is..."
> "Ed Malloy is here? Why?"
> "This is part of his group. He came with Jimmy Cahill. He's actually a steamfitter, but he's the international representative for the United Association of Plumbers and Pipefitters, who have endorsed us..."
> "Wait, give me that again?"
> He repeats this information, along with a further elaboration on the union family tree.
> "Can I have a pen, please?"
> Percoco rummages around, finds him one.
> "Okay. Ed Malloy, Jimmy Cahill, Jack Torpey."
> "Right," says Percoco. They chat a few minutes more, then head inside. The joint's jumping. Cuomo makes his way through the crowd with an easy vigor, hugging people, grabbing them by their arms, giving two-part handshakes. He

[170] Fredric U. Dicker, "Unemployed Andy Revs Up Gov Bid," *The New York Post*, January 22, 2001.
[171] Confessore, "In Cuomo Corner," cit.
[172] At the time of the Cuomo-Kennedy separation, when a statement by Cuomo's lawyer that she had "betrayed" him unleashed tabloid gossiping that could damage Andrew's political ambitions, the press cited Percoco as his spokesman, the man who would tell the press "We're not going to have any comment until further notice." See Marc Humbert, "Cuomo-Kennedy separation statement draws fire," *The Associated Press*, July 1, 2003.
[173] Confessore, "In Cuomo Corner," cit.
[174] Jimmy Vielkind, "Martens Draws Praise As Dec Pick," *The Times-Union*, January 5, 2011.

climbs onto the stage. "I can't tell you what an honor it is to be here," he tells the crowd. "Jack Torpey, Jimmy Cahill, I see here Eddie Malloy. All the big shots came out tonight, boy..."[175]

In a campaign, in sum, Joe Percoco functions as the shadow counselor who knows everyone on the ground, keeps track of everything that is said and done, and suggests which strings to pull and how. These qualities also made him a most valuable "special assistant" to the attorney general in the following years. He was the only one in the close group of Andrew's aides to have longstanding ties to the Cuomo family and, among a staff of lawyers and former prosecutors, "one of the few with deep political experience." And indeed his role in the attorney general's office was eminently political, which—as a reporter aptly noted—was "not only appropriate but inevitable, given that the attorney general is also an elected official."[176] There are indeed few specific *policy* cases Percoco is known to have dealt with, and even then his major contribution came from his eminently *political* ability to work his shadow network of personal relationships to "help shepherd a measure" and "make a bill sail" through the legislature, overcoming whatever resistance lawmakers might initially feel.[177]

In the Backstage

This brings us to Percoco's controversial penchant for behind-the-scenes maneuvering and deal-making.[178] This emerged in the press in late 2008, after President Obama nominated Hillary Clinton as secretary of state and Governor Paterson was to hand-pick a successor to her U.S. senatorial seat. Andrew Cuomo was rumored to be interested in the job, along with a group of other contenders. Among these was Caroline Kennedy, the cousin of Andrew's ex-wife. Shortly before Kennedy embarked on an upstate tour to introduce herself to the public and the political establishment, Percoco—then "assistant to the attorney general"—allegedly contacted labor leaders, party officials, and city mayors trying to derail her Senate bid. Sources quoted in the *New York Times* hinted that Percoco had suggested they give Kennedy a cold reception, questioning her experience, knowledge, and understanding of upstate New York. Although the Cuomo office denied such rumors as "false gossip," one source indicated a more credible version of the

---

[175] Jennifer Senior, "The Name of the Father; In his race for attorney general, Andrew Cuomo has as much to live down as he does to live up to," *New York Magazine*, March 27, 2006.
[176] Confessore, "In Cuomo Corner," cit.
[177] Ibid.
[178] According to a Cuomo aide quoted in "The Main Players On Team Cuomo," cit.

events: Percoco would not speak specifically of Kennedy, nor would he openly say that Cuomo was interested in the job; it was more like a "I can't say he wants you to tell people he wants it, but you should, *wink-wink, nudge-nudge*, know that he kind of wants it" kind of conversation, the paper reported.[179]

Rumors that Percoco played this kind of game resurfaced again during the 2010 campaign. He was seen as the man managing the months-long Cuomo-Paterson "shadowboxing," speaking unofficially to black leaders to gauge their opinion on Paterson's chances, and letting them know that if Paterson declined to run "we're very interested...[.] And if [he does] not, then we'll have a conversation at a later date."[180] Months later, Percoco was also said to be helping Andrew to influence the choice of his successor as attorney general by informally contacting labor officials and urging them not to endorse State Senator Eric Schneiderman in the primaries.[181] When these episodes emerged in the press, Andrew Cuomo's adversary Carl Paladino released a letter asking State Inspector General Joseph Fisch to investigate Joseph Percoco, described as a "political bully who intimidates perceived adversaries. [...] I find this behavior a flagrant abuse of Mr. Percoco's position and a serious violation of the state's code of ethics."[182]

Percoco, in sum, could aptly be described as Andrew Cuomo's "shadow whip": the man who—with good or bad manners, and always keeping a low profile—organizes and maintains political support, deters opponents, and reins in party mavericks, elected officials, labor leaders, and reporters alike.[183] Understandably, this gives him enormous influence in Andrew's circle. Even his harsh inclination towards bypassing formal lines of authority is accepted by those who know his symbiotic relation with Andrew. A final episode that may clarify this aspect comes from a reporter who was at the Democratic State Convention in June 2010. Lamenting the overall secrecy of the Cuomo campaign, he recalls that, when Andrew's running mate for Lieutenant Governor Bob Duffy, in a rare display of openness, began to talk to reporters "Cuomo's aide, Joe Percoco, rushed to convey that his comments were not authorized. 'Shut it down!' he said."[184]

---

[179] Nicholas Confessore, "Cuomo Aide Is Said to Try to Slow Kennedy Bid," *The New York Times*, January 7, 2009.

[180] Nicholas Confessore, "On Governor's Race," *The New York Times*, August 3, 2009.

[181] Nicholas Confessore, "Behind Scenes, Cuomo Tries to Influence Who Will Be His Successor," *The New York Times*, May 21, 2010.

[182] Robert J. McCarthy, "Paladino under fire for e-mails; Forwarded pornographic, racist depictions to friends," *Buffalo News*, April 13, 2010.

[183] Danny Hakim and Jeremy W. Peters, "The Inner Circle Behind a Run for Governor," *The New York Times*, May 28, 2010.

[184] Jimmy Vielkind, "In Dark on Cuomo Schedules," *The Times-Union*, October 18, 2010.

It is, therefore, no wonder that Percoco was perceived as the "informal" campaign manager. Indeed, even though a deputy campaign manager had been hired, no such announcement had been made for the post of campaign manager. This can be `attributed to the well-known fact that Andrew—like his father—wanted to be in charge of even the minor details of the campaign. And the only person with whom he would share day-to-day decision-making in this realm was Joe Percoco, who "appears to function less as a chief executive than as an extension of Mr. Cuomo's will."[185] If nothing else, Percoco's crucial role in the campaign was indirectly confirmed weeks later by his presence on the transition team (along with two other members of Mario's inner circle, DelGiudice and Zambelli), by his nomination as executive deputy secretary to the governor, and by getting the largest "victory bonus" as compared to all other senior campaign advisors: $90,000 (professional pollster Zambelli came second with $80,000).[186]

As State Senator and Percoco's fellow Staten Islander Diane Savino once said: "He doesn't seek the limelight. He gets the job done."[187] He certainly did.

CONCLUSION

During the 2010 campaign, the American media easily caught the differences between the two candidates in terms of personal and political styles, somehow marveling at their common ancestry as they saw Carl Paladino as the most folkloric, stereotypical Italian American, while portraying Cuomo as a colder character, almost WASP-styled and definitely un-Italian. But ethnicity-politics relations, it turns out, are a more serious business. The Paladino and Cuomo campaigns did have one important characteristic in common, and it was the presence, in both cases, of an Italian-American inner circle at their core.

Proceeding from such an observation, the first research goal of this essay was to find out who these people were and what role did their ethnicity play in their being at the core of Cuomo's inner circle. The answer must necessarily be multifaceted since the ethnic factor seemed to have different weight and meaning in the two settings.

In the case of the Paladino team, the Italian-American presence at the helm of the campaign organization is too evident to be a mere coincidence; at the same time, however, common ancestry was not associated with pre-existing personal

---

[185] Vielkind, "Cuomo Welcomed," cit.
[186] Nicholas Confessore, "Cuomo Campaign Aides Receive 5-Figure Bonuses," *The New York Times*, January 19, 2011.
[187] Judy L. Randall, "Cuomo Names Islander," cit.

bonds among those in the inner circle and between them and the candidate, which somehow lowers the relevance of the ethnic factor. Paladino's team was picked by Stone and, indirectly, by Golisano, and what held it together was a shared conservative-populist attitude and an overall anti-establishment sentiment. In the familiar terms of New York politics, their strategy could be described as focusing on the upstate/downstate divide. But seen in a broader light, their political biographies and behavior seemed to appeal to a more general sense of frustration and estrangement typical of people in the periphery of the social-political system when they look at those in the center. This is where their upstate rural-suburban populism coalesced with downstate conservative strands of urban populism that can be found in New York City's heavily multiethnic boroughs such as Queens, where the campaign established its downstate headquarters. After all, one should not forget that the principal aim of the Paladino team was to win the GOP primary against the establishment candidate Rick Lazio—himself an Italian American, a former congressman, and a lobbyist for J.P. Morgan. It is understandable that, having won that battle against expectations, that insurgent crew of Italian-American underdogs felt that they were well-poised to defeat the other side of the (Italian) American socio-political universe, the Manhattan elite par excellence assembled around the golden child of an (Italian) American dynasty.

In sharp contrast with the opposing team, Cuomo's Italian-American inner circle was less visible, but comprised of men who had always been there: personal friends of Mario and Andrew who had not only served the former governor, but had worked for over two decades to pass the torch from father to son. In this respect, the role of the ethnic factor is more clearly recognizable here. It could be pictured by drawing a series of concentric circles around the candidate: family, friends, fellow ethnics, the Democratic Party, and the socio-political elite of New York City. The first three circles overlap, with common ancestry clearly representing the ideal bridge between the personal and the political. These people came to constitute a rock-solid "ethnic" nucleus around the Cuomo family and, although often operating behind the scenes, they were all crucial in Andrew's career up to his 2010 victory.

This brings us closer to an answer to our second point. That these two inner circles reflected the social, political, and cultural differences among the candidates is very telling indeed. By observing the different paths through which descendants of Italian immigrants traveled their way into American society and ended up on the opposite sides of an all-Italian battle for the governorship of New York, we are reminded that internal differentiation and complexity are signs of the richness and maturity of an immigrant community. That the Italian-American community appears to be a microcosm of America's socio-political world need not be viewed as a mere sign of passive assimilation; it can also be seen as a sign of its capacity to *incorporate* the structure of the host society within its own body politic, with all its divisions, conflicts, and alliances. If the "intra-ethnic" race of 2010 demonstrated anything, it is that Italian-American politicians and their "friends" can—without having to downplay their ancestry—monopolize a state-wide campaign and make themselves elected to the top office in a state where their fellow ethnics are a minority of the electorate, albeit a sizable one.

With this we come to our third and final question: How profound are the Italian signs in New York politics? How exhaustive a political portrait of New York can we get by connecting the Italian-American dots in the puzzle? Answering this question is a most complex exercise, one that can only be sketched here based on the most relevant political figures that surfaced from the biographies of those in the inner circles. Incomplete as such an exercise may seem, it nevertheless offers interesting insights into three decades of New York's political history.

Our first dot is, of course, the governor's father Mario, the first elected Italian-American governor of New York (1982-93), three terms in office and a man of presidential stature who had revived a tradition of Italian-American liberalism that had "remained dormant" for decades after it's peak under Fiorello LaGuardia and Vito Marcantonio. (Shefter, 1994: 221). On the other side, Paladino's political godfather Tom Golisano, founder of the Independence Party of New York, and its gubernatorial candidate on three occasions (in 1994, 1998, and 2002)—the closest source of inspiration for the Paladino campaign and the man indirectly responsible for the selection of its Italian-American inner core.

We have also met two lieutenant governors, Mario Cuomo himself (1977-82) and Alfred DelBello (1982-85); two Democratic Party chairmen, Dominic Baranello (1977-1982) and John Marino (1989-93); founder and president of the Conservative Party of New York, Serf Maltese, later the head of the Queens County Republican machine and an influential state senator (1989-2008); two Republican Senate majority leaders, Ralph Marino (1989-94) and Joseph Bruno (1994-2008); one U.S. Senator from New York, Alfonse D'Amato (1981-99); a famous if controversial mayor of New York City, Rudolph Giuliani (1994-2001), who later attempted a primary bid for the Republican presidential nomination (2008); a Republican Congressman from Long Island (1993-2001), Rick Lazio, who lost to Hillary Clinton in the 2000 race for New York's U.S. Senate seat and became the party favorite for governor in 2010, but lost the primary to Paladino; and Geraldine Ferraro, a Democratic Congresswoman (1979-85) who in the mid-1980s was the first woman—and the first Italian-American—vice-presidential candidate for a major American party.

These people only constitute the tip of the Italian-American iceberg in this state, but they have been the protagonists of major political developments in New York politics over three decades. Such developments included harsh political confrontations, the most significant perhaps taking place in 1991 when Mario Cuomo, after much hesitation, was "forced" to renounce a Democratic primary that many thought he might have easily won. On that occasion, Cuomo and his inner circle put the blame on Alfonse D'Amato's and Ralph Marino's tactics, which involved stalling the budget negotiations in Albany to ensure that the governor would not leave office to engage in a national campaign.

Italian-American politicians, however, have also forged innovative cross-party alliances, like the "Italian deal" of 1994, when Mayor Giuliani endorsed Governor Cuomo in his bid for a fourth term—a move masterminded by Democratic Chairman John Marino, which received the enthusiastic blessing of President Clinton. It is hard not to see the ethnic factor at work here, though it was of course mingled with other factors: the deal was meant, in part at least, to appeal to diverse immigrant communities that could defect to the Cuomo camp, though it was also based on a policy affinity between Cuomo and Giuliani, both of whom had also been elected on the Liberal line.

That episode ignited an intra-party conflict among New York Republicans where Italian Americans again figured prominently. It pitted Mayor Giuliani against conservative-Republican Senator D'Amato, who had handpicked his protégé George Pataki as the anti-Cuomo candidate. After defeating the Italian deal at the polls, in fact, D'Amato and Pataki began cleaning up the GOP and removing their opponents: at the highest levels, this involved replacing Senate Majority leader Ralph Marino, a moderate, with the more conservative Joe Bruno; at the lower levels it involved ousting Giuliani forces from the New York City party machine, as happened in Queens in 1995, with a coup orchestrated by D'Amato's associate Serf Maltese and his ally Tom Ognibene. Intra-party conflicts, however, were not lacking on the other side, as when Governor-elect Cuomo fired Dominic Baranello as the Democratic Party chairman for endorsing Ed Koch over him in the 1982 primary; or when Lieutenant Governor DelBello found he was incompatible with Cuomo and left the administration in 1985.

Last but not least, our sample of Italian-American politicians has also engaged in more traditional attempts to play the ethnic card by pitting fellow ethnics against each other in order to split the Italian-American vote. This happened in 1992, for instance, when Governor Cuomo and Party Chairman John Marino supported Geraldine Ferraro in the Democratic primary to select the candidate who would oust D'Amato from the U.S. Senate. Ferraro, a Congresswoman from Queens who had famously been Walter Mondale's vice presidential running mate against Ronald Reagan in 1984, was considered a dangerous challenger for D'Amato precisely because she could cut into his Italian-American electoral base.

In conclusion, seen in this broader context, the all-Italian race of 2010 appears to be only the latest episode—though certainly one of the most relevant—in a long history of Italian-American penetration into the body politic of New York. Or, put in different terms, it is the most recent confirmation that a complex, multifaceted Italian-American body politic exists in the most Italian of the American states, and that it incorporates and interacts with the major dynamics of the political system. It clearly does not act, simplistically, as a cohesive "ethnic" political bloc, just as the Italian-American electorate does not behave as a monolithic voting bloc. But it does comprise a recognizable component of the political class of New York—one that, for better or worse, has made and will continue to make a difference in the life of this state.

WORKS CITED

Ceaser, James W. and Andrew Busch (1993), *Upside Down and Inside Out: The 1992 Elections and American Politics*, Lanham, MD: Rowman & Littlefield Publishers.

Cappelli, Ottorino (2011), "Re-Interpreting Italian-American Politics: The Role of Ethnicity," in Jerome Krase, editor, *The Status of Interpretation in Italian American Studies*, Stony Brook, NY: Forum Italicum Publishing (Center for Italian Studies, State University of New York at Stony Brook).

Carroll, Thomas W. (1994), "Status Cuomo," *The Policy Review*, Spring.

Cuomo, Andrew (2003), editor, *Crossroads: The Future of American Politics*, New York: Random House.

Cuomo, Mario M. (1984), *Diaries of Mario M. Cuomo. The Campaign for Governor*, New York, Random House, 1984.

Cuomo, Mario M. (1994a), *More Than Words: The Speeches of Mario Cuomo*, New York: St. Martin's Press.

Cuomo, Mario M. (1994b), The New York Idea, an Experiment in Democracy, New York: Crown.

D'Amato, Alfonse (1995), *Power, Pasta, and Politics*, New York: Hyperion.

Glazer, Nathan and Patrick D. Moynihan (1963), *Beyond the Melting Pot. The Negroes, Puerto Ricans, Jews, Italians, and Irish of New York City*, Cambridge, Mass: MIT Press.

Koch, Edward I. (2000), with Daniel Pasner, *I'm Not Done Yet*, New York, William Morrow.

Loevy, Robert D. (1995), *The Flawed Path to the Presidency 1992: Unfairness and Inequality in the Presidential Selection Process*, Albany: State University of New York Press.

Morehouse, Sarah McCally (1998) *The Governor As Party Leader: Campaigning and Governing*, Ann Arbor, MI: University of Michigan Press.

Mosca, Gaetano (1982), *Teorica dei governi e governo parlamentare* [1883], in *Scritti Politici*, ed. Giorgio Sola, Torino: UTET.

Murtaugh, John Brian, Antoinette Pole, and Edward V. Schneier (2009) *New York Politics: A Tale of Two States*, M.E. Sharpe.

Pecorella, Robert F. and Jeffrey M. Stonecash (2006), editors, *Governing New York State*, New York: State University of New York Press.

Shefter, Martin (1994), *Political Parties and the State. The American Experience*, Princeton, NJ: Princeton University Press.

Siegel, Fred (2005), *The Prince of the City: Giuliani, New York and the Genius of American Life*, San Francisco, CA: Ecounter Books.

Soffer, Jonathan (2010), *Ed Koch and the Rebuilding of New York City*, New York: Columbia University Press.

Spitzer, Robert J. (2006), "Third Parties in New York," in Robert F. Pecorella and Jeffrey M. Stonecash, editors, *Governing New York State*, New York, State University of New York Press.

Sullivan, Timoty J. (2009), *New York State and the Rise of Modern Conservatism*, Albany, NY: State University of New York Press.

Zimmerman, Joseph F., (2008) *The Government and Politics of New York State*, Albany, NY: State University of New York Press.

II. Historical Perspectives

THE 1950 ELECTION
A Classic Intra-Ethnic Struggle

Salvatore J. LaGumina
NASSAU COMMUNITY COLLEGE

WHEN NEW YORK WAS ITALIAN

The succession of New York City immigrant and ethnic groups that have re-sided there over the centuries and thus temporarily became predominant clusters in the nation's largest city is a striking phenomenon. The spectacle manifested it-self in sanguine statements, which adumbrated that a boastful New York had the largest German or Irish population outside of Germany or Ireland and it likewise lent itself to writing ballads highlighting the singularity. Accordingly, it was under-standable to maintain that there was a given point in history when New York was Italian. Moreover, the following statistics can easily be adduced to confirm the impression (Miranda and Rossi, 118):

Table 1. Italian Foreign Stock Living in New York by Decades (first and second generation)

YEAR	NUMBER
1900	219,597
1910	455,178
1920	807,048
1930	1,070,355
1940	1,095,000
1950	1,028,980
1960	858,601
1970	682,013

Foreign stock referred only to first and second generations; however, when additional generations are included they result in more impressive statistics.

*Table 2. Italian Americans of All Generations in New York City
by Decades (approximate figures)*

YEAR	NUMBER
1900	219,000
1910	862,000
1920	1,272,700
1930	1,511,800
1940	1,716,900
1950	1,951,300
1960	1,739,700

These statistics demonstrate the rapidity with which the city's population of Italian descent increased from a minor cohort early in the twentieth century to the city's major ethnic group by mid-century. They would come to populate Manhattan "Little Italies" on Mulberry Street or in East Harlem neighborhoods that previously had been the locus for other ethnic groups and where now Italians lived their lives, where they raised children, where they went to school, where they shopped and sometimes worked, and where they worshipped. While for many Italians these familiar neighborhoods meant home for generations of family members, for others these enclaves were way stations before they moved to other parts of the city where they established newer "Little Italies" in Brooklyn, Queens, the Bronx and Staten Island.

The early Italian immigrant generation partook of limited involvement in American political practices, in part because of the disadvantage due to their relative ignorance of the English language, in part because of lack of citizenship—either because of a return migration phenomenon to the home country that was more substantial than most immigrant groups, or because of their preoccupation with earning a livelihood for themselves and their families. Notwithstanding this background, there were small but noteworthy steps at entering the political arena in the pre-World War I era although it meant for all practical purposes that they would have to be content to accept elective office primarily within characteristic Italian enclaves and to settle for minor posts such as coroner or deputy police commissioner. Despite their limited conspicuousness in public office during the entry period, Italian-American political leaders were acculturating American political practices, including that of organizing the ethnic group. James March (Maggio) and Paul Vaccarelli, for instance, achieved considerable success and clout by recruiting thousands of immigrants into political clubs within their New York Italian communities, thereby commanding attention of the major political parties.[1] Establishment of this groundwork became an immense benefit to aspiring politicians who reached the peak of their power in the next phase of political maturation. The 1920s and 1930s may be called the *striving* phase as Italian Americans vigorously contended for more prestigious political posts including election to the New York State Assembly, the State Senate, and in the person of Fiorello H. LaGuardia, New York City mayor. Born in New York City and brought up as a Protestant in western army camps, LaGuardia proffered a half Jewish, but all Italian background and became the hybrid politician par excellence. Firmly embracing an Italian identity, which struck responsive chords within his heavily Italian district in New York City's Lower East Side, where LaGuardia initially had won public office as a congressman in 1916 and then subsequently was elected to Congress repeatedly from East Harlem, in its time the nation's largest Little Italy. Ascending to the New York City mayoralty in 1933 and winning re-election twice, he established a merited reputation as a progressive, caring government official who worked steadfastly on behalf of constituents confronting the nation's worst depression. He is generally regarded as New York City's greatest twentieth-century mayor.

THE 1950 SPECIAL ELECTION

By mid-twentieth century, New York City Italian Americans had emerged to become a formidable political presence. Ranging from left-wing Congressman Vito Marcantonio, who ran unsuccessfully for mayor in 1949 on the American Labor Party ticket, to Carmine DeSapio, who became Tammany Hall's leader at a time when that Democratic political club was the most powerful organization in the state, to Generoso Pope, who had become the richest Italian American in the city via his ownership of the Colonial Sand and Gravel Company, and as publisher of the Italian language daily newspaper *Il Progresso Italo-Americano*, Italian Americans can be said to have arrived politically.[2]

New York City mayors are ordinarily elected for four-year terms on odd numbered years. Incumbent Mayor William O'Dwyer, for example, had succeeded La-Guardia by winning election in 1945 and was re-elected in 1949, presumably tenured in office until 1953. However, when in September 1950 O'Dwyer resigned

---

[1] For more on this topic see LaGumina (1994, 200–216; 1996, 24–45).
[2] Paul David Pope details numerous instances demonstrating Generoso Pope's political involve-ment, especially in chapters 9–13.

his mayoral position to accept assignment as President Truman's ambassador to Mexico this necessitated a special election for November 1950. According to the City Charter, City Council President Vincent R. Impellitteri, became acting mayor during the interim September to November period thereby setting the stage for unique intra-ethnic contest between Impellitteri, Ferdinand Pecora, and Edward Corsi. The fact that each one of them was born in Italy and that each was designated to run by their respective parties says volumes about the coming of age of the ethnic group in the city. Power brokers were clearly aware that the Italian ethnic assemblage was the city's largest element—one that could not be denied attainment of the highest municipal post.

SELECTION OF CANDIDATES

However one answers the question as to whether or not the three major candidates—Impellitteri, Pecora, and Corsi—were chosen because of their ethnicity, there is much to confirm the notion that all possessed cigar-smoking reflecting quality candidates. Ferdinand Pecora, the oldest of the three was born in Nicosia, Sicily in 1882 and emigrated to the United States with his parents Louis and Rose in 1886. His father, a shoemaker, eked out a livelihood for the family that had settled in a neighborhood that was outside of the traditional Italian enclave, an experience that would shape Ferdinand's life. His father's decision to become a Protestant also influenced Ferdinand who became an Episcopalian seminarian until he had to leave at age fifteen to assume the role of main breadwinner for the family following his father's work accident (LaGumina, 1992, 41-42; Perino, 28-30). He continued his education, graduated from the New York Law School in 1904, and in 1918 was appointed assistant district attorney in New York, thus initiating his long public career. He would win acclaim as "the most brilliant cross-examiner in New York" in the District Attorney's office and was named chief assistant district attorney, the second in command in the celebrated office (Perino, 40). A believer of the Progressive philosophy espoused by Theodore Roosevelt, he nevertheless joined the New York Democratic Party, then ably run by Tammany Hall leader Charles Murphy whose stewardship spawned the careers of Progressive Democrats like Alfred E. Smith and Robert Wagner. Pecora's appointment as counsel to the U. S. Senate Committee on Banking and Currency in 1934 would bring him national renown as "the hellhound of Wall Street" as he directed one of the most far-reaching and extensive inquiries into the sordid side of American financial practices that led inexorably to the stock market's Great Crash of 1929. The diminutive bronzed, swarthy-faced, cigar-smoking Italian American made an indelible impression as he extracted from chastened witnesses the sad story of stock manipulation by greedy millionaires at the expense of small investors. The end result of the investigation was that Congress enacted laws designed to eliminate various evils and violations of fiduciary responsibilities, including the creation of the Securities and Exchange Commission to which he received appointment as one of five members. In 1935, New York Governor Herbert H. Lehman appointed Pecora a justice of the New York Supreme Court, a position he continued to maintain in 1950.

Born in 1895 in Capestrano, Italy, Edward Corsi was the bearer of an illustrious name as the son of Filippo Corsi, an Italian deputy, an agrarian reformer, a union organizer, editor, and disciple of Giuseppe Mazzini, the Italian nationalist and patriot leader of the *Risorgimento* (Federal Writers Project, 109). On Filippo's death, in 1907 the Corsi family immigrated to the United States where the economic struggle facing the family required all to make sacrifices including Edward, who went to work even before teenage-hood while simultaneously continuing his schooling. Even as he worked his way through St. Francis Xavier College and earned a law degree from Fordham University in 1922, he also was interested in social work, journalism, and politics, and worked professionally in all these areas. As director of the Harlem House on East 116th Street in New York City, at a time when East Harlem was the center of a vibrant Italian enclave, he met and interacted with two other Italian-American political luminaries: Fiorello LaGuardia and Vito Marcantonio, and like them, joined the local Republican Club. As Corsi explained, "In my case it was the influence of Theodore Roosevelt that led me to spurn the conventional Tammany advances. Also, I did not particularly like the shady characters and overweight politicians who hung around the Tammany table in my district.[3] Corsi's writing talents were evident in undertakings as editor of an Italian language weekly newspaper *La Settimana*, as a correspondent in both Mexico and Italy for English language newspapers and journals such as *Outlook* and *Reader's Digest*, and in his books *In the Shadow of Liberty* and *Pathways to the New World*.

In 1931, Republican President Herbert Hoover appointed Corsi U.S. Commissioner of Immigration and Naturalization, a position he continued to hold under Democratic President Roosevelt until 1934, when in the dire straits of the Depression Mayor LaGuardia appointed him director of the Emergency Relief Bureau in New York, the nation's largest welfare department (Ascoli, 34). Corsi ran an unsuccessful race for city councilman in 1937, was equally unsuccessful in his

---

[3] Edward Corsi, Speech to Young Republican Club, Edward Corsi Papers, (January 25, 1946).

1938 race as Republican nominee for the U.S. Senate, played a leading role in New York State's revision of its constitution, and in 1943 was appointed by Governor Thomas Dewey to head the New York Department of Labor—in sum a formidable record of public service.

In 1900, Vincent Richard Impellitteri was born in Isnello, Sicily, a desolate, impoverished, forgotten town nestled in the Madonie mountain chain in the north-central part of the island that was virtually inaccessible except for animals and narrow vehicular traffic. Its disengagement left an indelible impression with novelist Carlo Levi. "It is a village of shepherds, of peasants who are landowners in the smallest possible scale, the ground being divided into microscopic sections, of craftsmen whose crafts are now fallen into decay..." (Levi, 34).[4] In 1901, Vincent emigrated to America with the entire Impellitteri clan of seven children. Like Pecora's father, Vincent's father also sought to earn a living via his inherited shoemaker trade.[5] After a short stay in Manhattan, the Impellitteri family moved to Ansonia, Connecticut where Vincent was raised and where he was educated, first in the local parochial school, then in public school and Ansonia High School, where he excelled in athletics and where he demonstrated organizing skills including managing the school basketball team. He also participated extensively in the debating society.

His plans to go to college were frustrated by the family's financial straits and by America's entry into the Great War. Succumbing to the blandishment of a nationwide enlistment campaign, Vincent joined the Navy and saw action on board a ship that protected conveys from submarines. Upon the termination of military service, Impellitteri moved to New York City and attended Fordham University Law School where he associated with students who had political inclinations like future Republican leader Thomas Curran, and a larger number of students who sided

---

[4] Levi visited Isnello on the occasion of Mayor Impellitteri's good will tour in behalf of the U.S. Department of State in 1951.

[5] Shoemaking, it might be added, historically was a respectable trade in the pre-industrial age. In Italy, where it enjoyed a position as an indispensable factor in the life of the community, the shoemaker could learn the craft only through long apprenticeship, and when mastered, guaranteed the master a fairly secure economic existence. The classically trained shoemaker was involved in all aspects of making the shoe from the selection of leather, to the insertion of shoe laces, along with knowledge of the human anatomy. In a word the Italian shoemaker was an Old World craftsman participating in a centuries-old trade. By contrast, the evolution of mass shoe production in the United States meant the shoemaker was involved merely in shoe repairing. The experience is best described by Henry Tolino, an actual participant. "I began to learn the shoemaking trade in Italy when I was six years old. The craft of shoemaking was learned from the bottom up. An apprentice, I would have to take shoes apart to learn how to make the pattern for women, children and men. Each aspect of shoemaking was a specialty in itself" (LaGumina, 1979, 54).

with the Democratic Party that was linked with Tammany Hall such as classmate Alfred E. Smith, Jr., son of the famous New York governor. Vincent accordingly joined the Democratic Party and upon receiving his law degree and worked as a lawyer in the private and public spheres. One of the positions that provided high visibility was that of assistant district attorney in the important New York County District Attorney's office, where as head of the rackets bureau he handled some of the most notorious and difficult cases of that time (LaGumina, 1992, 69). In private law practice with some of New York's most capable defense attorneys, Impellitteri enjoyed considerable successes including a case before Kings County Judge William F. O'Dwyer that so impressed the jurist that when the latter ran for mayor in 1945, he enlisted Impellitteri to run for City Council president. Impellitteri's designation to the City Council position was the source of differing interpretations ranging from the Democratic Party's realization that a high profile position as a sop to Italian ethnic demands was extremely important, to a deal supposedly made with a notorious underworld figure, to the implausibility of the selection as the result of an accidental thumbing through the city's Green Book—a reference manual of city officials. The believability of the latter position that was advanced by journalist Warren Moscow (63), an anti-O'Dwyer advocate, renders the account hardly credible.[6]

THE CAMPAIGN

Even though for months there had been advanced rumors that Mayor O'Dwyer would resign his post, it was not officially announced until August 15, and immediately set into motion steps that, according to the City Charter, would be required for a special election for New York City mayor in 1950—assuring a hurried affair of little more than two months. As they geared up for the election the Democratic, Republican, and American Labor parties began to select their tickets. The smallest of the three, the American Labor Party that designated Paul Ross as it candidate, was not much of a factor, thus leaving the real contest to be decided by the three Italian-born candidates. As both major parties prepared for their respective nominating conventions set for September 9, speculation abounded that O'Dwyer favored City Comptroller Lazarus Joseph to succeed him, however, O'Dwyer's departure from the city on September 1 meant he would not control the selection process that now fell into the hands of Carmine DeSapio, the first

---

[6] Moscow was accorded credibility because of his reputation as a reporter whose articles appeared in the *New York Times*; however, he was also politically partisan and actively worked against Impellitteri.

Italian American to become leader of influential Tammany Hall. Taking note that the Republicans seemed about to name Edward Corsi for nomination to a high state office, DeSapio urged an Italian American as a candidate for city mayor, presumably Judge Pecora, should he fail to gain nomination for governor. Infighting between leading elements in New York City's Democratic Party, including an old feud between O'Dwyer and DeSapio, the prestige attached to the Pecora name, and the fact that the jurist already had been considered for a high state office persuaded the Tammany leader to reject Impellitteri for the mayoral nomination in favor of Pecora whom the Democrats nominated officially on September 10, a nomination that also gained Liberal Party endorsement. On the same day, the Republicans officially designated Corsi for mayor while Impellitteri did what he had threatened to do—run as an independent on his newly formed Experience Party line. Not surprisingly, the early prognosis projected a Pecora victory in view of the huge Democratic Party plurality in registration in contrast to Impellitteri, compelled to count on voters searching for his name on the Experience Party line that was near the bottom of the ballot, in addition to the complexity of ticket-splitting that voting for him required. Accordingly, not too much attention was given to the acting mayor in the first few days of the campaign.

But the election prophets were to be mistaken once the campaign began in earnest. The contrast in personalities between Impellitteri and his opponents was evident—he possessed a winning smile and was acknowledged to be a most likeable and friendly figure. By contrast, his Republican opponent Edward Corsi proffered the figure of a deceptively pugnacious looking man whose receding hairline and searching eyes were supported by bulging flesh in the upper cheeks as he sought to convey an image of an upright, no-nonsense campaigner in the LaGuardia tradition. Unfortunately for Corsi, as much as he tried to link himself with the popular late mayor, he was no LaGuardia when it came to politicking—he lacked the theatrics and vibrancy of the "Little Flower" and left the public with the image of a serious, soft-spoken, colorless, and humorless figure. In a word, he lacked the charisma, the intangible chemistry of rapport with the public that was an absolute necessity in populist politics. He also received little more than lip service support from Republican Governor Thomas Dewey who was said to be in collusion with Impellitteri, and that as governor he would do little campaigning for the Republican mayoralty candidate (LaGumina, 1992, 112-113).

At age 68, Pecora the oldest of the three Italian-American candidates, had to contend with the fact that the public saw in him someone from an older generation compared to the youthfulness and vigor of his opponents, especially Impellitteri. A capable and forceful public speaker, who brought an estimable dossier to the contest, Pecora ingenuously sought to counter the generational differences among the candidates by attempting to convert chronological liability into electoral asset, namely that his election to the mayoralty would be the culmination of a career rather than a stepping stone for higher office that would tempt younger office seekers. He labored to present a picture of a vigorous, sprightly, hard-working nominee who demonstrated that he possessed the stamina required as he progressed through a round of activities: reviewing mail, greeting groups of supporters, recording radio speeches, conducting live television appearances, giving speeches throughout the city, etc. Democratic public relations people circulated the story that young reporters assigned to cover Pecora's sixteen hour campaign days were physically unable to keep up with the diminutive jurist who, needing only six hours of sleep, went non-stop, only occasionally stopping to sip from a flask of honey, glycerin, and lemon juice to keep his vocal chords viable (LaGumina, 1992, 114).

It was Pecora's unfortunate fate to bring a mixed record to the contest. Although the bearer of impeccability because of his sterling record of public service on state and national levels, his probity and uprightness in office, and a strong image of integrity, he also had accepted the nomination for mayor through the influence of the tainted Tammany leadership with the result that it quickly used up the reservoir of good will that had been extended to him by virtue of his earlier career. Pecora was vulnerable also in the art of politicking and projecting himself as an ordinary man-in-the-street New Yorker. The sole election experience he possessed was that of running for state judgeship that he had won handily but which entailed a minimum of partisanship. The feisty race for mayor required more than an iteration of New Deal social welfare and pro-labor issues; it necessitated a much more arguable, rough-hewn, brusque, and blunt approach that portrayed a candidate comfortable with rank and file voters. When early polls indicated that he was not making the desired impact, Pecora was faced with costly defections that benefited Impellitteri.

According to many observers, the 1950 mayoral election was one of the dirtiest political campaigns in recent history—a phenomenon that was ironic considering the generally positive reputations the three major candidates enjoyed. Among the disquieting incidents that could be attributed to competing camps were attempts by vandals to intimidate workers at Impellitteri campaign headquarters, insinuations of anti-Semitism, underworld involvement, smearing candidates, etc. "The general approach of the candidates was negative rather than positive, destructive rather than positive, personal rather than ideological or programmatic," concluded one study (Montalto, 84). Major newspaper endorsements were split: Although having good words to say about all the Italian-American candidates, the

New York Times and the *New York Herald Tribune* urged the election of Corsi; the *New York Daily News* supported Impellitteri, while the *New York Post* and *Il Progresso Italo-Americano*'s potentially critical endorsement given its daily circulation of over 200,000, went to Pecora. Firmly ensconced as the Democratic Party bastion, the Italian language paper, in a betrayal of its journalistic responsibility virtually ignored Corsi, while giving only token coverage to Impellitteri as it concentrated on promoting Pecora. This pro-Pecora largesse extended into the Pope family-owned Italian radio stations.

By mid-September it was clear that the regular Democrat Party mayoral candidate did indeed have something to worry about: needing only 7,500 signatures for an independent party run for mayor, Impellitteri presented over 67,000 signatures as an impressive indication of broad support. The aid of Martin Lacey, head of the Central Trades and Labor Council of the city-based United Labor Committee, a unit of the American Federation of Labor and the Congress of Industrial Organizations, for Impellitteri presented another worrisome concern. The decision of the AFL-CIO not to endorse a candidate for mayor was in effect a victory for Impellitteri. Normally backers of Democrat candidates, organized labor split between Pecora and Impellitteri in 1950, while a substantial number of unions gave their backing to Corsi, the Republican.[7] On September 30, a unit of Tammany Hall, headed by Third Assembly District leader Frank J. Sampson, former leader of the Tammany organization, publicly split with DeSapio in order to back Impellitteri. Within the next several days, Harry Brickman, Robert Blaikie, and Morris Schiffino, leaders of Democratic Assembly districts and political clubs formally bolted from Pecora's candidacy in favor of Impellitteri, while former Sheriff Dan Finn of Greenwich Village, who had previously been ousted by DeSapio, rendered the availability of his local Democratic club to function as Impellitteri headquarters.[8]

The 1950 mayoralty race enmeshed leading Italian-American putative power brokers, including underworld figure Frank Costello who was openly active in city politics and *Il Progresso Italo-Americano* publisher Gene Pope, Jr. In disputing an accusation that he had sought nomination to a judgeship as the price of withdrawing from the contest against Pecora, Impellitteri charged that DeSapio and Costello overtly conferred about candidates for high office that led to the selection of Pecora as Democratic mayoralty candidate. "I am not questioning Judge Pecora's character. He has been a member of the bench for many years. But I do say he is nothing more than a respectable front for the lowest, vilest elements this town ever

[7] *New York Times*, October 8, 1950.
[8] *New York Times*, October 11, 1950, October 15, 1950.

saw." Impellitteri identified Gene Pope, Jr. as a frequent visitor to City Hall who admitted that his influential Italian language newspaper would endorse his father's old friend Pecora for mayor especially at Costello insistence. According to Impellitteri, when he asked which candidate he was going to endorse, Gene Pope said, "Costello told me he's going along with Pecora, so I am going along with Pecora too."[9] The first straw vote of a small group of executives augured well for the acting mayor who won 103 to 41 for Pecora and 24 for Corsi.

IMPELLITTERI THE WINNER

In choosing to run for mayor, Impellitteri faced truly momentous odds. Historical precedent illustrated that the last Democratic insurgent mayoral candidate Joseph V. McKee had run a respectable but losing race in 1933, and that in fact no city candidate had won the mayor's office without major party backing. Running as an independent was a daunting task with huge disadvantages: absence of major party endorsement, organization apparatus, manpower and machinery, the lack of sufficient capital to finance a credible campaign, and a mere two months to put together the manifold elements of a successful race for a major office. Nevertheless, Impellitteri had several important assets in his favor beginning with the assemblage of a dedicated campaign team, including the Scotch-Irishman businessman and theatrical entrepreneur William Shirley as campaign manager, Herman Hoffman, chief fund raiser and contact with the Jewish community, and William Donoghue, his executive secretary and expert strategist (LaGumina, 1992, 118). Impellitteri's appointments to major positions while acting mayor also proved to be positive especially choosing as police commissioner former Federal prosecutor Thomas Murphy, who gained fame for his vigorous prosecution in the notorious Alger Hiss case. Not lost on the public was the fact that Murphy's brother was the popular pitcher Johnny "Fireman" Murphy of the New York Yankees. Hardly less popular was Impellitteri's decision to retain the capable and versatile Robert Moses in his multiple administrative roles. Arguably the single most important political weapon in the Impellitteri campaign arsenal was the assertion that he had flatly rejected blatant efforts to try to bribe him with a judgeship, a charge to which he

[9] *New York Times*, October 25, 1950. Gene Pope, Jr.'s tenure as *Il Progresso Italo-Americano* publisher was short-lived due to an intra-family squabble that led to his banishment from the Pope family business. Gene Pope, Jr. resurfaced as the publisher of the newly created tabloid *National Inquirer* that despite its initial financial struggle eventually became a very profitable venture. It received an infusion of funds that allowed it to overcome its early money problems from Frank Costello on the condition that Gene would agree to reconciliation with Impellitteri (Pope, 224).

returned unceasingly and that was readily interpreted as Tammany Hall's effort to buy him off. Attribution of the offer to Tammany Hall boss DeSapio served to further discredit the political machine, while Impellitteri's spurning of the offer struck responsive chords with cynical New Yorkers who had come to believe the worst about political bosses and now had further proof of their unsavory machinations. Impellitteri now ran as the "unbossed and unbought candidate."

Another Impellitteri asset was his success in garnering an array of endorsements from within and without the Democratic Party including former Postmaster James Farley, the previously mentioned Daniel Finn, and Robert Moses. In addition to blessings from professional politicians, Impellitteri had the backing of some popular sports personalities such as Joe Louis, former heavyweight boxing champion whose photograph graced a wall of Impellitteri's bedroom. As a Navy veteran and active past commander of Catholic War Veterans and other veteran groups, Impellitteri had a background that none of his opponents could meet and naturally enjoyed the backing of various organizations of military veterans. In addition, as we have seen, he had considerable assistance from labor organizations. Finally, there was Impellitteri's personality. At five feet nine inches, with brown eyes and black hair that was only beginning to thin out and just slightly graying, he presented the visage of a trim, amiable, slightly olive-skinned man whose ready and winning smile put people at ease. His attractive blond wife, a former model of Irish ancestry was another asset. Thus, he offered a contrast between a friendly, humble man with a sense of humor with the overly austere rectitude of Judge Pecora and the seemingly aloof Corsi. The combination of assets were effective and well expressed in the strong support he received from the *New York Daily News*, at the time the most popular newspaper in the city, that summed up the campaign on the eve of the election commenting, "we think the independent, boss-free, courageous and experienced man is the best fitted of the four men for the job."[10] Nor was this mere boasting as most polls confirmed that Impellitteri "has stolen the show." Election Day tallies confirmed the prognostications as they revealed that Impellitteri had received 1,156,060 votes to Pecora's 937,060 and Corsi's 382, 785 and Ross who was last with 149,182 votes. Impellitteri made history by being the first independent candidate who had not been the designee of a major party to win election as mayor of New York City in the twentieth century. In defiance of the experts, the odds, and history itself, the unpretentious shoemaker's son had been elected to the second most prestigious administrative position in the world's most powerful coun-

---

[10] *New York Daily News*, November 6, 1950.

try without the aid of either major political party. The 1950 special mayoral election was also the pinnacle of Italian-American prominence in New York City—the only time in history when the three major candidates for mayor were Italian born and chosen in large part because of their ethnic background. It would not happen again.

The 1950 election was also a positive account of American democracy, providing an example of a nation where an immigrant could become hugely successful politically. That phenomenon was the message Impellitteri took with him to Italy in behalf of the State Department then in the throes of the Cold War and concerned about the rise of Communism in Europe, especially Italy where it had made serious inroads. As the most prominent Italian-American elected office-holder who was of Italian birth, Impellitteri toured Italy and promoted democracy in a successful effort to thwart Communist Party electoral victory, contrasting the totalitarian Communist appeal with the virtues of democracy. One example was his address to the townspeople in the town of his birth.

> I am the son of a poor shoemaker who left Isnello without two pennies in his pocket, with five sons, and then a girl arrived: here they were all boys and in America a girl. It goes to show that, with democracy, it is possible for these lads who are here now to become mayor of Rome tomorrow, or the head of the Italian state or the mayor of New York like me. That is democracy and freedom. I was baptized here and now I am mayor of the greatest city in the world. Long live Sicily, long live Italy, long live the United States of America (Levi, 50).

WORKS CITED

Ascoli, Max. "My Ninety Days in Washington." *The Reporter Reader*. New York: Doubleday & Co., Inc., 1969.

Federal Writers Project. *The Italians of New York*. New York: Random House, 1938. 109.

LaGumina, Salvatore J. *The Immigrants Speak: Italian Americans Tell Their Story*. New York: Center for Migration Studies, 1979. 54.

Salvatore J. LaGumina, *New York at Mid-Century, The Impellitteri Years*. Westport, CT: Greenwood Press, 1992. 41–42.

LaGumina, "March and Vaccarelli: Turn of-the-Century Political Bosses," *Italian Americans in a Multicultural Society*, Proceedings of American Italian Historical Association, 1994. 200–216.

Salvatore J. LaGumina, "Paul Vaccarelli: The Lightning Change Artist of Organized Labor," *Italian Americana*, 16.1 (Winter 1996): 24–45.

Levi, Carlo. *Words Are Stones Impressions of Sicily*. New York: Farrar, Straus, & Cudahy, 1958. 34.

Edward J. Miranda and Ino Rossi, *New York City's Italians*. New York: Italian American Center for Urban Affairs Inc., 1976.

Montalto, Nicholas V. "The Influence of Ethnicity on the Political Behavior of the New York City Community Since World War II." Thesis Master of Arts, Georgetown University, 1969. 84)

Moscow, Warren. *The Last of the Big-Time Bosses, The Life and Times of Carmine DeSapio and the Fall of Tammany Hall*. New York: Stein and Day.

Perino, Michael. *The Hellhound of Wall Street*. New York: The Penguin Press, 2010.

Pope, Paul David. *The Deeds of My Fathers*. Lanham, MD: Rowman & Littlefield, 2010.

WHEN EAST HARLEM'S POLITICS
WAS AN ITALIAN-AMERICAN MATTER
The Lanzetta-Marcantonio Congressional Races, 1934-1940[1]

Stefano Luconi
UNIVERSITY OF ROME "TOR VERGATA"

INTRODUCTION

As historian Andrew Rolle has pointed out, "Harlem's electorate once sent more [c]ongressmen of Italian origin to Washington than did any other district in the United States" (Rolle 1980, 141). Indeed, from 1923 through 1950, the member of the U.S. House of Representatives from the East Harlem constituency (initially the Twentieth Congressional District, which changed to the Eighteenth after New York State's 1944 reapportionment) was always a politician of Italian ancestry: Fiorello H. LaGuardia (1923-1933), James J. Lanzetta (1933-1934 and 1937-1938), as well as Vito Marcantonio (1935-1936 and 1939-1950). In those years, only four other Italian Americans throughout the United States served in Congress. They also remained in office for shorter periods than LaGuardia and Marcantonio: Louis J. Capozzoli from the nearby Thirteenth District in New York City's Lower East Side (1941-1944), Peter A. Cavicchia from Newark, New Jersey (1931-1936), Thomas D'Alessandro, Jr. from Baltimore, Maryland (1939-1947), and Anthony F. Tauriello from Buffalo, New York (1949-1950). All of these congressmen were preceded on Capitol Hill by as few as two of their fellow ethnics: Francis B. Spinola from New York City (1887-1891) and Anthony J. Caminetti from Jackson, California (1891-1895), besides LaGuardia himself who had also represented the Fourteenth Congressional District from 1917 to 1919 (U.S. Congress 1961, 652, 660, 676, 772, 1184-1185, 1193, 1262, 1561-1162, 1690, 1639).

No other urban district in the United States could have more properly let Italian Americans exert their hold on a Congressional seat than East Harlem (LaGumina 1969, 2). Located on the East Side of Manhattan, in the interwar years this

[1] Research for this essay was made possible in part by a grant from the Roosevelt Study Center, Middelburg, The Netherlands. The following abbreviations are used for frequently cited sources: FHLGP = Fiorello H. LaGuardia Papers, microfilm edition, Roosevelt Study Center; IPIA = Il Progresso Italo-Americano; NYT = New York Times; VMP = Vito Marcantonio Papers, New York Public Library, New York City.

area "happened to have the largest Italian population of any community in America."[2] Newcomers from Polla, in the province of Salerno, began to settle there in 1878. An increasing number of fellow countrymen—primarily from other areas of Campania, Sicily, and Calabria—joined them in the subsequent years and slowly displaced the Irish residents. In 1930, at the peak of the Italian presence, East Harlem was home to about 89,000 first- and second-generation Italian Americans. They made up more than 80 percent of the total population and concentrated primarily in the eastern areas of the district, between Third Avenue and the East River. The heart of this Little Italy was 116th Street (Meyer 1999, 57-58). The western section was inhabited mainly by Puerto Ricans, who were over 10,000 and clustered in the El Barrio neighborhood, and—to a lesser extent—by African Americans and the remnants of a previously sizeable Jewish presence (Venturini 1990, 45-59). Jews had been the second largest ethnic group in East Harlem in the early 1920s, but they had undergone a decline since then as many of them moved principally to the South Bronx under the pressure of the arrival of new residents of color. The local Jewish community numbered about 3,000 residents in 1930 (Gurock 1979; Bayor 1982, 90-93).[3]

Between 1934 and 1940 the beneficiary of the Italian-American virtual monopoly over the East Harlem seat in the U.S. House of Representatives resulted from four election campaigns that consecutively pitted Lanzetta against Marcantonio. Lanzetta, who had beaten LaGuardia in 1932 and was the incumbent when Marcantonio first challenged him in 1934, won only once and suffered defeat three times. This essay examines such races and their context, placing the latter in the long-term perspective of Italian Americans' early stages in their slow accommodation within New York City's politics.

The contests between Lanzetta and Marcantonio in the 1930s were the indirect consequence of Fiorello H. LaGuardia's abrupt political breakthrough into East Harlem's Congressional politics during the previous decade. Indeed, it was LaGuardia's successful bids for the U.S. House of Representatives in the 1920s that paved the way for the transformation of this district into an Italian-American electoral bulwark in the 1930s and 1940s.

---

[2] Charles Fama, untitled speech at the Fifth Convention of the Columbian Republican League, 1931, Anthony Maisano Papers, box 2, folder 2, Balch Institute Collection, Historical Society of Pennsylvania, Philadelphia, PA.
[3] For Jewish and Italian mobility in New York City in the pre-World War I decades, see also Kessner (1977).

PRELUDE TO THE 1930S

As is well known and does not need further elaboration here, the rise of politicians from Italian background underwent a significant delay in the United States even in New York City, although this place was the leading destination of fluxes from Italy in the decades of mass immigration from the late 1870s to the early 1920s and, thereby, home to the largest Italian-American community nationwide (Martellone 1983; Baily 1999, 209–211). In this respect, Spinola was not only a forerunner but quite an exception as well. Indeed, a veteran of the Civil War, he won election to Congress when the Italian-American settlement was too small to deliver a sizeable quantity of votes to him (LaGumina 1986; Pagano 2009).

Although the number of Italian immigrants considerably increased in the subsequent years, their growing presence was to little avail for their fellow ethnic political hopefuls. Italian newcomers revealed a negligible interest in elections at the beginning of their stay in the United States because hardly any of them was accustomed with the meaning of electoral democracy. On the one hand, few had been involved in politics before leaving their native land. The great bulk of the turn-of-the-century immigrants were southern peasants and workers who, due to property requirements, were barred from Italy's electorate until the 1912 enforcement of universal male suffrage in their country of origin. There Italian women were disenfranchised even longer. It was only as late as 1946 that they were allowed to cast their votes (Piretti 1995, 165–182, 327). On the other hand, until the enactment of the U.S. restrictive legislation on immigration in the 1920s, many Italian newcomers had a sojourner mentality. They planned to enjoy in Italy the money they anticipated making in their host country. Indeed, 63.2 percent of the total number of Italian immigrants repatriated in the 1910s and as many as 76,910 went back to their motherland in 1919 alone (Livi Bacci 1961, 35; Cerase 1971, 90). Longing for repatriation with their savings, few applied for naturalization. In turn, lacking U.S. citizenship, most newcomers were not entitled to register for the vote and were unable to cast their ballots (Martellone 1992, 173–174). Italian Americans' failure to master English further interfered with electoral participation since prospective electors found it difficult to comply with the bureaucratic procedures for inclusion in the voter lists and were in part shielded from the stimuli that could have resulted from the thrills of the political debate (Martinelli 1982, 219; Barone 1985, 379). Specifically, the Italian–American turnout did not exceed 4 percent in New York City before World War I (LaGumina 1977, 89). Even the cohorts of the Italian immigrant population who were most committed to politics—the socialists, the anarchists, and other left-wing radicals—usually deserted the polls because most of them contended that elections were a fraud against the working class under the

U.S. bourgeois regime (Martellone 1978, 191-193; Vezzosi 1991, 103-105, 179-180, 183-184, 197). For instance, Italian Americans accounted for as little as 1 percent of New York City's Socialist registered voters in 1915 (Leinenweber 1981, 43, 46).

Italian Americans' condition as latecomers to the United States in terms of succession of immigrant waves from Europe further interfered with the political rise of the leaders of the Little Italies. When Italians began to arrive en masse in their adoptive country, other ethnic groups that had started to land earlier in America controlled the hierarchies of both major parties. In particular, the Irish were well entrenched in the ranks of the Democratic Party at the local level in many metropolises of the East Coast—including New York City—and intended to retain their power in urban politics by marginalizing other minorities such as the Italian Americans (Bugiardini 2006). They resorted to ethnic brokers among saloonkeepers, small businessmen, and officers of ethnic clubs to secure the immigrant vote, but they hardly ever backed their lieutenants when the latter coveted elective offices (Henderson 1976). The very few exceptions included Antonio Zucca, the president of the Italian-American Democratic Association, who was successfully slated for coroner in 1897 (Baily 1999, 210-211; Bugiardini 2001, 586-587, 595-596).

As future Congressman Alfred E. Santangelo recalled of his youth, "Staten Island, where I grew up, was dominated by the Irish. The [c]ongressman, the [s]enator and one of the two [a]ssemblymen were Irish. [...] All the judges were Irish. No judge was of Italian descent. No Italian American was considered for public office, although the Italian Americans constituted about 25 percent of the Staten Island population" (Santangelo 1969, 7). Actually, the Irish hold over Democratic candidacies for elective offices and the consequent ostracism of Italian Americans, except for very few lesser positions of token meaning, in New York City added to LaGuardia's distaste for political corruption. This situation was among the reasons why he chose to align himself with the GOP and became a member of the Madison Republican Club when he decided to get involved into politics in 1906 (LaCerra 1997, 87). Other Italian-American leaders had previously shared his views about how to position themselves for political openings. Most prominent among them was James March (alias Antonio Michelino Maggio), an immigrant from Lucania and a labor contractor for the Erie Railroad, who bolted to the Republican Party out of frustration because of his failure to move upwards through the ranks of the Democratic machine. March was rewarded by the GOP with the election as leader of the Sixth Assembly District in 1894 and the subsequent appointment as warden of the port of New York City (LaGumina 1994, 200-204).

Besides having served as a U.S. consular agent in Budapest as well as Fiume and worked as an interpreter for immigrants landing at Ellis Island, LaGuardia was an admirer of Theodore Roosevelt and a labor lawyer who made a name for himself during the clothing workers' strike of 1912-1913 (Mann 1959, 53; Speroni 1993, 9-16, 54-58, 62-70; Jeffers 2002, 25-44). His own political agenda, therefore, was much more liberal than the platform of the GOP circa World War I. Nonetheless LaGuardia was fully aware that he would have had very few chances of gaining a place on the ballot if he had sought any nomination for the Democratic Party because the latter's organization in New York City, the notorious Tammany Hall, was dominated by Irish politicians (Bayor 1993, 24). The first district leader of Italian extraction in the Democratic machine, Albert Marinelli, was elected in Manhattan's Greenwich Village as late as 1931 (Tricarico 1984, 59). As a result of the Irish command, for instance, Italian Americans held only an aldermanic office out of forty-nine elective positions in Brooklyn in 1920 (Krase 1985, 194).

As a matter of fact, there were not many opportunities within the Republican Party either. LaGuardia's first significant reward came in 1914 when he was slated for Congress. Yet New York County's GOP organization endorsed him for the U.S. House of Representatives in the Fourteenth District only because this constituency in Greenwich Village was regarded as a Democratic stronghold and no other member of the Republican Party was willing to waste his time and money in mounting an allegedly hopeless challenge to the Irish incumbent, Michael Farley (LaGuardia 1948, 103).

Despite his eventual defeat, LaGuardia made an impressive showing, which entitled him to a second bid against Farley on the Republican slate two years later. This time he won and, thereby, the 1914 accidental candidate became a congressman in 1916 (Zinn 1959, 7-10). After re-election in 1918, LaGuardia's popularity as an effective legislator who cared for his constituents' needs induced the GOP to endorse him for president of New York City's Board of Aldermen in 1919. The campaign led to another victory and an emboldened LaGuardia broke with the local Republican establishment to launch a fruitless campaign for the GOP nomination for mayor in 1921 (Kessner 1989, 69-78).

His subsequent debacle at the polls in the primary election could have spelled the end of LaGuardia's political career. Yet the dynamics of maneuverings within the Republican Party offered him a second chance at the federal level in 1922. Populist newspapers mogul and Democratic maverick William Randolph Hearst endeavored to run for the U.S. Senate on a progressive slate and hinted that such a ticket would include LaGuardia as his own running mate for governor of New York State.[4] LaGuardia himself mentioned that he was considering an independent bid for governor in case the GOP had nominated a conservative for the State House and drew a progressive platform of his own to that purpose.[5] In fact, he had no chances of success. But his candidacy was likely to woo liberal voters among the prospective supporters of incumbent Republican Governor Nathan L. Miller, to split the GOP electorate, and to cause the victory of the regular Democratic candidate. Worried about the outcome of the gubernatorial race, the State leadership of the Republican Party made a deal with LaGuardia. If he did not challenge Miller, the GOP organization would support his candidacy for Congress in the Twentieth District, which spread in East Harlem from Fifth Avenue to the East River and from 99th Street to 120th Street. Notwithstanding his proverbial distaste for machine politics, LaGuardia accepted the offer and was returned to the U.S. House of Representatives (Limpus and Leyson 1938, 133).

LaGuardia ran in the Fourteenth Congressional District in 1914, 1916, and 1918 because he was a resident of Greenwich Village. He was also born to an Italian father and a Sephardic mother from Trieste, a port city that was still under Austrian rule at that time (Jeffers 2002, 9–10). His multiethnic background helped him with the Italian and Jewish working-class voters in the eastern section of the constituency, but it was not an issue in LaGuardia's selection. Polyglot LaGuardia did play on his multiple ancestries at least in his successful 1916 campaign "by speaking Yiddish to the Jews and Italian to Italians" (Goldman 1952, 199). On that occasion, he also exploited the nationalistic claims of immigrant voters in the wake of the outbreak of World War I. As he later recalled, "in my talks on the East Side I dismembered the Hapsburg Empire and liberated all the subjugated countries under that dynasty almost every night" (LaGuardia 1948, 124). Talking about the war to the publishers of an influential German-language and Democratic-oriented newspaper, Victor and Bernard Ridder, owners of New York City's *Staats-Zeitung*, he even pointed out that "German Americans have as much a right to be for Germany as the Plymouth Rockers have to be for England" (LaGuardia as quoted in Mann 1959, 68).

Yet ethnic politicking was not in the mind of Republican leaders when they initially accepted LaGuardia's candidacy for Congress. Rather, at the very beginning, his foreign-sounding name was even regarded as a drawback in the 1914

[4] "W. R. Hearst Denies He Is a Candidate," *NYT*, May 24, 1922, 3. For the background of Hearst's aims, see Nasaw (2000, 328-332).
[5] "Seeks Legislature Pledge for Hearst," *NYT*, June 21, 1922, 14.

campaign. "Oh, hell, let's get someone whose name we can spell," a Republican official objected before the County Committee agreed to slate LaGuardia (LaGuardia 1948, 103). After all, not only recent immigrants from Eastern and Southern Europe lived in the Fourteenth Congressional District. The latter's western part around Washington Square was home to affluent people of Anglo-Saxon stock who were suspicious of LaGuardia's liberalism and despised him because of his ethnic origin even after he had become their representative in Washington (Zinn 1959, 11). An anonymous correspondent, drawing upon a notorious anti-Italian stereotype, sent him a picture of an organ grinder and added in handwriting: "go to Italy and follow this occupation. You are more suited to it."[6] Another, after addressing LaGuardia with the ethnic slur "Dear Dago," continued his letter by stating that "observing a few newspaper pictures of yourself with that Mephisto-phelian grin on your map, I think Henry Mencken's observation, about the average [c]ongressman being but a hair's breadth above the criminal in character, is just about right."[7]

Contrary to the motivations for the Fourteenth Congressional District's choice in the mid- and late- 1910s, the preference for the Twentieth Congressional District as LaGuardia's constituency in 1922 involved ethnic considerations. At that time LaGuardia lived in Bronx and, consequently, was an outsider in East Harlem (Mann 1959, 142, 144). Yet the population of this area was predominantly Italian and Jewish (Corsi 1925). The retiring Republican [c]ongressman, Isaac Siegel, was himself a Jew and LaGuardia was regarded as an apt replacement in order to appeal to the Jewish electorate because of his Sephardic mother. At the same time, the candidate's Italianness on his father's side was considered an asset to attract Italian-American voters. Residents of Italian extraction had recently revealed their ethnic consciousness in politics and had made efforts to free themselves from Tammany Hall's control by forcing the Irish leadership to slate Salvatore A. Cotillo for the State Assembly in 1912 and for the State Senate four years later (Ferber 1938, 28-31, 42-43; Henderson 1979, 84-86, 88-89). It could be also suggested that LaGuardia's candidacy was conceived to reconcile Italian Americans and Jews politically under the Republican banner as the latter had previously joined forces with the Irish in keeping the former outside a local Tammany club on 116th Street (Swanberg 1976, 38). Therefore, LaGuardia's presence on the 1922 Republican

---

[6] Anonymous and undated piece of correspondence, *FHLGP*, reel 5, folder "Complaints, n.d."

[7] Roger Carman to Fiorello H. LaGuardia, n.p., n.d., *FHLGP*, reel 5, folder "Complaints, n.d." For "dago" and other anti-Italian epithets, see Tricarico (2000). For anti-Italian prejudice in the United States, see also Deschamps (2000).

slate in New York City was in part an example of an ethnically balanced ticket, namely a case in point for a strategy by which parties included immigrant leaders among their own candidates in order to lure the voters of their respective communities into supporting the whole party slate (Dahl 1961, 34). In New York City, it had been mainly the minority party, i.e. the Republicans, which had resorted to such a strategy since the 1890s in order to challenge the Democratic power by making inroads into immigrant constituencies (Lowi 1964, 41, 46). In this respect, Siegel's previous candidacies had offered a model for such an approach in the Twentieth Congressional District. Actually, the GOP successfully slated him between 1914 and 1920 to break Tammany Hall's fourteen years of control over the East Harlem Congressional seat and to snatch the Hebrew vote from the hands of the Jewish candidates of the Democratic and Socialist Parties (Gurock 1979, 79, 81).

A politician of both Italian and Jewish extraction, LaGuardia seemed the best candidate to manage the transition of East Harlem from a Jewish to an Italian community to the benefit of the Republican Party. After all, as historian Chris McNickle has suggested, "He was a balanced ticket all by himself" (McNickle 1993, 34).

LaGuardia's campaign focused on issues that were of particular interest to the Italian-American electorate, such as the repeal of prohibition and the liberalization of the U.S. restrictive legislation on immigration that had begun to be enforced since the enactment of the 1921 Quota Law.[8] Yet, according to New York City's Italian-language daily *Il Bollettino della Sera*, LaGuardia's ethnic background would be sufficient per se in order to enable the candidate to carry the Italian-American vote: "For the Italians, Major LaGuardia has no need of an expressed program. His name is the entire program" (as quoted in Mann 1959, 153). Even the more authoritative *New York Times* agreed that "Mr. LaGuardia, an Italian, [...] is expected to get the entire Italian vote."[9]

LaGuardia played the ethnic card with the Jewish electorate, too. For instance, he challenged his 1922 opponent, Democratic lawyer Henry Frank, to debate with him in Yiddish. LaGuardia knew that Frank could not speak this language and felt confident that his own linguistic skills would make Jewish voters in East Harlem see him as one of their own (Mann 1959, 156-157). He also took care of the specif-

---

[8] "LaGuardia Opens Congress Campaign," *NYT*, September 6, 1922, 7.
[9] "LaGuardia Placed on Congress Ticket," *NYT*, August 30, 1922, 12.

ic requests of Jewish organizations in his district such as the Hebrew Home for the Aged of Harlem.[10]

Ethnic identification with LaGuardia was particularly effective with Italian Americans. One of his supporters in the 1929 unsuccessful mayoralty race wrote to LaGuardia that New Yorkers had the tendency "to think that you could only get endorsements from Italians."[11] Many Italian Americans did vote for LaGuardia because they took pride in his achievements out of a sort of ethnic redress after a long time of political marginalization. One of LaGuardia's early supporters and aides, Louis Espresso, acknowledged that his own backing resulted from the awareness that "with a man like LaGuardia I was making a stepping-stone for the other Italians in this great city.... I wanted to do something for my forefathers that came to this country, understand, that their sons and daughters[,] etc. would get a better chance in politics because in those days the Italians was a nonentity" (Espresso as quoted in Mann 1959, 52–53). As late as the eve of the 1932 Congressional elections, another Italian American stated that his "main thought" when he cast his ballot for LaGuardia would be "the triumph of the Italian race at the polls."[12] At the end of that year, the editor of the Italian-language weekly *L'America* admitted that he had registered as a Republican voter for the only purpose of supporting his fellow ethnic candidate.[13]

LaGuardia demonstrated his skills as an effective vote getter after breaking again with the Republican Party. In 1924 he endorsed Progressive candidate Robert M. La Follette for the White House, instead of Republican incumbent President Calvin Coolidge. LaGuardia also ran for re-election to the U.S. House of Representatives on the slate of the Progressive Party with the backing of the Socialist Party, too, against both Democratic Frank and former Republican Congressman Siegel (Kessner 1989, 102–105). The Socialist and Progressive Parties established a joint committee to support LaGuardia's campaign.[14] Nevertheless once again LaGuardia paid specific attention to the Italian-American electorate and entrusted a young lawyer by the name of Vito Marcantonio with the task of pursuing

[10] I. Spira, superintendent, Hebrew Home for the Aged of Harlem, to Fiorello H. LaGuardia, New York City, August 24, 1927, *FHLGP*, reel 1, folder "General Corr. 1927, A-Z."

[11] Thomas Bennardo to Fiorello H. LaGuardia, New York City, July 24, 1929, *FHLGP*, reel 1, folder "General Corr. 1929, A-Z."

[12] Vincent Crafa to Fiorello H. LaGuardia, New York City, November 3, 1932, *FHLGP*, reel 3, folder "General Corr. 1932, A-L."

[13] Flavio Pasella to Fiorello H. LaGuardia, New York City, December 2, 1932, *FHLGP*, reel 5, folder "Constituents, Affairs of, 1932, P."

[14] Circular letter by Marie B. MacDonald, campaign manager of the Joint Twentieth Congressional Committee, New York City, October 13, 1924, *FHLGP*, reel 4, folder "Campaign 1924."

and cultivating his fellow ethnics' votes by assisting constituents in East Harlem (Bayor 1993, 77).

Conventional wisdom has it that LaGuardia met Marcantonio when the latter was still a high school student, was fascinated by his oratory skills in a speech advocating social security and old-age pensions, and established a long political relationship with him (Marcantonio 1956, 314-315; Covello 1958, 152-154; Berson 1994, 221). Marcantonio was a labor lawyer as well as a social worker involved in adult education at Haarlem House, a center of cultural activism in East Harlem, where he taught classes in English and other subjects for immigrants who planned to apply for U.S. citizenship. He was also a dynamic member of the neighborhood's Italian-American ethnic association Il Circolo Italiano. Marcantonio was placed in charge of the allocation of LaGuardia's Congressional patronage and laid the foundations of his mentor's personal machine, the Fiorello LaGuardia Political Club, which operated independently from the parties its leader happened to be affiliated with (Cuneo 1955, 155; Zinn 1959, 248; Caro 1974, 353-354; Meyer 1989, 15-17; Abt with Myerson 1993, 91).[15]

The outcome of the 1924 elections offered an early example of the strength of this embryonic organization. Notwithstanding La Follette's defeat both nationwide and in New York State as well as the opposition of the two major parties, LaGuardia retained his seat, gaining 10,756 votes as opposed to Frank's 7,141 and Siegel's 7,099 (Bayor 1993, 63-64).

After his remarkable success, the Republican Party rushed to make amends with LaGuardia and gave him the GOP nomination again in 1926. The desire to slate the incumbent congressman on the ticket was so strong that the initial Republican endorsee, Abraham Cohen, was induced to withdraw his candidacy in order to let LaGuardia replace him.[16] As a Jew, Cohen could appeal to the Jewish electorate only. Conversely, LaGuardia would be able to woo both Italian and Jewish voters. The *New York Times* observed that the county chairperson, Samuel S. Koenig, "was forced to adopt Mr. LaGuardia, not for the latter's sake, but in the hope to increase the Republican vote in the Harlem section of Manhattan," where Jews and especially Italians lived.[17] Receiving 9,121 votes, as opposed to 9,058 for his Democratic challenger and 1,049 for the Socialist candidate, LaGuardia was

---

[15] H.C. Leslie, report for the Federal Bureau of Investigation, New York City, August 4, 1930, FBI file no. 100-28126, "Vito Marcantonio," part 1, New York Public Library, New York City.

[16] "LaGuardia Returns to Republican Fold," NYT, August 25, 1926, 1.

[17] "A Forced Adoption," NYT, August 26, 1926, 18.

the only Republican who managed to defeat Tammany Hall in a Congressional race throughout New York City in 1926 (Zinn 1959, 165; Bayor 1993, 65).

A shrewd politician such as Tom Foley, one of the Irish bosses of Tammany Hall, could not fail to realize that LaGuardia's popularity with his fellow ethnics was siphoning away Italian-American votes from the Democratic Party and that the only viable strategy to counter such a trend was the accommodation of candidates from Italian background on the Democratic ticket. "Show me another LaGuardia," he reportedly exclaimed, "and I'll run him" (Elliott 1983, 108). After LaGuardia's four victories in a row regardless of his party ticket, Tammany Hall enforced this new strategy in 1930 when it eventually decided to slate another Italian American against LaGuardia (Bayor 1993, 67).

The choice of the Democratic leaders was Vincent H. Auleta, a member of the State Assembly. Although the *New York Times* assumed that Auleta was "popular" with his fellow ethnics in East Harlem and the newspaper expected him "to give Major LaGuardia a close race,"[18] the Democratic standard bearer in East Harlem was hardly the replica of LaGuardia that Foley had longed for. One could also suggest that Auleta was unlikely to wage a forceful campaign against the Republican incumbent. Actually, just a few months before receiving the Democratic nomination, Auleta had been a beneficiary of his own opponent's patronage like many other residents of East Harlem, including Marcantonio, who was appointed as assistant United States Attorney for the Southern District of New York in August 1930.[19] In February of the same year, LaGuardia had successfully recommended Auleta's son, August, as a midshipman to the U.S. Naval Academy at Annapolis thanks to his own Congressional privileges.[20]

The most influential Italian-language daily in New York, *Il Progresso Italo-Americano*, did not endorse LaGuardia and stressed his Democratic challenger's accomplishments in Albany (Ariel 1930).[21] The publisher of the newspaper, Generoso Pope, was a self-made man with close connections to Tammany Hall because he relied primarily on contracts with the city administration for his own building

---

[18] "Republicans Map Fight on Sirovich," *NYT*, August 24, 1930, 17.
[19] Charles P. Sisson, assistant attorney general, to Vito Marcantonio, Washington D.C., August 8, 1930, *VMP*, box 4, folder "Prominent People, Ltrs. from."
[20] Fiorello H. LaGuardia to Albert [*sic* for August] Auleta, Washington, D.C., February 20, 1930, *FHLGP*, reel 2, folder "General Correspondence, 1930, A-C."
[21] "I problemi cittadini alla cui soluzione l'On. Auleta portò il suo lavoro," *IPIA*, November 2, 1930, 13.

materials company (Cannistraro 1985). Nevertheless LaGuardia eventually thrashed Auleta by 9,934 votes to 8,217.[22]

ENTER LANZETTA

The year 1930 was a turning point in the history of Italian Americans' political rise in New York City. Since then, both major parties had always nominated a candidate from this minority group in the Congressional district that included East Harlem for a decade. Despite Auleta's defeat, the Democratic Party stuck to its ethnic strategy of nominating a candidate who belonged to the largest ethnic group living in that constituency. LaGuardia himself sought to secure the Democratic nomination for Congress in 1932. After roughly three years of hard times following the collapse of the stock market in late October 1929, most people held Republican President Herbert Hoover responsible for the longstanding economic depression and LaGuardia feared that his own GOP label—albeit nominal—would prove to be a major drawback at the polls. New York City's Democratic mayor, James J. Walker, whom LaGuardia had vainly challenged in the 1929 race for City Hall, was on trial in the aftermath of a corruption scandal that had involved the municipal administration (Mann 1965, 38-62; Fowler 1973, 159-328; Walsh 1974; Mitgang 2000).[23] Therefore, placing a progressive such as LaGuardia on its ticket was likely to be beneficial to the reputation of the Democratic Party in the eyes of independent voters who did not depend on the patronage of Tammany Hall. Moreover, his re-election to Washington would keep LaGuardia out of local politics in case Walker was forced to resign, which he did on September 1. New York City's Democratic officials such as John McCooney and national leaders like Senator Robert F. Wagner had no objections to LaGuardia's nomination for Congress. But the boss of Tammany Hall, Jimmy Hines, refused to endorse LaGuardia (Cuneo 1955, 147-149). As a result, after Auleta in 1930, the 1932 Italian-American candidate of the Democratic Party in the Twentieth Congressional District was James J. Lanzetta, a young second-generation lawyer who also held a degree in engineering from Columbia University and served on New York City's Board of Aldermen as East Harlem's representative.[24]

The outcome of the 1932 campaign was a reversal of the 1930 elections. Lanzetta defeated LaGuardia by 16,447 votes to 15,227, while Socialist Frank Poree

---

[22] "Record Plurality for Governor Here," *NYT*, November 5, 1930, 3.
[23] For Judge Samuel Seabury, the mastermind of the investigation against Walker, see Mitgang (1963).
[24] "Farley Aide Slated to Run for Sheriff," *NYT*, August 19, 1932, 7.

lagged a distant third with as few as 464 (Board of Elections of the City of New York 1932, 110). It could be easily suggested that, against the backdrop of Franklin D. Roosevelt's landslide, Lanzetta carried the Twentieth Congressional District on the Democratic presidential candidate's coattails (Cuneo 1955, 106; Rodgers and Rankin 1948, 118). Since the number of ballots cast in the Twentieth Congressional District increased by about 77 percent between 1930 and 1932, Roosevelt definitely mobilized a significant number of new electors, most of whom were likely to vote a straight Democratic ticket. Yet the Republican debacle in the presidential contest per se does not account for LaGuardia's defeat.

The fact that Roosevelt received over 20,000 votes in the Twentieth Congressional District means that LaGuardia managed to make inroads into the presidential candidate's plurality because of his own progressive record in the U.S. House of Representatives—where several of his bills and proposals foreran the New Deal legislation—and criticism of the Hoover administration succeeded in part in distancing him from the discredit that affected the GOP nationwide (Zinn 1959, 175-230). In addition, LaGuardia's stand reflected many concerns of the Italian-American electorate. For instance, besides coming out once more against Prohibition, he reprimanded the Republican Party because of insufficient consideration toward Italian Americans in political appointments.[25] LaGuardia's platform and his legislative record were well known in East Harlem. The congressman had made a point of having a circular semi-annual newsletter distributed to each family living in East Harlem since his first term as the U.S. Representative from the Twentieth District in 1923.[26] He also reported his activities to his constituents on a yearly basis at a rally that was usually held in September.[27]

Listing the possible explanations for the 1932 election results in the Twentieth District, historian Ronald H. Bayor has stressed that the incumbent congressman failed to realize the changing demography of East Harlem, where Jews were leaving and Hispanics were replacing them, while "Lanzetta and Tammany [...] were ahead of LaGuardia in establishing contacts with Puerto Ricans migrating into the neighborhood" (Bayor 1993, 79). After becoming a congressman, Marcantonio definitely established a stricter relationship with East Harlemites from Puerto Rico

---

[25] "Representative F.H. LaGuardia Asks Secretary of State Stimson to Declare His Stand on Prohibition," press release, March 1, 1932, *FHLGP*, reel 3, folder "General Correspondence, 1932, S;" Anthony F. Minisi to Fiorello H. LaGuardia, Newark, N.J., March 18, 1932, ibid., reel 2, folder "General Correspondence, 1932, M-P."
[26] *FHLGP*, reel 4, folder "District Letters, 1923-1928."
[27] Fiorello H. LaGuardia to Circolo Corleone, Washington, D.C., September 16, 1932, *FHLGP*, reel 4, folder "Congressional District, Report to."

than his predecessor had done (Ojeda 1978; Vega 1984, 183-190). Yet LaGuardia did not overlook them either. He was an advocate of self-government for Puerto Rico and introduced a bill providing for the popular election of the governor of this territory as early as 1928 (Zinn 1959, 117-118). His stand was immediately commended by the Porto Rican Brotherhood of America and produced further political dividends in the subsequent elections.[28] It is sufficient to quote from a letter that a Puerto Rican constituent wrote to LaGuardia after the 1928 Congressional race: "Had I known earlier of your campaign for 'freedom' perhaps I would have gladly accomplished a little bit more than I did on your behalf. Nevertheless there will be another election. And by that time I will be unfettered [...] to devote unsparingly all my time and energy to your campaign for re-election."[29]

As had already happened two years earlier, in 1932—following Pope's appointment as the chairperson of the Italian Democratic Executive Committee of Greater New York—*Il Progresso Italo-Americano* failed again to endorse LaGuardia and published articles backing Lanzetta (Pope 1932).[30] In a critical letter to Pope, Vincenzo Crafa argued that it was necessary to re-elect LaGuardia to Congress for the sake of Italian-American prestige.[31] Yet ethnic pride was not enough to secure LaGuardia the vote of the residents of East Harlem's Little Italy. After all, to the members of that community, one of the assets resulting from the Italian-American political rise was the opportunity to access a larger share of political patronage. These positions became pivotal during the economic crisis, when LaGuardia's constituents needed primarily jobs (Bayor 1978, 17-19). For instance, Anthony A. Valenti wrote to LaGuardia and asked him for "a recommendation towards getting me employed as an 'extra' at any Post Office for the coming Christmas holiday rush." In return, he promised that "I am favoring you with my vote."[32]

Scholars such as Thomas Kessner and Ronald Bayor have suggested that in 1932 LaGuardia was perceived as an absentee U.S. Representative who neglected his district in East Harlem to play—as the former has put it—"the statesman in

---

[28] Antonio Gonzales to Fiorello H. LaGuardia, New York City, March 20, 1928, *FHLGP*, reel 12, folder "Puerto Rico Governor's Bill."
[29] George M. Lago to Fiorello H. LaGuardia, New York City, November 18, 1932, *FHLGP*, reel 11, folder "Puerto Rico."
[30] For an example of Pope's editorial policy in support of Lanzetta, see "Il 20.o Distretto di Congresso eleggerà James J. Lanzetta," *IPIA*, October 20, 1932, 3. For Pope's stand in the 1932 Congressional race, see also Cannistraro (1985, 281-282).
[31] Vincenzo Crafa to Generoso Pope, New York City, n.d. [but 1932], *FHLGP*, reel 3, folder "General Correspondence, 1932, A-L."
[32] Anthony A. Valenti to Fiorello H. LaGuardia, New York City, October 18, 1932, *FHLGP*, reel 3, folder "General Correspondence, 1932, A-L."

Washington" (Kessner 1989, 194-195; Bayor 1993, 79). This contention was also one of the leitmotifs of Lanzetta's campaign since the Democratic candidate referred to his opponent as "the world's and not Harlem's [c]ongressman."[33] Indeed, in a letter to another constituent by the name of Giovanni Panza, who had asked for his free legal counseling, LaGuardia seemed to project himself beyond his district to the national level and stated that "my place is right in the House of Representatives in Washington representing the interests and welfare of the people who elect me. My official duties are such that I have been compelled to give up the practice of law. I devote all my time and energy to my legislative duties."[34]

Kessner himself has drawn upon these specific words to support his own argument (Kessner 1989, 194-195). Actually, LaGuardia's letter was in response to Panza's warning that he and five relatives would not cast their ballots for their incumbent congressman in 1932.[35] Yet LaGuardia's reference to "the interest and welfare of the people who elect me" meant that his presence on Capitol Hill was intended to be beneficial to his very constituents in East Harlem. After all, during the 1932 campaign, his machine was in full gear in the attempt at bringing out the vote of his district (Cuneo 1955, 153-177). However, in that year, LaGuardia could rely on fewer plums than he had used in previous election campaigns. For instance, he had to reply to Valenti that he was unable to help him because the postal service "will take only those who are on the Civil Service list."[36]

In 1930 employment with the federal government as enumerators for the decennial census of the United States offered LaGuardia a major source of patronage to get jobs for his constituents who had been dismissed in the aftermath of the economic crisis. People such as Leonard Vitti asked their congressman the endorsement for such positions stressing that "I voted for you every time you were a candidate."[37] Indeed, electoral allegiance was the main criterion by which LaGuardia decided whether or not to back such applicants. In the case of Vitti, the fact that he had been "very active during the recent campaign" was the only qualifica-

---

[33] "LaGuardia's Throne Is Shaky," unidentified and undated newspaper clipping, *FHLGP*, reel 5, folder "Complaints, n. d."

[34] Fiorello H. LaGuardia to Giovanni Panza, Washington, D.C., September 24, 1932, *FHLGP*, reel 2, "General Correspondence, 1932, M-P."

[35] Giovanni Panza to Fiorello H. LaGuardia, New York City, September 23, 1932, *FHLGP*, reel 2, "General Correspondence, 1932, M-P."

[36] Fiorello H. LaGuardia to Anthony A. Valenti, Washington, D.C., October 19, 1932, *FHLGP*, reel 3, folder "General Correspondence, 1932, A-L."

[37] Leonard Vitti to Fiorello H. LaGuardia, New York City, January 3, 1930, *FHLGP*, reel 4, folder "Census, Bureau of."

tion that LaGuardia cared to mention while recommending him for the appointment with the Bureau of the Census.[38]

The hiring was channeled through LaGuardia's fellow ethnic and partisan associate, Edward Corsi, who was the supervisor in New York City's Twenty-Third Census District (Department of Commerce 1930, unpaginated). LaGuardia was very specific about the procedure for the distribution of positions. He wrote to Corsi: "Lest there may be any misunderstanding later on, I want to repeat the arrangement for the appointment of enumerators. [...] I have three election districts within the Assembly districts. As to the 19th, 15th, 16th and 17th, you will consult with me first and I will take then the matter up with you through the [c]ounty [c]hairman. Now, for all the territory which goes beyond my Congressional district in any of the Assembly districts, you will confer with me on all the appointments in all of these districts."[39] So unrelenting was LaGuardia in his requests of employment for stalwart voters and political cronies that Corsi resented such pressures because, as he tried to explain to the congressman, "my only concern is to do a good job and to get the best men available."[40] But LaGuardia, whose political survival was at stake, insisted that "I expect you to give preference to residents of my district as every other member of Congress is doing. Hope we have no difference on this point."[41] Corsi, who had been the director of Haarlem House and was himself a Republican political appointee (Corsi 1935, 28-29; Marazzi 2006, 271-272), eventually yielded and quickly learned to apply the rules of ethnic balancing to the hiring of his own staff. After LaGuardia had recommended two additional Italian Americans, in order not to antagonize other sizeable ethnic groups in the constituency Corsi took the liberty to wire: "Amoroso and Cioffi OK. Send names of one Portorican [sic], one Jewish clerk preferably."[42]

All these beneficiaries rewarded their mentor at the polls. As one of them remarked in matter-of-fact language that LaGuardia could not fail to appreciate, "I am indeed grateful and hope to show my appreciation at the polls instead of

---

[38] Fiorello H. LaGuardia to Charles Largy, Washington, D.C., January 8, 1930, *FHLGP*, reel 4, folder "Census, Bureau of."

[39] Fiorello H. LaGuardia to Edward Corsi, Washington, D.C., January 23, 1930, *FHLGP*, reel 4, folder "Census, Bureau of."

[40] Edward Corsi to Fiorello H. LaGuardia, New York City, February 5, 1930, *FHLGP*, reel 4, folder "Census, Bureau of."

[41] Fiorello H. LaGuardia to Edward Corsi, Washington, D.C., March 18, 1930, *FHLGP*, reel 4, folder "Census, Bureau of."

[42] Edward Corsi to Fiorello H. LaGuardia, New York City, March 27, 1930, *FHLGP*, reel 4, folder "Census, Bureau of."

through a lengthy letter which might not mean anything anyway."[43] Nonetheless this largesse was no longer available to LaGuardia two years later. The census had already been completed and, with the city administration still in the hands of Tammany Hall, LaGuardia found himself with a significantly reduced patronage in 1932. To him it was hard even to find a job for Dominick Russillo, a cousin of his own aide Marcantonio.[44] The number of his plums had shrunk to such an extent that, in the early summer of 1932, while his eyes were still set on the Democratic nomination, LaGuardia ironically did not refrain from advising one of his postulants to report to the person who would become his opponent a few weeks later. As he wrote to a Francesco Renta, "I would be very glad to give you a letter to the Hon[orable] John J. Delaney for work in the Eighth Avenue Subway, but regrettably this is a City matter and one over which I have no jurisdiction. I would suggest the [sic] you call on Alderman James J. Lanzetta, who I am sure will be glad to help you."[45]

Thanks to Tammany Hall's hold over the city patronage, Lanzetta did help and, therefore, could reap his political crops on Election Day. He also profited from his service on the Gibson Unemployment Relief Committee, a charity agency that operated until early 1932 with funds of $31,000,000 (Brock 1988, 91).[46] But it was the Democratic distribution of jobs and assistance among the destitute which eventually enabled Lanzetta to defeat LaGuardia. In particular, the Tammany Hall machine was instrumental in delivering the Puerto Rican areas to Lanzetta. For instance, in the Eighteenth Assembly District, the heart of El Barrio, voters were threatened with the loss of municipal relief unless they voted for the whole Democratic ticket (Mann 1959, 319). LaGuardia claimed that his prospective supporters had been intimidated and coerced into casting their ballots for Lanzetta. On this ground, he endeavored to make the U.S. House of Representatives refuse to seat Lanzetta, but his efforts were to no avail in a Congress in which the Democrats were the majority party and most of them had cheerfully resorted to heavy-handed methods and traditional machine-style instruments in order to get elected.[47]

---

[43] Herman Sirota to Fiorello H. LaGuardia, New York City, February 14, 1930, *FHLGP*, reel 4, folder "Census, Bureau of."

[44] Fiorello H. LaGuardia to Vito Marcantonio, Washington, D.C., June 19, 1932, *FHLGP*, reel 3, folder "General Correspondence, 1932, A-L."

[45] Fiorello H. LaGuardia to Francesco Renta, Washington, D.C., n.d. [but June 1932], *FHLGP*, reel 3, "General Correspondence, 1932, Q-R."

[46] "LaGuardia's Throne Is Shaky," unidentified and undated newspaper clipping, *FHLGP*, reel 5, folder "Complaints, n. d."

[47] "LaGuardia to Fight Election of Rival," *NYT*, January 10, 1933, 1; "Few Errors Found in LaGuardia Vote," *NYT*, January 11, 1933, 15.

New York City and East Harlem were no exception. Unlike LaGuardia, Tammany Hall still enjoyed plenty of plums. Governor Roosevelt had negotiated a truce with New York City's Democratic officials by which the latter retained command of most State appointments in their hometown. Furthermore, notwithstanding a significant increase in the budget deficit, the city administration refrained from dismissing its political cronies even during the Depression (Bellush 1952, 281). As Robert A. Caro has argued, "the city payroll had become the payroll of the Tammany political machine, and while a city might reduce the numbers of its employees or their salaries, it was less easy for a political machine to throw its retainers off the payroll or substantially reduce their stipends" (Caro 1974, 326–327).

Actually, the Democratic plums continued to influence how New Yorkers cast their ballots for at least another year. The 1933 mayoral race to replace Walker at City Hall offered a case in point. That year LaGuardia was elected mayor on a GOP-City Fusion ticket, a combination of anti-Tammany Democrats and progressive Republicans. Still, the surviving control of Tammany Hall over the municipal patronage enabled LaGuardia's Democratic opponent, John Patrick O'Brian, to carry those working-class districts where the unemployment rate was high, with the only exception of the Italian-American neighborhoods (Mann 1959, 154–155).

CHANGE OF THE GUARD IN WASHINGTON

LaGuardia's election to City Hall ruled out a rematch with Lanzetta in 1934. Yet the new mayor made a point of designating his own heir as the Republican candidate in the Twentieth Congressional District. As Italian Americans continued to be the largest cohort of voters in East Harlem and to complain that they were "not represented politically in proportion to their numerical and moral strength" (Bacigalupi 1933, 216), there was no objection to slate another member of their community on the GOP ticket against Lanzetta. Marcantonio had brought out the Italian-American vote for LaGuardia in the 1933 race, showing his skills as an effective campaigner and deserving a significant political reward. As a result, not only did LaGuardia maneuver into securing Marcantonio the nomination for the U.S. House of Representatives of both the Republican and City Fusion Parties along with the support of minor progressive forces such as the Knickerbocker Democrats and the Liberal Party (Rubinstein 1956, 2; Schaffer 1966, 24), he also publicly endorsed Marcantonio's candidacy a few days before the elections. As he stated, "I have confidence in you and that you will join with the progressive forces of the House for good government and progressive social welfare laws. I know that you will support the President in his efforts to bring about proper economic readjustment."[48] Indeed, Marcantonio had previously outlined a detailed electoral program that was also likely to appeal to ethnic minorities in East Harlem. His platform included support for the New Deal labor and social legislation, the introduction of unemployment insurance, the increase in expenses for public works, and the exemption from duties on all imports from Puerto Rico.[49]

While singing Marcantonio's praises, LaGuardia's words referred implicitly to Lanzetta's ambiguous political stand. Scholars agree that Lanzetta was not an impressive congressman. As a Democrat, he was supposed to back President Roosevelt's New Deal, but in fact he voted against some of its provisions, including the Economy Act of 1933. He was absent from Congress at the time of the vote on other measures. His major legislative achievement was an amendment to the Federal Home Loan Bill that protected the interests of tenement landlords because the measure allowed them to borrow money from the federal government in order to repair their properties. On the floor of U.S. House of Representatives Lanzetta even pitied homeowners who had not evicted their tenants despite the latter's failure to pay their rent (Schaffer 1966, 23; Meyer 1989, 23).

Yet it seemed that reality hardly matched Lanzetta's rosy depiction of the landlord-tenant relationship. During the Depression, evictions were quite frequent and the consequent resentment toward the proprietors was widespread in East Harlem (Orsi 1985, 43). In addition, housing conditions continued to be poor. One dweller out of two did not have a private toilet, almost seven out ten were without a tub or a shower, and more than eight out of ten lacked central heating. Furthermore, most buildings had been built prior to the enforcement of the 1901 Tenement Act that had imposed some security standards (Meyer 1999, 58). Therefore, in such a working-class district as East Harlem, where most voters were slum tenants, Lanzetta seemed to be on the wrong side of the social and political divide notwithstanding his attempts at justifying his Congressional record.[50]

Actually, numerous labor unions endorsed Marcantonio. Most prominent among them were the Amalgamated Clothing Workers of America (ACWA) and the International Ladies' Garment Workers' Union (ILGWU).[51] The latter was particularly influential in East Harlem, where its membership had undergone a remarkable increase since the enactment of the New Deal labor legislation after a

---

[48] "Support of Roosevelt Asked by LaGuardia in Endorsing Republican in His Old District," NYT, October 30, 1934, 1; "LaGuardia voterà per Marcantonio," IPIA, October 31, 1934, 2.

[49] "Vito Marcantonio ed il 'New Deal,'" IPIA, October 26, 1934, 2.

[50] "Lanzetta illustra i suoi precedenti," IPIA, November 2, 1934, 2.

[51] "Le Unioni dei sarti per la candidatura di Marcantonio," IPIA, October 18, 1934, 8.

decline in the wake of the Depression (Montana 1975, 141-143). In 1935, Italian Dress and Waistmakers' Union Local 89 and Italian Cloak, Suit, and Skirt Makers' Union Local 48 had respectively 8,191 and 37,998 members, most of whom worked in New York City's garment industry and resided in East Harlem (Corbella 1972, 375; Berkowitz 1987, 74; Guglielmo 2010). Specifically, Luigi Antonini—the head of Local 89, the first vice president of the International Ladies' Garment Workers' Union as well as the leader of New York City's United Labor Committee—came out for Marcantonio in his "Voice of Local 89," a weekly radio program that he started on the airwaves of stations WEVD and WHOM in 1934 and conceived as the Italian-language version of President Roosevelt's fireside chats for Italian-American workers (Tintori 2005, 202-203). Antonini called Marcantonio "a disciple and continuator of LaGuardia" as well as "a proven friend of the labor movement," repeatedly urging Italian-American voters to cast their ballots for him.[52] Other union leaders such as Joseph Salerno of the Amalgamated Clothing Workers of America joined Antonini in endorsing Marcantonio.[53]

Yet Marcantonio did not enjoy the monopoly of labor support. The Democratic incumbent secured the backing of William Green, the president of the conservative American Federation of Labor, a move that Antonini criticized on the ground that Marcantonio was much closer to the unions and workers than his opponent.[54] Lanzetta was also quite skillful at playing on ethnic politics. To the benefit of Italian Americans and other ethnic minorities, he introduced a bill that would have allowed the naturalization of those immigrants who had arrived in the United States before February 6, 1917 even if they failed to meet the literacy requirements that were necessary for the acquisition of American citizenship pursuant to the provisions of the 1906 Basic Naturalization Act.[55] Congress tabled the bill, which offered Lanzetta a further opportunity to call for a liberal reform of naturalization procedures and to show off his empathy toward immigrants.[56] Moreover, Lanzetta

---

[52] "Ieri i messaggi della Locale 89, Ilgwu," *La Stampa Libera*, October 14, 1934, 2; "Il messaggio settimanale della Locale 89," *IPIA*, October 21, 1934, 2; "Un appello di L. Antonini per l'avv. V. Marcantonio," *IPIA*, October 30, 1934, 2; "Un discorso elettorale di Antonini," *IPIA*, November 2, 1934, 13; "Nel campo del lavoro," *IPIA*, November 4, 1934, 2; "Antonini per Marcantonio," *IPIA*, November 5, 1934, p. 2.

[53] "Il comitato delle Unioni Operaie per la candidatura di Marcantonio," *La Stampa Libera*, November 4, 1934, 2.

[54] "W. Green appoggia l'On. J.J. Lanzetta," *IPIA*, October 26, 1934, 2; "Un telegramma di Antonini a Green per l'elezione dell'avv. Marcantonio," *La Stampa Libera*, October 27, 1934, 2.

[55] "Why Congressman James J. Lanzetta Should Be Reelected," *Il Grido della Stirpe*, October 27, 1934, 10; "Lanzetta acclamato a diversi comizi," *IPIA*, November 4, 1934, 11.

[56] "L'On. Lanzetta denuncia l'opposizione dell'House alla riforma immigratoria," *IPIA*, October 31, 1934, 3.

championed the cause of Puerto Rico. In particular, he introduced an amendment to the Agricultural Adjustment Bill to the effect that discriminatory restrictions on raw and refined sugar imported from the Caribbean island would be repealed (Schaffer 1966, 23). Such a stand won Lanzetta the support of Senator Antonio Barcelo of Puerto Rico, who made his way to East Harlem's El Barrio in October 1934 to offer his own backing of the Democratic congressman's re-election bid at a rally of roughly 2,000 voters held under the auspices of the Puerto Rican Political Association of East Harlem.[57]

When the ballots were counted, it turned out that, forging an ethnic coalition of Italian-American and Puerto Rican voters with the support of the dwindling Jewish electorate, Marcantonio had defeated Lanzetta by 13,083 votes to 12,483. Since Marcantonio received 12,428 ballots as the Republican candidate, what made the difference and sent him to Washington were the 655 votes he obtained on the City Fusion ticket on which LaGuardia had been instrumental in placing his protégé's name (Meyer 1989, 24, 45).

The mayor's contribution to the results of the Congressional contest went far beyond his formal endorsement of Marcantonio's candidacy. Most effective for Lanzetta's defeat was the fact that LaGuardia placed his own machine behind Marcantonio's bid for the U.S. House of Representatives. In this respect, the 1934 campaign was a reverse of the 1932 contest against the backdrop of the worsening economic conditions of East Harlem's voters. Actually, the district had witnessed the return of a number of individuals who had moved to prosperous areas of New York City by the late roaring 1920s but could no longer afford to remain there during the Depression (Orsi 1985, 42). With LaGuardia at City Hall, it was now Tammany Hall's turn at being short of patronage (Barry 2009, 89). Marcantonio contended that Lanzetta intimidated postal workers in the final days of the campaign.[58] The accusation might even sound plausible since his Democratic opponent had the formal backing of Postmaster General James A. Farley, who was President Roosevelt's "patronage czar" in New York State (Krase and LaCerra 1991, 52).[59] Conversely, Marcantonio's charge that Lanzetta also threatened the recipients of city relief with discharge from the welfare rolls unless they voted for him was just a campaign stunt that failed to account for the change of the administra-

---

[57] "Arrives to Aid Lanzetta," NYT, October 16, 1934, 12.
[58] "L'On. Marcantonio è pel Presidente," IPIA, November 1, 1934, 2.
[59] "Lanzetta elogiato da James A. Farley," IPIA, November 3, 1934, 2.

tion.[60] Contrary to 1932, in 1934 the new mayor, LaGuardia, was perhaps Marcantonio's most outstanding and influential supporter.

Indeed, Lanzetta's federal plums were no match for LaGuardia's machine. Specifically, New York City's welfare commissioner, William Hodson, and the director of the Home Relief Bureau, Edward Corsi, allegedly mobilized their resources to seek votes for Marcantonio within East Harlem's sizeable cohort of the unemployed.[61] Lack of jobs affected specifically Italian Americans. According to historian Selma Berrol, "in 1934 about 50 percent of workers on relief were from trades in which Italians had formerly been employed" (Berrol 1997, 117).

Corsi's agency undeniably was key to the survival of numerous residents of East Harlem during the Depression. Helen Harris, a social worker, stated that "without the Home Relief Bureau, people would have starved" (as quoted in Orsi 1985, 43). However, the level of politicking in the operation of this agency is controversial. Progressive newspapers such as the Socialist-oriented *La Stampa Libera* argued that these charges were an attempt by Lanzetta to discredit his challenger (Astrologo 1934). One of Marcantonio's biographers, Alan Schaffer, has similarly contended that such accusations were little more than innuendos (Schaffer 1966, 26). Nevertheless, Kessner's study of the LaGuardia administration has concluded that, under Hodson, the relief programs "were simply not run well, or honestly" (Kessner 1989, 382). After all, even some readers of *La Stampa Libera* stated that rewarding voters who had contributed to the defeat of the Democratic "corrupt organization" was "not a crime" and Corsi had already allowed political pressures to interfere with his own work when he had been the Census supervisor in New York City's Twenty-Third District four years earlier (De Caro 1934). Furthermore, although Marcantonio denied that political considerations affected the distribution of welfare, he admitted that personal services to Italian-American and Puerto Rican voters were key to the success of his campaign for Congress: "It is true that people came to us at our political club with relief problems, and we did help them when we could, showing them how they could get relief."[62]

Indeed, besides committing himself to the New Deal, Marcantonio based his election strategy on Lanzetta's supposed failure to deliver services to his constituents. He dubbed the incumbent Congressman "Jimmy Next Week," claiming that

[60] "Una imponente dimostrazione delle associazioni ed unioni per l'Avv. Marcantonio," *IPIA*, November 4, 1934, 11.
[61] "Hodson Is Accused of Relief Politics," *NYT*, August 31, 1934, 1-2; James J. Lanzetta to Fiorello H. LaGuardia, Washington, D.C., October 8, 1934, *FHLGP*, reel 17, folder "L;" "Relief Politics Charged," *NYT*, October 10, 1934, 3.
[62] "Lanzetta Fights for House Seat," *NYT*, January 3, 1935, 16.

his Democratic opponent routinely answered "I'll take care of it next week" to people asking for his help and eventually did nothing for them. Consequently, LaGuardia urged voters to "fill the empty" seat in the U.S. House of Representatives (Meyer 1989, 23, 100–1).[63] *La Stampa Libera* still called Lanzetta the *Onorevole Scaldapanca* (Honorable Benchwarmer) as late as 1935, when the latter was no longer in Congress.[64] As for Italian-American voters in the Twentieth Congressional District, Local 89 also controlled jobs in the garment industry and, thereby, could exploit such positions to consolidate the allegiance of part of the working-class electorate of Italian background to Marcantonio (Tintori 2005, 177). Furthermore, according to Angelo Paliotto, Lanzetta's campaign manager, threatening dismissal, Antonini supposedly coerced the members of his union into contributing to Marcantonio's campaign chest (LaGumina 1972, 376). One, therefore, can reasonably conclude that patronage, more than the political stands and platforms of the candidates, shaped the outcome of the 1934 Congressional race.

LANZETTA REBOUNDS

Lanzetta's 1934 defeat on the Democratic ticket in the only twentieth-century mid-term elections before 1998 that witnessed a gain in seats by the incumbent [p]resident's party was rather anti-climatic (Busch 1999). Conversely, his 1936 re-election on the occasion of Roosevelt's landslide reflected the general trend of the nation. Schaffer has argued that "it was undoubtedly Roosevelt, not Lanzetta, to whom Marcantonio lost in 1936" (Schaffer 1966, 55). This argument has its merits. Italian Americans, who continued to be the largest ethnic group in East Harlem, were also the main recipients of employment with the Works Progress Administration in New York City. About one in five was engaged in federal projects. Jews came next with 12 percent (Wenger 1996, 17). The political gratitude of these two minorities to Roosevelt and the Democratic Party, therefore, was quite obvious. Actually, the [p]resident received 78.7 percent of the Italian-American vote and 87.5 percent of the Jewish vote in New York City in 1936 (Bayor 1978, 147). Roosevelt's large political following benefited the other Democratic candidates as well. For instance, Cesare Rizzo argued that, when Italian-American candidates ran against one another, he felt free to cast a straight ballot for the party that was closer to his needs (Rizzo 1936). Similarly, Carmelo Pantò and Onorio Giunta declared

---

[63] "Vito Marcantonio ed il 'New Deal,'" *IPIA*, October 26, 1934, 2; Vito Marcantonio, "My Answer to a Very Filthy and False Attack Made on Me by Luigi Antonini, Emperor Tripe Tyrant of New York Dressmakers and Labor Racketeer," n.d. [but 1940], 5, *VMP*, box 1, folder "Anonymous Letters."
[64] "L'avv. J. Lanzetta perde la testa in corte," *La Stampa Libera*, April 5, 1935, 1.

that they were "proud to support President Franklin D. Roosevelt and the man who will certainly help the development of the New Deal, the Hon[orable] James J. Lanzetta" (Pantò and Giunta 1936).

Nevertheless, as had already happened in 1932, Roosevelt's coattails only partly explain Lanzetta's victory four years later. Some cracks among Marcantonio's 1934 backers also contributed to the outcome of the 1936 race for the U.S. House of Representatives.

In two years the support of labor unions for Marcantonio underwent a decline. In particular, the leadership of the International Ladies' Garment Workers' Union turned its back on him. On the one hand, Marcantonio's stand in Congress was so radical that, contrary to his previous campaign pledge, he refused to play the New Deal legislator. For instance, he abstained on some public works provisions because they stipulated for a threshold on salaries that, in his opinion, was too low to ensure workers' decent living standards. Likewise, Marcantonio backed the Communist-sponsored Frazier-Lundeen Bill that provided for a much broader system of unemployment, sickness, old-age, maternal, and industrial accident insurance than the 1935 Social Security Act that President Roosevelt considered the "cornerstone of his administration," as his own Labor secretary Frances Perkins put it (Perkins 1946, 301; Schaffer 1966, 32-34).[65] To Congresswoman Caroline O'Day, such a shaky record on the administration's bills was enough to make her withdraw her backing of Marcantonio and endorse Lanzetta as "a loyal Democrat and a staunch supporter of President Franklin D. Roosevelt and the New Deal."[66] On the other hand, Marcantonio feared isolation within his own nominal party and, in view of his 1936 bid for a second term, endeavored to develop his own network of partisan endorsements. Therefore, he aligned himself with the All People's Party, a new and supposedly grass-roots political organization that the Communist Party was instrumental in establishing in East Harlem in the summer of 1936 (Naison 1983, 231).

Marcantonio's gradual approach to Communism was perhaps more pragmatic than ideological. He became a fellow traveler because the party shared his own idea of social justice and the means by which a fairer society was to be achieved.[67] Nonetheless, such a political journey caused a split with his 1934 prominent sup-

---

[65] "L'On. Marcantonio contro i progetti che ribassano il tenore degli operai," La Stampa Libera, April 3, 1935, 4.

[66] "Mrs. O'Day for Lanzetta," NYT, September 26, 1936, 2.

[67] For the details of Marcantonio's complex relationship with the Communist Party, see Meyer (1989, 53-86).

porter Antonini, who had become a staunch and fervent anti-Communist in the mid-1920s after his previous militancy in the Workers' (Communist) Party in the wake of the Bolshevik Revolution (Tintori 2005, 177–178; Zappia 1986; Zappia 2003, 148–150). The leader of Local 89 had advised Marcantonio since April 1935 that he could not "expect to get the approval and count on [l]abor [o]rganizations" because of his radical leaning.[68] A few months later Antonini restated his warning that, unless the congressman severed his connections to Communism, their alliance would come to an end. "You placed me in an awkward position," Antonini wrote to Marcantonio. "My and your friends cannot find a reason for your love for the Communists. [...] The purpose of this letter is not to interfere with the evolution or involution of your political thought, but simply to protect my personal dignity and that of my organization. It is up to you, you must decide after thinking that one cannot stand by the Devil and the holy water at the same time."[69] Similarly, after Marcantonio had addressed a rally with Communist leader Earl Browder, Italian-American Socialist organizer Girolamo Valenti—the editor of *La Stampa Libera*—complained to him that "in the next campaign for your re-election many friend of yours in the trade union movement will have a hard time to explain your present flirting with the Communist [P]arty. [...] *Il Progresso*, the *Hearst* and other reactionary newspapers will remind the voters in your constituency your appearances on the same platform with the Benjamins and the Browders of Mr. Stalin's Communist [P]arty."[70]

Marcantonio did not intend to sever his ties to the International Ladies' Garment Workers' Union. But he did not want to reshape his stand and compromise his political ideals either, in order to please Antonini. As Marcantonio answered back:

> I am very glad to stand by both Luigi Antonini and Local 89 against the entire world, but [...] I am willing to make common cause with anyone who joins with me to fight for American civil liberties and religious freedom, irrespective of the politics of the person. Red baiting and Communist baiting is the assault of the force of dictatorial reaction. Those of you who profess to be liberal place us in the same category as the reactionaries when you try to persecute anyone because

---

[68] Luigi Antonini to Vito Marcantonio, New York City, April 25, 1935, VMP, box 52, folder "International Ladies' Garment Workers' Union."

[69] Luigi Antonini to Vito Marcantonio, New York City, August 12, 1935, VMP, box 1, folder "Antonini, Luigi."

[70] "Browder, Marcantonio, Butler to Speak on Bonus Bill," *Daily Worker*, June 11, 1935, 4; Girolamo Valenti to Marcantonio, New York City, June 11, 1935, VMP, box 5, folder "V." For Valenti, see Vezzosi (2001, 128-129).

of his ideas. Persecution of the Communists and other radicals in America on the part of organized labor will give aid and comfort to the exploiters of labor and to those who would bring about a tyrannical dictatorship in our country. [...] I fully realize that one needs guts to pursue such a course. I also thought you had them. I trust that you have not recently undergone an operation.[71]

Marcantonio's tone was no different in his reply to Valenti. As the congressman put it, "I have your letter and I am very much amused by it. The fact that a Communist or a Democrat speaks on the same platform as me does not mean that I am a Communist or a Democrat. [...] My political affiliations remain the same."[72]

Consequently, Marcantonio's relations with Antonini and the Socialists soured. In 1936, Antonini and other union leaders such as David Dubinsky of the IL-GWU and Sidney Hillman of the ACWA created the American Labor Party. This new political force was based in New York State and intended to be a partisan house for those workers who wanted to re-elect Roosevelt but refused to cast their ballots for the whole Democratic slate (Piven and Cloward 1977, 162). To this purpose, the American Labor Party exploited New York State's peculiar electoral laws that allowed candidates to run on more than a slate and have all their votes counted together (Waltzer 1978). Antonini became the State chairperson of the American Labor Party (Tintori 2005, 217-218). When he campaigned in 1936, he stressed his endorsement of President Roosevelt. Yet, unlike what he had done in 1934, he never mentioned Marcantonio's name.[73] After a number of personal attacks on the congressman in early 1936, silence on the part of the leader of Local 89 was the result of a compromise by which—as one of his aides reported to Marcantonio—"Mr. Antonini will refrain from mention[ing] you in his radio-speechs [sic], providing you will do likewise. In other words you will have to ignore each other."[74]

The break with Antonini was more detrimental to Marcantonio than the rift with Valenti. Between 1934 and 1936 Marcantonio managed to increase the total number of his votes from 13,083 to 17,212. He received as many as 5,096 ballots as the candidate of the All People's Party. Such growth, however, could not match the much more significant rise in the votes cast for Lanzetta, which jumped from 12,483 to 18,772 in those two years (Meyer 1989, 45). As the labor movement was

---

[71] Marcantonio to Antonini, n.p., August 14, 1935, VMP, box 1, folder "Antonini, Luigi."
[72] Vito Marcantonio to Girolamo Valenti, Washington D.C., June 12, 1935, VMP, box 5, folder "V."
[73] "Luigi Antonini alla Wedv e Wov per Roosevelt," IPIA, Novembre 1, 1936, 2.
[74] Ernesto Caponetti to Vito Marcantonio, New York City, April 1, 1936, VMP, box 52, folder "International Ladies' Garment Workers' Union."

one of the main vehicles for the mobilization of the theretofore inactive voters in 1936, it can be reasonably assumed that Marcantonio suffered from the loss of support from the leadership of the ILGWU and specifically from the failure of the American Labor Party to endorse his candidacy (Klehr 1984, 293-294). Rumors also circulated to the effect that Antonini intimidated ILGWU voters and caused them not to cast their ballots for Marcantonio.[75]

Italian Americans made about 51 percent of the membership of the ILGWU which, in turn, was the major component of the American Labor Party (Meyer 1997, 38). Of course, not all the affiliates of this union shared Antonini's position or were influenced by him at the polls. For instance, when Antonini was involved in a mudslinging campaign against Marcantonio in early 1936, Santo Farina harshly criticized the head of his own local.[76] Moreover, LaGuardia endorsed Marcantonio's bid for Congress one more time because "his record of votes in the House during his first term justifies his re-election" and, therefore, endeavored to help the candidate consolidate his support among Italian Americans.[77]

The mayor's goal was not an easy task. Many voters of Italian extraction revealed some resentment, if not even hostility, toward Marcantonio that prevented them from casting their ballots for him on Election Day. The interwar years witnessed a remarkable surge in Italian Americans' ethnic consciousness. Voting for candidates who belonged to their immigrant minority was part of this phenomenon, but in 1936 Marcantonio did not seem to fit this pattern any longer.

After enduring prejudice on the grounds that they belonged to an inferior people, Italian Americans took pride in the alleged accomplishments of their native country during the Fascist dictatorship. The prominent international status Italy achieved under Benito Mussolini and his aggressive foreign policy for the supposed defense of Italian prestige abroad made individuals of Italian ancestry revel in the glory of their national origin. Prominent anti-Fascist exile Gaetano Salvemini stated that when "[Italians] arrived in America illiterate, barefoot, and carrying a knapsack, [...] they were treated with contempt by everybody because they were Italians. And now even the Americans told them that Mussolini had turned Italy into a mighty country, that there was no unemployment, that there

---

[75] "Un gruppo della Local 89" to Marcantonio, Brooklyn, n.d. [but 1936], VMP, box 52, folder "International Ladies' Garment Workers' Union."

[76] Santo Farina to Vito Marcantonio, New York City, March 30, 1936, VMP, box 52, folder "International Ladies' Garment Workers' Union."

[77] Fiorello LaGuardia to Morris L. Ernst, Non-Partisan Committee for the Re-Election of Congressman Vito Marcantonio, New York City, October 23, 1936, VMP, box 3, folder "LaGuardia, Fiorella [sic];" "Il sindaco LaGuardia appoggia Marcantonio," IPIA, October 26, 1936, 2.

was a bathroom in every apartment, that trains arrived on time, and that Italy inspired awe worldwide" (Salvemini 2002, 90).

Their sense of national pride climaxed when Italy invaded Ethiopia in October 1935, conquered the country, and established its own colonial empire in May of the following year (Pretelli 2010, 68–70). At that time, even anti-Fascists acknowledged that Mussolini "enabled four million Italians in America to hold up their heads" (Ware 1940, 63). As a quantitative demonstration of their identification with Fascism, during the seven months of the Italo-Ethiopian War, New Yorkers of Italian origin raised more than 700,000 dollars for the Italian Red Cross which, as Mussolini opponents denounced, was an ingenious way of funding the Duce's colonial venture under a humanitarian cover-up (Salvemini 1977, 208). Italian Americans also lobbied Congress to the benefit of the government of their ancestral country and contributed to preventing the passing of the Pittman-McReynolds Bill, which would have enabled President Roosevelt to restrict such U.S. exports to Italy as oil, trucks, and scrap iron that were key to Mussolini's military machinery in Ethiopia (Kanawada 1982, 75–89).

In the heart of Italian Harlem, the Morgantini Club was named after the first Fascist officer who had been killed in the Ethiopian campaign. There, cries of "Duce, Duce, Duce" welcomed the visit of Italian Ambassador Fulvio Suvich to celebrate the annexation of Ethiopia and the proclamation of Italy's empire (Goodman 1993, 237).

Only a handful of radicals were immune to that nationalistic euphoria (Guglielmo 2010, 217–218). Marcantonio was among them. On the eve of the outbreak of the war, Fascist sympathizer Luigi Criscuolo invited him to a meeting that aimed at preserving U.S. "strict neutrality" in the "impending developments" because "although we are all American citizens it is obvious that our sympathies go to Italy."[78] But Marcantonio excused himself: "Until Congress adjourns it is my intention to participate in no outside activities for I feel it is of vital importance to attend to my Congressional duties during this period in order to voice the people whom I represent, the vast majority of whom are of Italian extraction."[79] Similarly, unlike LaGuardia, he declined to participate in a mass rally at Madison Square Garden to boost donations to the Italian Red Cross. Marcantonio claimed once more that official duties kept him in Washington, but in fact he returned to East

---

[78] Luigi Criscuolo to Vito Marcantonio, New York City, August 7, 1935, VMP, box 2, folder "Co-Cz."
[79] Vito Marcantonio to Luigi Criscuolo, Washington, D.C., August 9, 1935, VMP, box 2, folder "Co-Cz."

Harlem and made a point of dining in a local restaurant and walking the streets of his constituency in order to stress his voluntary absence from such a pro-Fascist gathering (Kessner 1989, 404).[80] Conversely, a few weeks before Italy's aggression on Ethiopia in August 1935, Marcantonio had joined an anti-Fascist meeting (LaGumina 1969, 36). During the debate in Congress about the Pittman-McReynolds Bill, he eventually confined himself to making a very short and ambiguous speech that, without ever mentioning Ethiopia and Fascism, argued that Italian Americans "want peace" and "are opposed to any scheme which would make our Nation the tool of either the international racketeerism of the League of Nations or the imperialistic interests of any foreign nation."[81]

Such a vague address was not enough to reconcile Marcantonio with his fellow ethnic voters, even if one of his supporters, Edward Corsi, used his own weekly to circulate the news that the congressman was ready to launch an inquiry into British attempts at interfering with U.S. foreign policy to the detriment of Fascist expansionism in eastern Africa (A.B. 1936). Indeed, many Italian Americans regarded Marcantonio as a traitor of his "race" because he had not wholeheartedly supported Italy's aggression on Ethiopia. It was *Il Grido della Stirpe*—the most rabid pro-Fascist Italian-language newspaper in New York City—which made Marcantonio's stand on Mussolini's colonialism a campaign issue. The weekly called on Italian Americans to cast their ballots for Lanzetta because "while Italy was struggling to gain her place in the sun, while our vigorous youth was covering itself with glory in eastern Africa in a heroic fight, while Italian blood was shed on the sun-burnt Ethiopian land to strengthen the prestige of our nation in the world, Vito Marcantonio, who now unashamedly claims the Italian vote, stabbed Italy in the back."[82]

These kinds of appeals must not have fallen on deaf ears. Actually, constituents who had initially supported Marcantonio also backed the Fascist colonial venture. Santo Farina, who had previously defended him against Antonini, offered a case in point. The establishment of the Italy's empire made him proud and he found improper any attempt at interfering with Italian colonialism. For example,

---

[80] "Marcantonio Insults Italy and the Italian Intelligence," *Il Grido della Stirpe*, February 29, 1936, 1.

[81] Vito Marcantonio, "The Americans of Italian Extraction Expect Not Special Consideration but Justice," February 17, 1936, VMP, box 68, folder "Italian-Americans in the War, '36-'43."

[82] "L'antitalianità di Vito Marcantonio," *Il Grido della Stirpe*, October 31, 1936, 1. For *Il Grido della Stirpe* and its publisher and editor, Domenico Trombetta, see Joseph T. Genco, report for the Federal Bureau of Investigation, Washington, D.C., December 7, 1942, 865.20211/Trombetta Domenico/7, Department of State, Record Group 59, microfilm series LM 142, reel 41, National Archives II, College Park, Md.

he deeply resented that *La Stampa Libera* had stigmatized Italian Americans' celebration of the conquest of Ethiopia as a clownery. As Farina stated, "by hailing the
victory of our soldiers we intended to do our duty as real Italians. What the anonymous calls a clownery was nothing more than a legitimate outburst of the enthu-
siasm of our hearts because we do not believe that endangering the fate of our
motherland to fight Fascism is reasonable. Wishing Italy's defeat to displease Mussolini is ridiculous. We should not forget that governments pass away, but Italy will
remain forever" (Farina 1936).[83] Other Italian-American members of the ILGWU
shared Farina's stand. John Milazzo argued with dubious political consistency that
"I collected money for the Italian Red Cross twice in the factory where I work and
shall initiate additional fund-raisings until our beloved Duce orders our brothers
who are bravely fighting in Africa to lay their arms. [...] I am not and shall be never
a Fascist, but I am Italian, an unrepentant Italian" (Milazzo 1935).

Marcantonio tried to offset the defections among Italian-American voters with
Puerto Rican support, which he cultivated by resorting to Spanish-speaking activists in East Harlem (Meier and Stewart 1991, 47). He also backed a protest campaign against a report by the Chamber of Commerce of the State of New York that
contended that Puerto Rican students had "significantly lower IQs than American-
born white children" (Garza 1994, 97–98). Furthermore, contrary to proposals for
the transformation of the Caribbean island into a commonwealth, he introduced a
bill that would have immediately granted independence to Puerto Rico and mone-
tary indemnity for almost forty years of U.S. rule (Marcantonio 1956, 374–378).[84]
He attended a rally of Puerto Rican nationalists in New York City in March 1936
and allegedly stated that "Yankee imperialism has long been abusing the Puerto
Ricans."[85] He even flew to the Caribbean island to offer his legal counseling as an
attorney to Pedro Albizu Campos, the leader of the Puerto Rican Nationalist Party,
who had been convicted on charges of conspiracy to overthrow the government
(Schaffer 1966, 46–47; Thomas 2010, 123). As a result, Marcantonio received the
endorsement of Luis Muñoz Marin, a nationalist member of the island's legislature.[86]

Yet Lanzetta continued to enjoy the support of more influential Puerto Rican
politicians, such as Senator Barcelo, whose following was probably larger in East

---

[83] Farina's letter was a rejoinder to Un ennese (1936).

[84] Vito Marcantonio, "My Position on Puerto Rico," n.d. [but 1936], VMP, box 69, folder
"Speeches & Press Releases: Puerto Rico."

[85] Anthony F. Ferentz, report for the Federal Bureau of Investigation, New York City, March 2,
1945, 4, FBI file no. 100-28126, "Vito Marcantonio," part 2.

[86] "Il Senatore portoricano L. Marin per la rielezione di Marcantonio," *IPIA*, October 3, 1936, 2.

Harlem where few immigrants longed for separatism from the United States (Schaffer 1966, 47).[87] To that backing Lanzetta could also add the endorsement of pro-Fascist Italian-American newspapers such as *Il Grido della Stirpe*, which presented him as an individual who, unlike Marcantonio, was "proud of his Italian background" and ready to join all campaigns to defend his ancestral land (Tarangelo 1936).

MARCANTONIO RETURNS TO WASHINGTON

During the 1936 campaign, the most enthusiastic backing for Marcantonio came from groups of unemployed and destitute voters who were also the backbone of the Fiorello LaGuardia Political Club in East Harlem.[88] Therefore, planning to reclaim his seat in the House in 1938, Marcantonio did not discontinue his services to the residents of the Twentieth Congressional District in the following two years. His law practice as an attorney often interwove with the mechanics of his political organization.[89] Moreover, in 1937, he began to work with a Communist-inspired but self-proclaimed non-partisan coalition, the Harlem Legislative Conference, that aimed at lobbying for the people of the neighborhood in the State Assembly and had members primarily among Italian Americans, Puerto Ricans, and African Americans. Under pressure from George Charney, the district's Communist leader, Marcantonio eventually agreed to become the chairperson of this group (Naison 1983, 238–239). When he could not help East Harlemites on his own, he resorted to his former colleagues in Washington. In early 1938, for instance, he wrote U.S. Representative Emanuel Celler "in behalf of John Rizzo, whom I am very anxious to assist. Not being in a position to do so, I am calling on you in this case."[90]

Marcantonio also obviously exploited LaGuardia's aid to the hilt. The patronage of the city administration continued to be key to the people's welfare in East Harlem. Roughly three quarters of the residents of the district depended on the Home Relief Bureau to make a living in 1938.[91] Moreover, in this year, the mayor

---

[87] "Puerto Ricans Back Roosevelt," *NYT*, October 29, 1936, 18.

[88] See, e.g., "Calde accoglienza al Congressman Vito Marcantonio," *IPIA*, September 30, 1936, 2; "Comizio dei disoccupati per l'On. Marcantonio," *IPIA*, October 17, 1936, 2; "Una riunione in favore di Vito Marcantonio," *IPIA*, October 27, 1936, 3

[89] See, e.g., Vito Marcantonio to David Marcus, New York City, June 30, 1937, *VMP*, box 2, folder "F."

[90] Marcantonio to Congressman Emanuel Celler, New York City, February 8, 1938, *VMP*, box 4, folder "R."

[91] Leonard Covello, "Community-Centered School (1938-39)," Leonard Covello Papers, box 18, folder 2, Balch Institute Collection, Historical Society of Pennsylvania.

intervened to support his protégé not only in the fall elections but also in the primaries. Dissatisfied with the conservative turn of the GOP, Marcantonio registered
for the American Labor Party after his 1936 defeat (Meyer 1989, 26). But his increasing flirtation with Communism led Antonini to launch a campaign to prevent
Marcantonio from securing the endorsement of the American Labor Party for
Congress in 1938. Contending that Marcantonio was "a tool of the Communist
[P]arty" within a larger scheme "to dominate labor unions," the East Harlem club
of the American Labor Party backed Joseph Piscitello, a district manager of Local
89. He, too, was of Italian ancestry, a further demonstration of the extent to which
Italian Americans had secured the control of candidacies in this section. Actually,
a possible challenger to Piscitello, Bruno DeBiasi, was also an Italian American,
but he eventually withdrew in favor of Antonini's hand-picked candidate.[92] Yet a
showdown between Marcantonio and Piscitello was avoided, at least in 1938.
LaGuardia stepped in one more time in behalf of the former and succeeded in
having the State Executive Committee of the American Labor Party designate
Marcantonio as its candidate for the U.S. House of Representatives (Schaffer
1966, 59).

The endorsement, however, was not tantamount to election. In 1937, the
votes for LaGuardia on the slate of the American Labor Party accounted for 21
percent of the total ballots cast for him. This figure meant that LaGuardia would
not have been re-elected to City Hall without the support of the American Labor
Party (Meyer 1997, 34). Yet the same percentage also indicated that its backing
alone did not ensure LaGuardia enough votes to win a second term. Marcantonio
was fully aware that he had no chances of returning to Washington if he ran only
on the ticket of the American Labor Party in 1938. For this reason, he sought the
nominations of the Republican and Democratic Parties, too.[93] His entry into the
Democratic primaries prompted Lanzetta, who was again the endorsee of Tammany Hall, to compete for the nomination of the Republican and American Labor
Parties.[94] Marcantonio's alleged subservience to Communism became the paramount issue of the campaign especially among Italian Americans, who were supposed to be more conservative than Jews and Puerto Ricans because of their massive mobilization to back the Fascist invasion of Ethiopia. Specifically, on the eve
of the primaries, voters of Italian extraction received an apocryphal letter from an

[92] "Marcantonio Is Scored," NYT, July 16, 1938, 2; "Congressional Candidate," IPIA, July 17, 1938,
p. 8-S. For Piscitello, see Guglielmo (2010, 251-252).
[93] "Labor Plans Fight to Unseat Burton," NYT, July 8, 1938, 5.
[94] "Tammany's Slate Has No Surprises," NYT, July 22, 1938, 2.

alleged officer of the Italian consulate urging them not to cast their ballots for Marcantonio because he was a Communist.[95] Red-baiting was also the argument of Samuel Kupferman, the GOP chairperson in New York County, who tried to snatch the Republican nomination from Marcantonio's hands.[96]

All these efforts were to no avail. Marcantonio trounced Kupferman by 2,296 votes to 199 in the GOP primaries as well as Lanzetta by 1,759 votes to 170 for the nomination of the American Labor Party. Conversely, Lanzetta defeated Marcantonio by 4,252 votes to 1,930 for the place on the Democratic ticket (Meyer 1989, 45).[97]

As Lanzetta and Marcantonio faced each other in the fall campaign for the third time in a row, support for the New Deal returned to the foreground of the political debate. Drawing upon his previous record, each candidate claimed to be more loyal to Roosevelt's program than his opponent. Marcantonio contended that his own election was necessary to strengthen the presence of progressives in the House because Lanzetta had been part of the anti-New Deal and reactionary forces in Congress during his second term.[98] Conversely, Lanzetta trumpeted again Green's endorsement to show off that, in spite of partisan labels, he was a better friend of the workers than his challenger because he had "consistently show[ed] a willingness to favorably comply with any action in the interest of Labor requested by the American Federation of Labor."[99] Among Italian-American voters, Lanzetta also emphasized his legislative agenda for the liberalization of immigration provisions and campaigned on the slogan "save Harlem from Communism."[100]

Some Italian Americans contended that Marcantonio's radicalization undermined his political following in the Little Italy (Corsi 1936; Rosario Ingargiola, as quoted in LaGumina 1979, 185). But the son of local Communist leader Michele Salerno argued that East Harlem sent such a radical politician to Washington as Marcantonio because, regardless of his ideological stand, he was deeply interested in helping the immigrants with their everyday problems (Salerno 2001, 116). Indeed, as Guido Tintori has observed, "East Harlem's electorate did not care much about Marcantonio's political fluctuations," provided that he ensured his constitu-

---

[95] "'Fake' Letters Laid to O'Connor Aides," NYT, September 21, 1938, 20.
[96] "Communists Endorse Labor Candidates," NYT, September 23, 1938, 27.
[97] "Fay, sostenuto dal New Deal, ha sconfitto O'Connor alle Primarie," IPIA, September 22, 1938, 3.
[98] "Marcantonio Opens Drive," NYT, September 27, 1938, 4.
[99] "Green Endorses Lanzetta," NYT, November 1, 1938, 6; "William Green per l'On. J. Lanzetta," IPIA, November 2, 1938, p. 2.
[100] "Gli italiani di Harlem per la candidatura di J. Lanzetta," IPIA, November 1, 1938, 2; "Entusiasmo fra gli italiani per la candidatura Lanzetta," IPIA, November 7, 1938, pp. 2, 4.

ents the services they needed (Tintori 2005, 227). He was able to provide such assistance thanks to LaGuardia who, as had already happened in the past, gave Marcantonio not only his endorsement but also the support of his political organization. Indeed, even if the mayor sided with the right wing of the American Labor
Party, he committed his own patronage to Marcantonio in East Harlem (Garrett
1961, 275). Although LaGuardia and Marcantonio shared the same Italian ancestry, the latter followed a strict strategy of ethnic balance among Italian, Jewish, and
Puerto Rican constituents in his recommendations for appointments or relief. Actually, Italian- Jewish- and Hispanic-sounding names have the same ratio in the
correspondence between Marcantonio and the mayor's secretaries.[101]

The Fiorello LaGuardia Political Club had reached 5,000 members by 1938
and could, thereby, determine the outcome of off-year elections in the Twentieth
Congressional District, where the number of votes cast hardly exceeded 30,000
ballots (Workers of the Federal Writers' Project 1938, 98). Voters could easily per-
ceive access to relief, welfare programs, and personal assistance between the lines
of the banner reading "Mayor LaGuardia says 'Harlem Needs Vito Marcantonio In
Congress'" on the Labor–Republican candidate's campaign headquarters (Schaffer
1966, 63–65). Recalling the meaning and benefits of Marcantonio's election to
those unable to understand the small print was the task of the Communist volunteers whom Charney unleashed throughout East Harlem in order to bring out the
vote for the slate of the American Labor Party, especially among Puerto Ricans and
African Americans who were more likely to welcome Marxist activists than Italian
Americans (Klehr 1984, 294; Charney 1968, 113). The number of votes the
Communist Party had received statewide in the 1936 elections was not large
enough to qualify it for a place on the ballot two years later.[102] Consequently, pursuing a popular front strategy primarily out of expediency, a large number of
Communist members registered for the American Labor Party and supported the
latter's candidates in 1938 (Schaffer 1966, 95–96). Despite his own political antip-
athy, even Italy's Fascist consul general acknowledged the effectiveness of such
mobilization on the radical Left: "the Negro, Jewish, Spanish [sic for Puerto Rican]
and Italian subversives living in the constituency voted en masse for Marcantonio."[103]

[101] See, e.g., FHLGP, reel 29, folder "Mar-May."
[102] "Communists Lose Status as Party," NYT, November 5, 1936, 1.
[103] Gaetano Vecchiotti, Italian Consul General, to Minister of the Interior, New York City,
November 10, 1938, Records of the Ministry of the Interior, Casellario Politico Centrale, box 3019,
folder 39515, Archivio Centrale dello Stato, Rome, Italy.

In an off-year election, when Lanzetta could not profit from Roosevelt's coat-tails, it was this grass-roots recruitment of voters which enabled Marcantonio to win the day. Lanzetta's political following remained relatively stable between 1934 and 1938, as he received 12,483 and 12,376 ballots, respectively, in these two years. Conversely, Marcantonio's support on the Republican ticket fell from 12,428 to 10,059 votes. But the 655 ballots he had polled as the candidate of the City Fusion Party in 1934 were replaced by the 8,901 votes on the American Labor Party slate four years later (Meyer 1989, 45). As for the Italian-American electorate, which remained the leading force in the Twentieth Congressional District, Edward Corsi's candidacy for the U.S. Senate in New York State for the GOP contributed to curbing the drain of voters from the Republican column. In East Harlem, too, Italian-American voters were encouraged to cast straight ballots for the GOP in the eventually fruitless effort to help Corsi conquer the highest political position one of their fellow ethnics had been ever slated for by either major party nationwide (Masillo 1938).[104]

THE LAST CAMPAIGN

In anticipation of the demise of the off-year factor and the resurgence of the coattails effect when Roosevelt's name appeared again on the Democratic ticket in November, in 1940 Lanzetta succeeded in receiving Tammany Hall's endorsement for Congress for the fifth time in a row despite his 1938 defeat and Marcantonio's second attempt at competing in the Democratic primaries.[105] The choice seemed reasonable because Lanzetta had won in the previous two presidential years. None-theless, the political repercussions of the outbreak of World War II in Europe up-set the Democratic Party's plans and Marcantonio managed to secure a third term that had initially seemed unlikely on the grounds of the preceding voting trends in East Harlem.

Notwithstanding his bipartisan election in 1938, Marcantonio made a point of being listed in the Congressional Directory as the U.S Representative of the Amer-ican Labor Party only (Schaffer 1966, 65). In his opinion, the force that had ena-bled him to come out on top in 1938 was the future of U.S. politics. When one of his associates suggested that the denomination of the American Labor Party Club on 104th Street should be turned into Republican Party Club, Marcantonio an-swered that "it would be a most serious mistake to change the name, and to affili-

---

[104] "L'Ordine Ind. Figli d'Italia per Dewey e l'On. Corsi," *IPIA*, October 24, 1938, 2.
[105] "Marcantonio Files for Primary Race," *NYT*, August 14, 1940, 23.

ate yourself to any of the two old parties. [...] The American Labor Party is a grow-ing party, and the only progressive party in New York City."[106] Therefore, what looked ominous for Marcantonio at the beginning of the 1940 campaign was a deeper split than the 1938 division within the American Labor Party. Its right wing stigmatized the 1939 Molotov-Ribbentrop Non-Aggression Pact, which paved the way for the partition of Poland between Nazi Germany and the Soviet Union and for the absorption of the Baltic States by Moscow. Conversely, the Left and pro-Communist wing—led by Marcantonio himself—criticized the stand of the other faction of the party (Tintori 2005, 222-224).

This dispute further exacerbated the already strained relations between Anto-nini and Marcantonio. The leader of Local 89 of the ILGWU endeavored again to slate Piscitello against Marcantonio in the primaries of the American Labor Par-ty.[107] Yet Piscitello's petitions for nomination were ruled invalid in court and Mar-cantonio ended up on the ticket unopposed.[108] However, Antonini refused to give in to him. He encouraged ILGWU members in East Harlem not only to register for the American Labor Party, so as to prevent the Communists from taking over the laborite organization in this district, but also to cast straight Democratic ballots in November in order to unseat the *Onorevole Frittomisto* (Honorable Mixed Fry), as he had scornfully dubbed Marcantonio with reference to the multiplicity of his partisan affiliations over time.[109] In order to further discredit Marcantonio with the larger electorate, Antonini also penned an English-language pamphlet by which he accused him of flirtation, at the same time, with Communists, reactionary Re-publicans, and even Fascists (Antonini n.d.). But Eugene Connolly, the county chairperson of the American Labor Party, was among the first to defy Antonini's diktat and to endorse Marcantonio even before Piscitello was barred from the pri-maries.[110]

Marcantonio especially feared the retaliatory power that Antonini could exert on ILGWU members. In factories that operated under a closed shop agreement, workers risked dismissal from their jobs if they were expelled from the union to which they belonged when they had been hired. Therefore, Marcantonio intended

---

[106] Vito Marcantonio to Luigi Scarandino, n.p., January 23, 1939, *VMP*, box 44, folder "Assembly District 18th (1939-40)."

[107] "Piscitello Gets Support," *NYT*, August 12, 1940, 32.

[108] "Labor Right Winger Barred from Ballot," *NYT*, September 10, 1940, 16.

[109] "I salti di un campione di trapezio volante," leaflet, n.d. [but 1940], Records of the International Ladies' Garment Workers' Union, Luigi Antonini Correspondence, box 2, folder "American Labor Party, 1939-1941," Kheel Center, Cornell University, Ithaca, N.Y.

[110] "Bollettino politico," *IPIA*, August 10, 1940, 6.

to ensure his own prospective voters that "the ballot is a secret ballot. No one can compel you to vote against me. I will protect your right to vote as you see fit."[111] In any case, Antonini's appeal failed to influence a significant number of Italian-American voters. Actually, Marcantonio's correspondence contains a number of letters by constituents who declared their support for the congressman. For instance, Jack Emanuel wrote to him that "we Italians have our mothers, sisters, and girlfriends who are dressmakers, and know pretty well the abuses that this scoundrel commits to feed his belly. [...] We would be grateful to you even if the only achievement in your career were to get rid of Antonini. [...] We will be always your stalwarts and will do everything for your victory."[112] Another Italian American, Salvatore Politi, wanted Marcantonio to know that:

> Your answer to the racketeer Antonini came into my hands and I spread that answer as much as I could among the clothing and cloak workers in the Bronx. Nearly all of them are anxious to see this presumptuous vampire of the community done for and dethroned and are anxious to have a copy of your answer apiece. There are about a dozen honest workers who hope that you will be able to do what many other courageous people have not been able to do and do all possible to put an end to the camorra of this ignorant exploiting thief.[113]

Throughout the previous three years, Marcantonio had made a point of cultivating Italian-American voters, including Mussolini's fellow travelers whom he would blame for his 1936 defeat against Lanzetta sometime later.[114] Softening his attacks on the Duce's dictatorship was part of such a scheme. Soon after his 1938 re-election, Marcantonio was invited to a rally at the Manhattan Opera House to protest the passing of Italy's anti-Semitic legislation.[115] Actually, one of the organizers urged him to "come down and give Mussolini hell."[116] Marcantonio did attend the meeting and addressed it. However, when he took the floor, he spoke at length about the German situation and made only cursory remarks about what was hap-

---

[111] Marcantonio, "My Answer to a Very Filthy and False Attack Made on Me by Luigi Antonini," 7-8.
[112] Jack Emanuel to Vito Marcantonio, New York City, October 21, 1940, VMP, box 45, folder "campaign 1940 (2 of 2)."
[113] Salvatore Politi to Vito Marcantonio, October 22, 1940, VMP, box 45, folder "campaign 1940."
[114] "Both A.L.P. Wings Voice Confidence," NYT, August 10, 1942, 9.
[115] "Italians Don't Hate Jews," leaflet, n.d. [but November 1938], Covello Papers, box 100, folder 22; "Appunto per la Dir. Gen. Affari Transoceanici," Rome, December 12, 1938, Records of the Ministry of Foreign Affairs, Affari Politici, Stati Uniti, 1931-1945, box 47, folder 2, Archivio Storico del Ministero degli Affari Esteri, Rome, Italy.
[116] Robert Yaller to Vito Marcantonio, New York City, n.d. [but November 1938], VMP, box 4, folder "Il Popolo."

pening in Italy.[117] A few weeks later he excused himself from greeting the convention of the Committee for United Action against Fascism and Anti-Semitism.[118] He also refused to participate in a gathering against Mussolini's anti-Jewish measures in Philadelphia on February 3, 1939. First he resented that his name was inserted in the program without being consulted; then he claimed that he had previous engagements elsewhere; finally, he cancelled his speech on the grounds that he was too ill to travel to Philadelphia.[119]

Paradoxically, however, it was Marcantonio's pro-Communist stand on World War II which eventually reconciled the congressman with the pro-Fascist cohort of the Italian-American electorate in 1940. Until Germany invaded Russia in June 1941 and Moscow needed the U.S. arms supplies of the lend-lease program, in Congress Marcantonio was the staunchest advocate of Washington's neutrality in the European military conflict, following a line that closely reflected the position of the Communists and their increasing denunciation of the fighting as an "imperialistic war" (Ottanelli 1991, 185–192). He was so isolationist that in the summer of 1940 he was the only member of the House to vote against the Naval Ship Construction Bill and the Aviation Expansion Bill, contending that their purpose was to prepare the U.S. intervention in the war rather than strengthening the nation's defense and discouraging a foreign attack on the United States (Kaner 1968, 93–95; Cole 1983, 354; Doenecke 2000, 107). For the same reason, he opposed the Conscription Bill and, after its passing by a large majority, introduced another bill that aimed at repealing the draft (Schaffer 1966, 94; Montana 1975, 166). In his opinion, ending the Depression should remain the priority of the United States, regardless of the European events. To this end, few weeks after Nazi Germany had seized western Poland, Marcantonio was the co-sponsor of a mass rally to call for U.S. neutrality and to protest against dismissals in the Works Progress Administration.[120] His 1940 election campaign slogan was "the United States needs overalls not uniforms" (Meyer 2003, 224).

Though Communist-induced, Marcantonio's views about U.S. foreign policy made him extremely popular in East Harlem because they reflected the worries and

---

[117] Gaetano Vecchiotti to Giuseppe Cosmelli, officer of the Ministry of the Interior, New York City, November 21, 1938, Records of the Ministry of the Interior, Casellario Politico Centrale, box 160, folder 2113.

[118] M. Gertner to Vito Marcantonio, New York City, December 5, 1938, VMP, box 3, folder "Jewish People Committee;" Vito Marcantonio to M. Gertner, New York City, December 8, 1938, ibid.

[119] "Protest Anti-Semitism in Italy!" leaflet , n.d. [but January 1939], VMP, box 4, folder "Il Popolo;" Vito Marcantonio to Girolamo Valenti, Washington, D.C., January 30, 1939, ibid.; Vito Marcantonio to Philip De Luca, n.p., February 3, 1939, ibid.

[120] "Comizio di protesta," leaflet, n.d. [but September 1939], Covello Papers, box 77, folder 9.

reservations of most of his Italian-American voters, who feared a war between their native and adoptive countries and did not want to be enlisted to fight against their own relatives who had remained in the motherland (Campailla 1998, 61; Meyer 1989, 119–120). For instance, the anti-conscription stand let Marcantonio gain the endorsement of the Lower and East Harlem Youth Congress.[121] However, on the issues of the defense of U.S. neutrality and denunciation of Roosevelt's alleged imperialistic plans among Italian Americans, notwithstanding the endorsement of the Italian-language Communist mouthpiece *L'Unità del Popolo*, in 1940 Marcantonio ended up primarily on the side of those Fascist sympathizers who had gone over to Lanzetta in the aftermath of the controversy about the invasion of Ethiopia four years earlier (Sherman 2001, 58).[122]

Roosevelt's stigmatization of Italy's eleventh-hour declaration of war on France in June 1940 contributed to drawing additional Italian-American votes from the Democratic column into Marcantonio's camp. The [p]resident's metaphor—"the hand that held the dagger has struck it into the back of its neighbor"—was perceived as an anti-Italian ethnic slur that was likely to trigger off a wave of discrimination since the sentence seemed to be inspired by the prejudicial stereotype of Italian immigrants as a stiletto-prone people (Roosevelt 1941, 263; LaGumina 1973, 13). As reporter Warren Moscow remarked, "The Italian did not have to be a rooter for Mussolini to feel that his own pride was involved" (Moscow 1967, 132). Roosevelt's words also appeared as the first step toward the U.S. entry into the conflict against Italy. Referring to the looming war between Italy and the United States, the secretary of East Harlem's Italian Welfare League, Angela Carlozzi, admitted that "we all feel terrible about it" (as quoted in Mormino and Pozzetta 1999, 140). Even after the United States entered World War II, in the words of sociologist Joseph S. Roucek, "most American Italians looked for a mirage: American victory without Italian defeat" (Roucek 1945, 468).

In the fall of 1940, Democratic Party workers needed police escorts to campaign in New York City's Italian-American neighborhoods because of the residents' animosity toward the president (Roosevelt 1950, 1072). Republican activists seized this opportunity to warn Italian-American voters that Roosevelt re-election was tantamount to war against Italy and to urge them to cast their ballot for GOP presidential candidate Wendell L. Willkie. Urging his fellow ethnics to bolt the

---

[121] "Your Life Is in a Lottery," leaflet, n.d. [but 1940], *VMP*, box 45, folder "Campaign Miscellany (1 of 2)."

[122] "Our Position on the Election," *L'Unità del Popolo*, October 20, 1940, 6. For *L'Unità del Popolo*, see Meyer (2001).

Democratic Party, Anthony Maisano, the chairperson of the Columbian Republican League of New York State, specifically claimed that "Roosevelt and his third term mean war. We have made our choice. Our vote is for Wendell L. Willkie and for peace."[123] This propaganda stunt found a receptive audience in East Harlem and benefited Marcantonio, too, because he had again received the Republican nomination for Congress.[124] As an Italian American wrote to him, "I will campaign in Italian language in favor of Mr. Willkie [...]. I would like to cooperate with you for your re-election as [c]ongressman."[125]

Furthermore, Marcantonio came out against the 1940 Smith Act, which provided for the registration and fingerprinting of resident aliens (Marcantonio 1940; Meyer 2003, 214-215). Specifically, he charged that the new law would "turn the FBI into a Gestapo" persecuting newcomers who had not acquired U.S. citizenship.[126] Marcantonio, therefore, further ingratiated himself with the Italian-American electorate. Actually, the Smith Act increased the sense of insecurity in the Little Italy because it seemed the starting point of a campaign against the nearly 700,000 unnaturalized Italian immigrants (LaGumina 2006, 63). Marcantonio's work for the Communist-promoted American Committee for the Protection of Foreign Born offered Italian-American voters further evidence of his commitment to prevent the discrimination against ethnic minorities (Sherman 2001, 12, 63, 65-66).

Recipients of federal relief were potentially the largest cohort of Democratic supporters within the Italian-American electorate. Still, as Nathan Glazer and Daniel Patrick Moynihan have pointed out, "the Italian Americans became probably the most anti-Roosevelt of all low-income groups" in the wake of the president's criticism of the Fascist entry into World War II (Glazer and Moynihan 1963, 214). Indeed, the Italian-American vote for Roosevelt fell from 78.7 percent in 1936 to 42.2 percent in 1940 (Bayor 1978, 147). Conversely, in the same years, the votes for Marcantonio on the Republican ticket increased from 12,116 to 14,737 (Meyer 1989, 45-46). His additional support at the polls resulted in part from the straight GOP ballots cast by the Italian Americans who had followed Maisano's advice.

Reactions to Roosevelt's stab-in-the-back address also contributed to distancing Italian-American voters from Antonini and, consequently, from the latter's cam-

---

[123] Anthony Maisano, "Five Minute Talk," October 29, 1940, Maisano Papers, box 1, folder 5.
[124] "Leibowitz Wins in Primary Race," NYT, September 18, 1940, 1, 12.
[125] Benedetto Lo Casto to Vito Marcantonio, New York City, July 25, 1940, VMP, box 45, folder "Campaign 1940."
[126] Vito Marcantonio, "War Conscription Civil Liberties," leaflet, FBI file no. 100-28126, "Vito Marcantonio," part 1.

paign against Marcantonio's re-election. Undaunted by his own fellow ethnics' resentment toward Roosevelt's statement, Antonini rushed to praise the president by a telegram that repeatedly incorporated the same prejudicial expression. The leader of Local 89 of the ILGWU wired that:

> As an Italian immigrant and naturalized American citizen, and as one who has fought against Mussolini's [F]ascist regime since its inception, I wholehearted-ly congratulate you on your masterly speech of yesterday condemning Mussolini's criminal war against democracy. You said that on June tenth, nineteen forty Mus-solini's dagger stabbed a neighbor in the back. It is the same dagger which on June tenth, nineteen twenty-four stabbed Matteotti; the same dagger which on June tenth, nineteen thirty-seven stabbed the brothers Carlo and Bruno Rosselli, whose only crime, as in the case of Matteotti, was to oppose [F]ascism and to fight for a free Italy.[127]

Reprimands of Antonini characterized the election campaign among voters of Italian ancestry. For example, an ILGWU member charged him with selling him-self out to Roosevelt and forgetting that it had been "our Duce Musslino [sic]" who had won respect for Italian Americans in the United States.[128]

However, not all voters in East Harlem were from an Italian background, nor was foreign policy the only issue in the 1940 campaign for Congress. With the un-employment rate as high as 29 percent in the district (Waltzer 1978, 191), relief and welfare were paramount matters in the political debate.

Nevertheless, this was another field from which Marcantonio could draw more benefits than Lanzetta. The congressman's services were still key to the everyday life of many of his constituents. In his campaign literature, Marcantonio boasted that "I have been in my district every single Sunday, and have devoted every Sun-day dealing with the problems of the people of my district. I have made their prob-lems my problems, and I have handled over 12,000 of such cases."[129] In particular, the relief rolls of New York City's Department of Welfare for East Harlem and the membership of the Fiorello LaGuardia Political Club revealed close similarities and overlap (Meyer 1989, 91). The gratitude of East Harlem's residents had obvi-ous electoral implications. Sufficient to demonstrate this point is a sample of the

---

[127] Luigi Antonini to Franklin D. Roosevelt, New York City, June 11, 1940, Franklin D. Roosevelt Papers. Official File 233a, Franklin D. Roosevelt Library, Hyde Park, N.Y.

[128] "Una italiana" to Antonini, November 5, 1940, Antonini Correspondence, box 2, folder "American Labor Party, 1939-1941."

[129] Vito Marcantonio, circular letter to East Harlem voters, n.p., October 27, 1940, VMP, box 44, folder "East Harlem Italian Organizations."

letters Marcantonio received during the 1940 campaign. Clement Bertoni, for instance, thanked him for his help in getting an apartment in a public housing project and concluded by wishing for his re-election to Congress.[130] Edgard De Silvia, who had similarly profited from Marcantonio's services, wanted him to know that "I haven't forgotten you, and will do all in my power to assist you. My friends in your district assure me, they are quite contented with you as their representative."[131] Charles Lombardi was even more outspoken: "I certainly thank you sincerely for representing me with an attorney. Being grateful for what you have done for me, I in turn shall do my duty in casting my vote for you, as I have always done in the past."[132] Likewise, Ferrer Marchini, president of the Italian Welfare Association, in recognition of Marcantonio's efforts on behalf of the unemployed in East Harlem, committed his organization "to assure that the House of Representatives is honored again with your presence in the crucial coming two years."[133]

Since Mayor LaGuardia and President Roosevelt continued to prevent the access of Tammany Hall to patronage, Lanzetta had little in his hands to counter Marcantonio's plums, except for a reminder of his old bill to liberalize U.S. immigration laws and Green's usual letter of endorsement (Simon 2006, 43).[134] Yet, as the incumbent, Marcantonio could also show off a more appealing legislative record for East Harlem's voters that included securing funds for the East River public housing project and the construction of the new Benjamin Franklin High School.[135] After all, as further demonstration of Marcantonio's popularity over his challenger, he came as few as 238 votes short of defeating Lanzetta even in the Democratic primaries.[136]

---

[130] Clement Bertoni to Marcantonio, New York City, n.d. [but October 1940], VMP, box 45, folder "Campaign 1940 (2 of 2)."
[131] Edgard De Silvia to Vito Marcantonio, New York City, October 17, 1940, VMP, box 45, folder "Campaign 1940 (2 of 2)."
[132] Charles Lombardi to Vito Marcantonio, October 31, 1940, VMP box 45, folder "Campaign 1940 (2 of 2)"
[133] Ferrer Marchini to Vito Marcantonio, New York City, July 8, 1940, VMP, box 3, folder "Italian Associations (American) (1 of 2)."
[134] "Lanzetta chiude la campagna prevedendo la vittoria," IPIA, September 17, 1940, 2; "La candidatura Lanzetta approvata da Green," ibid., November 4, 1940, 2.
[135] Vito Marcantonio, circular letter to East Harlem voters, n.p., October 27, 1940. For Marcantonio's involvement in both projects, see also Meyer (1985, 58-60); Johanek and Puckett (2007, 181-197). For the East River public housing project, see Venturini (1996); Cinotto (2010).
[136] "Lanzetta Wins Recount," NYT, October 24, 1940, 11.

CONCLUSION

Lanzetta's astounding defeat in 1940, when he managed to poll as little as 37.5 percent of the votes in a presidential year (Meyer 1989, 46), swept him away forever from East Harlem's political scene. He resumed the practice of law, was appointed as a city magistrate in the postwar years, and no longer competed against Marcantonio (U.S. Congress 1961, 1193).[137] Yet Lanzetta's retirement from active politics did not mark the demise of Italian Americans' hegemony in the Twentieth Congressional District. Candidacies in East Harlem remained an Italian-American matter for two additional years. In 1942, both Marcantonio's contenders in the primaries—Frank J. Ricca for the Democratic nomination and A. Charles Mucciolo for the Republican as well as American Labor nominations—were of Italian extraction.[138]

However, Italian Americans' monopoly over Congressional candidacies in East Harlem was strictly linked to the fact that they were the largest ethnic group in the district. In 1942, Marcantonio was re-elected unopposed after securing the Republican, Democratic, and Labor Party nominations. His power seemed absolute and unchallengeable. As a coeval political analyst observed, "In East Harlem Marcantonio's name is a legend as 'the man who does things for people.' There is a joke that he would win if he ran on a laundry ticket. In his 'home territory' he is a political saint who intercedes with the bureaucratic gods, a Solon, a poor man's lawyer and an oracle of wisdom."[139]

Rumor had it that Marcantonio also struck a deal with underworld bosses, by which he exploited his clout in the municipal administration to offer East Harlem's gamblers, loan sharks, and dope peddlers protection from the police in exchange for gangsters' commitment to mobilize the district's voters in his behalf on Election Day (Lait and Mortimer 1952, 29; Sexton 1965, 108; Moscow 1971, 59). Yet his most authoritative biographer has found no evidence to corroborate such charges (Meyer 1989, 127–129), while a leading scholar of Italian Americans' involvement in organized crime has placed Marcantonio among such progressive politicians as LaGuardia who fought racketeers in New York City (Lupo 2008, 105).

---

[137] "James Lanzetta, Justice, 61, Dead," NYT, October 29, 1956, 25.
[138] "Barry Nominated," NYT, August 12, 1942, 1, 3; tabulation of the 1942 primary election returns, VMP, box 44, folder "Campaign Primary Results—1942."
[139] J. H. Stephenson, "Political Sociology of the Eighteenth Congressional District, New York City," n.d. [but mid-1940s], VMP, box 44, folder "Campaign, 1940—Hdqrs. Corresp. (1 of 2)."

In an alleged attempt at gerrymandering Marcantonio out of office,[140] in 1944 most of East Harlem was added to Yorkville in the recently reapportioned Eighteenth Congressional District. Such efforts to prevent Marcantonio's re-election were in vain. Thanks to the consolidation of the network of services that his political machine guaranteed to voters, Marcantonio succeeded in retaining his seat until his opposition to the U.S. intervention in the Korean War caused his defeat in 1950 (Marcantonio 1956, 352-355). Indeed, Marcantonio had become the quintessential machine politician who "knew East Harlem house by house and floor by floor" (Sasuly 1957, 147). But the merger of East Harlem and Yorkville radically changed the demography of Marcantonio's constituency. As the area was home to a significant number of Irish and German Americans, besides Puerto Ricans and African Americans, Italian Americans were no longer the more numerous cohort of voters in the district (LaGumina 1969, 85; Jackson 1983, 62-63). Consequently, Marcantonio's challengers in both the primaries and elections did not have vowel-ending last names any more (Meyer 1989, 46-47).

Marcantonio had sharpened the mechanics of his own political machine by the mid-1940s: "He and his assistants are nearly always available to the man with a problem, and render service without regard to the constituent's political usefulness. The problems he is called upon to solve run the full gamut of the tribulations and tragedies that a depressed area can produce—evictions, divorce, juvenile delinquency, discrimination, unemployment—even getting out of an insane asylum."[141] Richard H. Rovere similarly reported about Marcantonio that

> Every Saturday noon, when the House recesses, he flies home to New York. He may make as many as twenty speeches over the week end, but Sunday afternoon is reserved for oiling the machine. The scene in the LaGuardia Club after one o'clock on Sunday looks like nothing so much as a busy day in the clinic of a great city hospital. Marcantonio and three or four secretaries sit at desks on a platform in the front of the main hall. Before them on wooden camp chairs are about a hundred constituents, [...] as many as four hundred may come and go in an afternoon. [...] Mostly their problems concern money or jobs. During the Depression, the majority were relief applicants. [...] Today the same people are back for army dependency allotments. [...] Some need legal aid. [...] Marcantonio sees personally about thirty thousand [...] in the course of a Congressional term. So large an in-

---

[140] This is the opinion of Rubinstein (1956, 5) and Schaffer (1966, 142), but such an interpretation has been rejected by Meyer (1989, 207).

[141] Stephenson, "Political Sociology of the Eighteenth Congressional District."

vestment naturally pays huge dividends. [...] grateful constituents can win general elections (Rovere 1944, 395–396).[142]

Antonini's hand-picked candidate to challenge Marcantonio in the 1942 primaries of the American Labor Party was an implicit and indirect confirmation of the influence and power of the congressman's political machine. Mucciolo was a former secretary to Marcantonio, that is, somebody whose name East Harlem's voters were quite familiar with as the go-between for patronage in their district.[143] Since the mid-1930s, whenever Marcantonio was in Washington, the congressman had usually asked his constituents with problems to call on Mucciolo at the Fiorello LaGuardia Political Club.[144] It is therefore likely that, unable to defeat Marcantonio by other means, the right wing of the American Labor Party made an eventually fruitless attempt at exploiting this one asset to lure a few grateful voters who had secured jobs, relief, and assistance thanks to Mucciolo's intermediation.

However, except for Marcantonio, whose patronage enabled him to control the Republican organization in the district and even to make deals with Tammany Hall when the latter did not support him officially (Moscow 1971, 59–60; Garrett 1961, 306–307), Italian-American politicians still struggled for political positions in East Harlem. In the mid-1930s a student of local partisan organizations remarked that "undoubtedly the future of New York, at least the immediate future, belongs to the sons of Italy" (Peel 1935, 252). Nevertheless, Italian Americans failed to secure political power as an ethnic group. Their influence in the 1930s and early 1940s resulted from both the size of their cohort of voters within the total electorate of the Congressional district and the might of LaGuardia's and Marcantonio's personal machines. In spite of LaGuardia's hold on the mayoralty and Marcantonio's control of the Eighteenth Congressional District, Italian Americans' under-representation in public office continued at least throughout the 1940s. After Tammany Hall had refused to grant its own formal endorsement to Marcantonio and designated Irish-American Martin Kennedy against him in the 1944 primaries, an East Harlem resident of Italian extraction still complained about the Democratic Party that "according to voting representation, the Italo-Americans should have received nominations for four assembly seats, two state senators, and one [c]ongressman, but we got nothing! This year the nomination for

---

[142] For further and less impressionistic details about Marcantonio's machine, see Meyer (1989, 87-111). See also Murtagh (2010).

[143] "Marcantonio Maps 3 Primary Fights," NYT, June 7, 1942, 36.

[144] See, e.g., Vito Marcantonio to Angelina Letzia, Washington D.C., April 25, 1935, VMP, box 6, folder "L."

county judge was promised to an 'Italian American,' but when the time came the 'Party' gave it to an Irish American" (anonymous, as quoted in Bone 1946, 275).[145]

In 1950 New Yorkers of Italian extraction reached the climax of their political power. Carmine DeSapio had been the new boss of Tammany Hall since the previous year and three of their fellow ethnics were running for City Hall (Moscow 1971; Eire 1988, 122, 150, 171). They were Corsi on the GOP ticket, Ferdinand Pecora for the Democratic Party, and the acting mayor as well as eventual winner Vincent Impellitteri as an independent (LaGumina 1992, 106–130). Yet, as Italian Americans' numerical strength was watered down by the 1944 reapportionment of East Harlem, so was their political clout in the Eighteenth Congressional District. When Marcantonio decided not to run in 1952, Vito Magli made a hopeless bid for U.S. Representative on the ticket of the American Labor Party, receiving as few as 6,663 votes as opposed to Marcantonio's 36,095 two years earlier (Meyer 1989, 44, 111). But, in the Congressional races that followed Marcantonio's defeat, none of the candidates of either major party was from Italian background until Alfred A. Santangelo received the Democratic nomination and won election to the U.S. House from that district in 1956 (Santangelo 1999). Moreover, although he managed to retain his seat in Congress in 1948, in this year as well as in 1950 even Marcantonio himself was rejected by both the Republican and the Democratic Party establishment. Specifically, he was compelled to run only on the ticket of the American Labor Party under the provisions of New York State's 1947 Wilson-Pakula Act, which had outlawed open primaries for candidates and prevented any member of a specific party from competing for the nomination of another party without the consent of the latter's County Committee (Meyer 1989, 47; Shefter 1994, 216–218; Barry 2009, 231–233).

---

[145] "Tammany Rejects Marcantonio Bid," NYT, June 2, 1944, 1.

WORKS CITED

A.B. "Lettera da Washington." *La Settimana*, January 3, 1936: 14.

Abt, John J. with Michael Myerson. *Advocate and Activist: Memoirs of an American Communist Lawyer*. Urbana: University of Illinois Press, 1993.

Antonini, Luigi. *Vito Marcantonio: The Man on the Flying Trapeze*. New York: S. Romualdi and S.M. Levitas, n.d.

Ariel. "Vigilia elettorale." *Il Progresso Italo-Americano*, November 3, 1930: 6.

Astrologo. "Lanzetta ossessionato." *La Stampa Libera*, October 3, 1934: 4.

Bacigalupi, Evelyn M. "The Italian Americans in the Political Arena." *Atlantica* 4.2 (1933): 213-219.

Baily, Samuel L. *Immigrants in the Lands of Promise: Italians in Buenos Aires and New York City, 1870 to 1914*. Ithaca, N.Y.: Cornell University Press, 1999.

Barone, Michael. "Italian Americans and Politics." *Italian Americans: New Perspectives in Italian Immigration and Ethnicity*, edited by Lydio F. Tomasi. Staten Island, N.Y.: Center for Migration Studies, 1985. 378-384.

Barry, Francis S. *The Scandal of Reform: The Grand Failure of New York's Political Crusaders*. New Brunswick, N.J.: Rutgers University Press, 2009.

Bayor, Ronald H. *Neighbors in Conflict: The Irish, Germans, Jews, and Italians of New York City, 1929-1941*. Baltimore, Md.: Johns Hopkins University Press, 1978.

———. "The Neighborhood Invasion Pattern." *Neighborhoods in Urban America*, edited by Ronald H. Bayor. Port Washington, N.Y.: Kennikat Press, 1982. 86-102.

———. *La Guardia: Ethnicity and Reform*. Arlington Heights, Ill.: Harlan Davidson, 1993.

Bellush, Bernard. *Franklin D. Roosevelt as Governor of New York*. New York: Columbia University Press, 1952.

Berkowitz, Michael. "Americanization and Ethnicity in an Italian Community: Immigrants, Education, and Politics in East Harlem, 1920 to 1941." B.A. thesis, Princeton University, 1987.

Berrol, Selma. *The Empire City: New York and Its People, 1624-1996*. Westport, Conn.: Praeger, 1997.

Berson, Robin Kadison. *Marching to a Different Drummer: Unrecognized Heroes of American History*. Westport, Conn.: Greenwood Press, 1994.

Board of Elections of the City of New York. *Annual Report of the Board of Elections of the City of New York*. New York: Board of Elections of the City of New York, 1932.

Bone, Hugh A. "Political Parties in New York City." *American Political Science Review* 40.2 (1946): 272-282.

Brock, William R. *Welfare, Democracy, and the New Deal*. New York: Cambridge University Press, 1988.

Bugiardini, Sergio. "Notabilato e personale politico nella comunità italiana di New York tra Otto e Novecento." *L'Italia dei notabili: Il punto della situazione*, edited by Luigi Ponziani. Naples: Edizioni Scientifiche Italiane, 2001. 553-596.

_____. "'Stretti tra gli irlandesi e la non partecipazione...': Gli italo-americani di New York City e l'accesso in politica." *Storia e Problemi Contemporanei* 19.46 (2006): 115-135.

Busch, Andrew E. *Horses in Midstream: U.S. Mid-term Elections and Their Consequences, 1894-1998*. Pittsburgh: University of Pittsburgh Press, 1999.

Campailla, Sergio. "Little Italy." *Il sogno italo-americano: Realtà e immaginario dell'emigrazione negli Stati Uniti*, edited by Sebastiano Martelli. Naples: Cuen, 1998. 49-64.

Cannistraro, Philip V. "Generoso Pope and the Rise of Italia Americans in Politics, 1925-1936." *Italian Americans: New Perspectives in Italian Immigration and Ethnicity*, edited by Lydio F. Tomasi. Staten Island, N.Y.: Center for Migration Studies, 1985. 265-288.

Caro, Robert A. *The Power Broker: Robert Moses and the Fall of New York*. New York: Alfred A. Knopf, 1974.

Cerase, Francesco Paolo. *L'emigrazione di ritorno. Innovazione o reazione? L'esperienza dell'emigrazione di ritorno dagli Stati Uniti d'America*. Rome: Pubblicazioni della Facoltà di Scienze Statistiche Demografiche e Attuariali, 1971.

Charney, George. *A Long Journey*. Chicago: Quadrangle Books, 1968.

Cinotto, Simone. "A Place Called Home: Italian Americans and Public Housing in New York, 1937-1941." *Small Towns, Big Cities: The Urban Experience of Italian Americans*, edited by Dennis Barone and Stefano Luconi. New York: American Italian Historical Association, 2010. 52-73.

Cole, Wayne S. *Roosevelt and the Isolationists, 1932-1945*. Lincoln: University of Nebraska Press, 1983.

Corbella, Nicoletta Pardi. "Storia di un sindacato operaio italiano a New York (i sarti)." *Gli italiani negli Stati Uniti: L'emigrazione e l'opera degli italiani negli Stati Uniti d'America*, edited by Rudolph J. Vecoli et al. Florence: Istituto di Studi Americani, 1972. 365-381.

Corsi, Edward. "My Neighborhood." *Outlook*, September 16, 1925: 90-92.

_____. *In the Shadow of Liberty: The Chronicle of Ellis Island*. New York: Macmillan, 1935.

_____. "Vigilia elettorale: Doveri da compiere." *La Settimana*, October 23, 1936: 3.

Covello, Leonard. *The Heart Is the Teacher*. New York: McGraw-Hill, 1958.

Cuneo, Ernest. *Life with Fiorello: A Memoir*. New York: Macmillan, 1955.

Dahl, Robert. *Who Governs? Democracy and Power in an American City*. New Haven, Conn.: Yale University Press, 1961.

De Caro, Giuseppe. "Ancora della mossa di Lanzetta contro Corsi." *La Stampa Libera*, October 5, 1934: 4.

Department of Commerce, Bureau of the Census. *Fifteenth Census of the United States: Supervisors' Districts, New York*. Washington, D.C.: U.S. Government Printing Office, 1930.

Deschamps, Bénédicte. "Le racisme anti-italien aux États-Unis (1880-1940)." *Exclure au nom de la race (États-Unis, Irlande, Grande-Bretagne)*, edited by Michel Prum. Paris: Syllepse, 2000. 59-81.

Doenecke, Justus D. *Storm on the Horizon: The Challenge to American Intervention, 1939-1941*. Lanham, Md.: Rowman & Littlefield, 2000.

Eire, Steven P. *Rainbow's End: Irish Americans and the Dilemmas of Urban Machine Politics, 1840-1985*. Berkeley: University of California Press, 1988.

Elliott, Lawrence. *Little Flower: The Life and Times of Fiorello La Guardia*. New York: Morrow, 1983.

Farina, Santo. "Letter to the Editor." *La Stampa Libera*, May 19, 1936: 6.

Ferber, Nat J. *A New American: From the Life Story of Salvatore A. Cotillo, Supreme Court Justice, State of New York*. New York: Farrar & Rinehart, 1938.

Fowler, Gene. *Beau James: The Life and Times of Jimmy Walker*. Clifton, N.J.: Kelley, 1973.

Garrett, Charles. *The La Guardia Years: Machine and Reform Politics in New York City*. New Brunswick, N.J.: Rutgers University Press, 1961.

Garza, Hedda. *Latinas: Hispanic Women in the United States*. New York: Franklin Watts, 1994.

Glazer, Nathan and Daniel Patrick Moynihan. *Beyond the Melting Pot: The Negroes, Puerto Ricans, Jews, Italians, and Irish of New York City*. Cambridge, Mass.: M.I.T. Press, 1963.

Goldman, Eric Frederick. *Rendezvous with Destiny: A History of Modern American Reform*. New York: Vintage Books, 1952.

Goodman, Madeline J. "The Evolution of Ethnicity: Fascism and Anti-Fascism in the Italian-American Community, 1914-1945." Ph.D. dissertation, Carnegie Mellon University, 1993.

Guglielmo, Jennifer. *Living the Revolution: Italian Women's Resistance and Radicalism in New York City, 1880-1945*. Chapel Hill: University of North Carolina Press, 2010.

Gurock, Jeffrey S. *When Harlem Was Jewish, 1870-1930*. New York: Columbia University Press, 1979.

Henderson, Thomas M. *Tammany Hall and the New Immigrants: The Progressive Years*. New York: Arno Press, 1976.

_____. "Immigrant Politician: Salvatore Cotillo, Progressive Ethnic." *International Migration Review* 13.1 (Spring 1979): 81-102.

Jackson, Peter. "Vito Marcantonio and Ethnic Politics in New York." *Ethnic and Racial Studies* 6.1 (1983): 50-71.

Jeffers, H. Paul. *The Napoleon of New York City: Mayor Fiorello La Guardia*. New York: John Wiley & Sons, 2002.

Johanek, Michael C. and John L. Puckett. *Leonard Covello and the Making of Benjamin Franklin High School: Education as if Citizenship Mattered*. Philadelphia: Temple University Press, 2007.

Kanawada, Jr., Leo V. *Franklin D. Roosevelt's Diplomacy and American Catholics, Italians, and Jews*. Ann Arbor, Mich. UMI Research Press, 1982.

Kaner, Norman Jay. "Towards a Minority of One: Vito Marcantonio and American Foreign Policy." Ph.D. dissertation, Rutgers University, 1968.

Kessner, Thomas. *The Golden Door: Italian and Jewish Immigrant Mobility in New York City, 1880-1915*. New York: Oxford University Press, 1977.

_____. *Fiorello H. La Guardia and the Making of Modern New York*. New York: McGraw-Hill, 1989.

Klehr, Harvey. *The Heyday of American Communism: The Depression Decade*. New York: Basic Books, 1984.

Krase, Jerome. "The Missed Step: Italian Americans and Brooklyn Politics." *Italians and Irish in America*, edited by Francis X. Femminella. Staten Island, N.Y.: American Italian Historical Association, 1985. 187-198.

Krase, Jerome, and Charles LaCerra. *Ethnicity and Machine Politics*. Lanham, Md.: University Press of America, 1991.

LaCerra, Charles. *Franklin Delano Roosevelt and Tammany Hall of New York*. Lanham, Md.: University Press of America, 1997.

La Guardia, Fiorello H. *The Making of an Insurgent: An Autobiography, 1882-1919*. Philadelphia: J.B. Lippincott, 1948.

LaGumina, Salvatore J. *Vito Marcantonio: The People's Politician*. Dubuque, Ia.: Kendall Hunt, 1969.

_____. "Vito Marcantonio: A Study in the Functional and Ideological Dynamics of a Labor Politician." *Labor History* 13.3 (1972): 374-399.

_____. "Introduction." *WOP! A Documentary History of Anti-Italian Discrimination in the United States*, edited by Salvatore J. LaGumina. San Francisco: Straight Arrow Books, 1973. 9-19.

_____. "American Political Process and Italian Participation in New York State." *Perspectives in Italian Immigration and Ethnicity*, edited by Silvano M. Tomasi. New York: Center for Migration Studies, 1977. 85-102.

_____. *The Immigrants Speak: Italian Americans Tell Their Story*. New York: Center for Migration Studies, 1979.

_____. "Francis Barreto Spinola, Nineteenth Century Patriot and Politicians." *The Italian Americans Through the Generations*, edited by Rocco Caporale. Staten Island: American Italian Historical Association, 1986. 22-34.

_____. *New York at Mid-Century: The Impellitteri Years*. Westport, Conn.: Greenwood, 1992.

_____. "March and Vaccarelli: Turn-of-the-Century Political Bosses." *Italian Americans in a Multicultural Society*, edited by Jerome Krase and Judith N. DeSena. Stony Brook, N.Y.: Forum Italicum, 1994. 200-216.

_____. *The Humble and the Heroic: Wartime Italian Americans*. Youngstown, N.Y.: Cambria Press, 2006.

Lait, Jack and Lee Mortimer. *U.S.A. Confidential*. New York: Crown, 1952.

Leinenweber, Charles. "The Class and Ethnic Bases of New York Socialism." *Labor History* 22.1 (1981): 31-56.

Livi Bacci, Massimo. *L'immigrazione e l'assimilazione degli italiani negli Stati Uniti secondo le statistiche demografiche americane*. Milan: Giuffrè, 1961.

Lowi, Theodore J. *At the Pleasure of the Mayor: Patronage and Power in New York City, 1898-1958*. New York: Free Press, 1964.

Lupo, Salvatore. *Quando la mafia trovò l'America: Storia di un intreccio intercontinentale, 1888-2008*. Turin: Einaudi, 2008.

Limpus, Lowell M. and Burr W. Leyson. *This Man LaGuardia*. New York: Dutton, 1938.

Mann, Arthur. *La Guardia: A Fighter against His Times, 1882-1933*. Philadelphia: J.B. Lippincott, 1959.

_____. *La Guardia Comes to Power, 1933*. Philadelphia: J.B. Lippincott, 1965.

Marazzi, Martino. *Voices of Italian America: A History of Early Italian American Literature with a critical Anthology.* Madison, N.J.: Fairleigh Dickinson University Press, 2006.

Marcantonio, Vito. *The Registration of Aliens.* New York: American Committee for the Protection of Foreign Born, 1940.

_____. *I Vote My Conscience: Debates, Speeches and Writings of Vito Marcantonio,* edited by Annette T. Rubinstein. New York: Vito Marcantonio Memorial, 1956.

Martellone, Anna Maria. "Per una storia della sinistra italiana negli Stati Uniti: riformismo e sindacalismo, 1880-1911." *Il movimento migratorio italiano dall'unità nazionale ai giorni nostri,* edited by Franca Assante. Geneve: Librairie Droz, 1978. 181-195.

_____. "La presenza dell'elemento etnico italiano nella vita politica degli Stati Uniti: Dalla non partecipazione alla post etnia." in Fondazione Giacomo Brodolini, *Gli italiani fuori d'Italia: Gli emigranti italiani nei movimenti operai dei paesi d'adozione,* edited by Bruno Bezza. Milan: Angeli, 1983. 345-358.

_____. "Italian Immigrants, Party Machines, Ethnic Brokers in City Politics, from the 1880s to the 1930s." *The European Emigrant Experience in the U.S.A,* edited by Walter Hölbling and Reinhold Wagnleitner. Tübingen: Gunter Narr Verlag, 1992. 171-187.

Martinelli, Phyllis Cancilla. "Italian-American Experience," *America's Ethnic Politics,* edited by Joseph S. Roucek and Bernard Eisenberg. Westport, Conn.: Greenwood, 1982. 217-231.

Masillo, Cosimo. "Per le elezioni." *Il Progresso Italo-Americano,* November 8, 1938: 6.

McNickle, Chris. *To Be Mayor of New York: Ethnic Politics in the City.* New York: Columbia University Press, 1993.

Meier, Kenneth J. and Joseph Steward, Jr. *The Politics of Hispanic Education: Un Paso Pa'lante y Dos Pa'tras.* Albany: State University of New York Press, 1991.

Meyer, Gerald. "Leonard Covello and Vito Marcantonio: A Lifelong Collaboration for Progress." *Italica* 62.1 (1985): 54-66.

_____. *Vito Marcantonio: Radical Politician, 1902-1954.* Albany: State University of New York Press, 1989.

_____. "The American Labor Party and New York City's Italian American Communities: 1936-1950." *Industry, Technology, Labor, and the Italian-American Communities,* edited by Mario Aste et al. Staten Island, N.Y.: American Italian Historical Association, 1997. 33-49.

_____. "Italian Harlem: Portrait of a Community." *The Italians of New York: Five Centuries of Struggle and Achievement,* edited by Philip V. Cannistraro. New York: New York Historical Society and John D. Calandra Italian American Institute, 1999. 57-67.

_____. "*L'Unità del Popolo*: The Voice of Italian American Communism, 1939-1951." *Italian American Review* 8.1 (2001): 121-55.

_____. "Italian Americans and the American Communist Party." *The Lost World of Italian American Radicalism: Politics, Labor, and Culture,* edited by Philip V. Cannistraro and Gerald Meyer. Westport, Conn.: Praeger, 2003. 205-227.

Milazzo, John. "La locale 89." *Il Progresso Italo-Americano,* November 25, 1935: 6.

Mitgang, Herbert. *The Man Who Rode the Tiger: The Life and Times of Judge Samuel Seabury.* Philadelphia: J.B. Lippincott, 1963.

_____. *Once Upon a Time in New York.* New York: Free Press, 2000.

Montana, Vanni B. *Amarostico: Testimonianze euro-americane*. Leghorn: Bastogi, 1975.

Mormino, Gary R. and George E. Pozzetta, "Italian Americans and the 1940s." *The Italians of New York: Five Centuries of Struggle and Achievement*, edited by Philip V. Cannistraro. New York: New York Historical Society and John D. Calandra Italian American Institute, 1999. 139-153.

Moscow, Warren. *What Have You Done for Me Lately? The Ins and Outs of New York City Politics*. Englewood Cliffs, N.J.: Prentice Hall, 1967.

_____. *The Last of Big-Time Bosses: The Life and Times of Carmine DeSapio and the Decline of Tammany Hall*. New York: Stein and Day, 1971.

Murtagh, Matthew. "Politician, Social Worker, and Lawyer: Vito Marcantonio and Constituent Legal Services." May 18, 2010. Accessed September 9, 2010. http://www.vitomarcantonio. com/oa_political_socialworker_lawyer.html.

Naison, Mark. *Communists in Harlem during the Depression*. Urbana: University of Illinois Press, 1983.

Nasaw, David. *The Chief: The Life of William Randolph Hearst*. Boston: Houghton Mifflin, 2000.

Ojeda, Felix Reyes. *Vito Marcantonio y Puerto Rico: Por los trabajadores y por la nación*. Rió Piedras: Huracán, 1978.

Orsi, Robert Anthony. *The Madonna of 115th Street: Faith and Community in Italian Harlem, 1880-1950*. New Haven, Conn.: Yale University Press, 1985.

Ottanelli, Fraser M. *The Communist Party of the United States: From the Depression to World War II*. New Brunswick, N.J.: Rutgers University Press, 1991.

Pagano, Alessandro. "Barreto Spinola, Francis." in Fondazione Casa America, *I primi italiani in America del Nord: Dizionario biografico dei liguri, piemontesi e altri: Storie e presenze italiane tra Settecento e Ottocento*. Reggio Emilia: Diabasis, 2009. 68-69.

Pantò, Carmelo and Onorio Giunta. "Una rettifica." *Il Progresso Italo-Americano*, November 1, 1936: 2.

Peel, Roy V. *Political Clubs of New York City*. Port Washington, N.Y.: Friedman, 1935.

Perkins, Frances. *The Roosevelt I Knew*. New York: Viking Press, 1946.

Piretti, Maria Serena. *Le elezioni politiche in Italia dal 1848 a oggi*. Rome and Bari: Laterza, 1995.

Piven, Frances Fox and Richard A. Cloward. *Poor People's Movements: Why They Succeed, How They Fail*. New York: Pantheon Books, 1977.

Pope, Generoso. "Per una nomina." *Il Progresso Italo-Americano*, October 19, 1932: 1.

Pretelli, Matteo. *Il fascismo e gli italiani all'estero*. Bologna: Clueb, 2010.

Rizzo, Cesare. "Solidarietà italiana." *Il Progresso Italo-Americano*, October 31, 1936: 6.

Rodgers, Cleveland and Rebecca B. Rankin. *New York: The World's Capital City*. New York: Harper, 1948.

Rolle, Andrew. *Italian Americans: Troubled Roots*. Norman: University of Oklahoma Press, 1980.

Roosevelt, Franklin D. *The Public Papers and Addresses of Franklin D. Roosevelt*, vol. 9: *War and Aid to Democracies*, edited by Samuel I. Rosenman. New York: Macmillan, 1941.

_____. *F.D.R.: His Personal Letters, 1928-1945*, edited by Elliott Roosevelt. New York: Duell, Sloane and Pearce, 1950.

Roucek, Joseph S. "Italo-Americans and World War II." *Sociology and Social Research* 29.6 (1945): 465-471.

Rovere, Richard H. "Marcantonio: Machine Politician, New Style." *Harper's Magazine* 188.1127 (1944): 391-398.

Rubinstein, Annette T. "Vito Marcantonio, Congressman." Vito Marcantonio, *I Vote My Conscience: Debates, Speeches and Writings of Vito Marcantonio*, edited by Annette T. Rubinstein. New York: Vito Marcantonio Memorial, 1956. 1-34.

Salerno, Eric. *Rossi a Manhattan*. Rome: Quiritta, 2001.

Salvemini, Gaetano. *Italian Fascist Activities in the United States*, edited by Philip V. Cannistraro. New York: Center for Migration Studies, 1977.

_____. *Dai ricordi di un fuoruscito*, edited by Mimmo Franzinelli. Turin: Bollati Boringhieri, 2002.

Santangelo, Alfred E. "Presentation." *Ethnicity in American Political Life: The Italian American Experience*, edited by Salvatore J. LaGumina. Staten Island, N.Y.: American Italian Historical Association, 1969. 6-15.

Santangelo, Betty L. *Lucky Corner: The Biography of Congressman Alfred E. Santangelo and the Rise of Italian-Americans in Politics*. New York: Center for Migration Studies, 1999.

Sasuly, Richard. "Vito Marcantonio: The People's Politician." *American Radicals: Some Problems and Personalities*, edited by Harvey Goldberg. New York: Monthly Review Press, 1957. 145-163.

Schaffer, Alan. *Vito Marcantonio: Radical in Congress*. Syracuse, N.Y.: Syracuse University Press, 1966.

Sexton, Patricia Cayo. *Spanish Harlem: Anatomy of Poverty*. New York: Harper and Row, 1965.

Shefter, Martin. *Political Parties and the State: The American Historical Experience*. Princeton, N.J.: Princeton University Press, 1994.

Sherman, John W. *A Communist Front at Mid-Century: The American Committee for Protection of Foreign Born, 1933-1959*. Westport, Conn.: Praeger, 2001.

Simon, John J. "Rebel in the House: The Life and Times of Vito Marcantonio." *Monthly Review* 57.11 (2006): 25-46.

Speroni, Gigi. *Fiorello La Guardia: Il più grande italiano d'America*. Milan: Rusconi, 1993.

Swanberg, W.A. *Norman Thomas: The Last Idealist*. New York: Charles Scribner's Sons, 1976.

Tarangelo, Victor. "A chi il nostro voto? All'Onorevole James J. Lanzetta." *Il Grido della Stirpe*, October 24, 1936: 7.

Thomas, Lorrin. *Puerto Rican Citizen: History and Political Identity in Twentieth-Century New York*. Chicago: University of Chicago Press, 2010.

Tintori, Guido. "Amministrazione Roosevelt e 'Labor etnico': Un caso italiano: Luigi Antonini." Ph.D. dissertation, University of Milan, 2005.

Tricarico, Donald. *The Italians of Greenwich Village: The Social Structure and Transformation of a Community*. Staten Island, N.Y.: Center for Migration Studies, 1984.

_____. "Labels and Stereotypes." *The Italian American Experience: An Encyclopedia*, edited by Salvatore J. LaGumina et al. New York: Garland, 2000. 319-321.

Un ennese. "Si sono ubriacati tutti." *La Stampa Libera*, May 14, 1936: 6.

U.S. Congress. *Biographical Directory of the American Congress, 1774-1961*. Washington, D.C.: U.S. Government Printing Office, 1961.

Vega, Bernardo. *Memoirs of Bernardo Vega: A Contribution to the History of the Puerto Rican Community in New York*. New York: Monthly Review Press, 1984.

Venturini, Nadia. *Neri e italiani ad Harlem: Gli anni Trenta e la Guerra d'Etiopia*. Rome: Edizioni Lavoro, 1990.

_____. "Nascita di un complesso di edilizia popolare a New York: East River Houses." *Storia Urbana* 20.75 (1996): 53-83.

Vezzosi, Elisabetta. *Il socialismo indifferente: Immigrati italiani e Socialist Party negli Stati Uniti del primo Novecento*. Rome: Edizioni Lavoro, 1991.

_____. "Radical Ethnic Brokers: Immigrant Socialist Leaders in the United States between Ethnic Community and the Larger Society." *Italian Workers of the World: Labor Migration and the Formation of Multiethnic States*, edited by Donna R. Gabaccia and Fraser M. Ottanelli. Urbana: University of Illinois Press, 2001. 121-138.

Walsh, George. *Gentleman Jimmy Walker: Mayor of the Jazz Age*. Westport, Conn.: Praeger, 1974.

Waltzer, Kenneth Alan. "The American Labor Party: Third Party Politics in New York, 1936-1954." Ph.D. dissertation, Harvard University, 1978.

Ware, Caroline. "Cultural Groups in the United States." *The Cultural Approach to History*, edited by Caroline Ware. New York: Columbia University Press, 1940. 61-89.

Wenger, Beth S. *New York Jews and the Great Depression: Uncertain Promise*. New Haven, Conn.: Yale University Press, 1996.

Workers of the Federal Writers' Project. *The Italians of New York*. New York: Random House, 1938.

Zappia, Charles A. "Unionism and the Italian American Worker: The Politics of Anti-Communism in the International Ladies' Garment Workers' Union in New York City, 1900-1925." *The Italian Americans through the Generations*, edited by Rocco Caporale. Staten Island, N.Y.: American Italian Historical Association, 1986. 77-87.

_____. "From Working-Class Radicalism to Cold War Anti-Communism: The Case of the Italian Locals of the International Ladies' Garment Workers' Union." *The Lost World of Italian American Radicalism: Politics, Labor, and Culture*, edited by Philip V. Cannistraro and Gerald Meyer. Westport, Conn.: Praeger, 2003. 143-159.

Zinn, Howard. *La Guardia in Congress*. New York: Norton, 1959.

III. Empirical Analyses

HOW DO ITALIAN AMERICANS VOTE—AND DOES IT MATTER?
Testing the 'Symbolic Rewards Hypothesis' in the U.S. House of Representatives

Rodrigo Praino
UNIVERSITY OF CONNECTICUT

INTRODUCTION

Currently the American state with the "most Italian" congressional delegation is Wyoming. In fact, two thirds of its entire congressional delegation is of Italian ancestry. According to the latest data available by the U.S. Census Bureau, there are a little over 11,600 people in the state of Wyoming who claim Italian ancestry, for a grand total of about 2.35 percent of the population of that state. True, Wyoming's congressional delegation is composed of only three people, but both senators elected in that state, Michael B. Enzi and John A. Barrasso, are Italian Americans. This strange case leads us to a number of important questions: Is the election of an Italian American more likely in places with large concentration of Italian-American voters? Does an Italian-American ethnic vote even exist in the United States? Other than affiliation to an ethnic group, is there any other socioeconomic factor that makes the political success of an Italian-American politician any more likely? This essay attempts to provide answers to these questions by analyzing a great amount of empirical data pertaining to elections of the U.S. House of Representatives between 1972 and 2008. The time frame is dictated by availability of data: before the 1970 census, there is no data gathered by congressional districts, and only starting in 1980 did the U.S. Census Bureau include questions about ancestry in its surveys. The choice to focus the analysis on the U.S. House of Representatives was dictated by methodological concerns. Being entirely renewed every two years, the House represents the best possible statistical laboratory available to political scientists, first because the number of cases available in the time frame—over eight thousand observations—allows the comfortable use of parametric methods of analysis, second because it provides an overall view of the country at large that analyses centered in specific states simply cannot provide.

At its very core, this work deals with political representation. Much has been written in political science about this topic, including some interesting works focused on ethnic or racial groups, their demands, their preferences, and the people who represent them in American institutions. Very little, however, has ever been written about Italian Americans and all the other important ancestry groups that exist in the United States. Interestingly enough, the work that probably inaugurated the entire political science sub-field of voting behavior, Berelson, Lazarsfeld, and McPhee's *Voting* (1954), paid great attention to Italian Americans as a politicized ethnic group. Successively, it is as if the literature got divided in two separate and seldom connected branches, with scholars interested in voting behavior completely forgetting about Italian Americans, and scholars dedicated to ethnic studies concentrating their efforts more on racial than ethnic groups, and studying, for the most part, African Americans and Hispanic Americans. This work starts to fill an immense gap within the political science literature, by providing some interesting insights on the dynamics of the political behavior of Italian Americans.

In the first part of this essay, I will provide a comprehensive review of the works dealing with political representation that are relevant to my analysis. I will then develop a comprehensive analytical framework for the study of ethnic politics in the United States. Once the theoretical framework is set up, I will briefly present the original dataset that I built for this work, and use it as empirical evidence against which the hypotheses formulated in the theoretical part will be tested. In conclusion, I will discuss my findings and present some interesting avenues for future research.

Political Representation and Ethnic Groups: Class or Ethnicity?

Since Nathan Glazer and Daniel Patrick Moynihan completed their seminal work *Beyond the Melting Pot* (1963), the idea of ethnic politics became intrinsically related to the idea of a group asking for material and tangible rewards. In other words, ethnic groups became groups sharing not only ethnicity, but also, to a great extent, socioeconomic conditions. According to this interpretation, ethnic groups are used by modern governments, be it the American version of the welfare state or the European version of social democracy, to distribute more tangible benefits to smaller groups than large social classes and, in exchange, obtain their political support (Glazer and Moynihan 1975, 8-9). Roughly along the same lines was the explanation given by Michael Parenti (1967, 725) about the persistence of ethnic identity and its relationship to ethnic politics:

> [The politician] in dealing with a mass of data must find some means of ordering it into meaningful and more manipulatable categories. More specifically, he must find means of making his constituency accessible to him in the most economical way. Given the limited availability of campaign resources and the potentially limitless demands for expenditure, the candidate is in need for a ready-made formal and informal network of relational sub-structures within his constituency. He dis-

covers that "reaching the people" is often a matter of reaching particular people who themselves can reach, or help him reach, still other people.

Such outcome-related interpretation finds its apotheosis in the realm of African American studies, where the idea of a "black linked fate" (Dawson 1994), this feeling among the members of an ethnic group that the destiny of all members of the group is tied together, became mainstream political knowledge.

A different interpretation was provided by Hanna Pitkin (1967), according to whom political representation can take the form of representation as "standing for" or representation as "acting for." In Pitkin's work (1967, 102), representation as "standing for" is a kind of political representation where the acts of the person representing a larger group are seldom of any importance, since this person represents the group "by definition." As Talcott Parsons (1975, 56) put it, this idea is sociologically different from the idea of a group with specific functions, for group membership, in this case, "characterizes what the individual *is* rather than what he *does*." According to Pitkin (1967, 113):

> Where the representative is likened to a descriptive representation or a symbol, he is usually seen as an inanimate object and not in terms of any activity; he represents by what he is or how he is regarded. He does not represent by doing anything at all; so it makes no sense to talk about his role or his duties and whether he has performed them.

In brief, the dilemma that must be solved seems to be whether a member of an ethnic group represents well his/her ethnic group only because he/she is a member of the group or because the group largely shares socioeconomic conditions and, therefore, the actions of the member of the group who is chosen to represent the others will almost certainly benefit the entire group. Apparently these two scenarios are not necessarily in contradiction, but in essence they are. Most scholars interested in ethnic politics have focused their works either on the ability of legislators to put on the legislative agenda policies which are considered important to the ethnically-based community (cf. Bratton and Haynie 1999; Haynie 2001; Haynie 2002), or on the ability of these legislators to influence legislative outcomes (cf. Cameron, Epstein, and O'Halloran 1996; Lublin 1997; Nelson 1991; Preuhs 2001; Swain 1993). However, an interesting alternative to this policy-centered framework does exist within the literature. Even Pitkin (1967, 214-5), drawing from Burkean and Liberal theory, had to deal with this dilemma and decided to establish a clear distinction between private and public representation. She argued that a political representative "has a constituency rather than a single principal;

and that raises problems about whether such an unorganized group can even have an interest for him to pursue, let alone a will to which he could be responsive, or an opinion before which he could attempt to justify what he has done," justifying her assessment with the general apathy, ignorance, and malleability of most members of such constituency. Much more recent empirical research seems to confirm Pitkin's intuitions by arguing that in reality people "care surprisingly little about most policies," and "would like very much to avoid politics" (Hibbing and Theiss-Morse 2005, 229). In the following section, I will present a theoretical framework that tries to distance itself from a policy-centered vision of ethnic politics, emphasizing its descriptive and symbolic elements.

REDISCOVERING "STATUS POLITICS"

The core of the problem when it comes to the analysis of ethnic politics, as Anne Phillips (2000, 162-164) pointed out, is that with the entry of concepts such as race, gender, and ethnicity in the American political arena, the classical and exclusive causal relation between class and difference became much more complicated, and "notions of 'typical' or 'mirror' or 'descriptive' representation have then returned with renewed force." In fact, analyses of the concept of representation within African American voters at the federal congressional level have shown that voters usually express higher levels of satisfaction when their representative is of their own race (Tate 2001). Some of these analyses have reached amazing levels of sophistication, with studies that go as far as elaborating the ideal criteria for the selection of descriptive representatives (cf. Dovi 2002). In essence, scholars tend to agree that "descriptive representation has a negative, significant and important effect on political alienation" (Pantoja and Segura 2003, 455) and even that "descriptive representation leads to political responsiveness," being more important than party allegiance, at least "outside of highly racialized political contexts" (Preuhs 2006, 598). Jane Mansbridge (1999, 628) provides an interesting conceptual synthesis, arguing that while descriptive representation is not always necessary, sometimes its benefits may exceed its costs, since it can provide four major functions to minoritarian groups: (1) adequate communication in contexts of mistrust; (2) innovative thinking in contexts of uncrystallized, not fully articulated, interests; (3) the creation of a social meaning of "ability to rule" for members of a group in historical contexts where that ability has been seriously questioned; (4) the increase of the polity's de facto legitimacy in contexts of past discrimination.

An interesting theoretical framework that can be used to consolidate the Glazer and Moynihan (1963; 1975) and the Pitkin (1967) approaches was developed by Richard Hofstadter (1963) and Seymour Martin Lipset (1963). While Hofstadter introduces the idea that in the United States people are generally anxious about their own status within society, Lipset brings the analysis to a different level by distinguishing between *class politics* and *status politics*. Given the fact that class politics is interrelated to the well-established concepts of class struggle and class conflict, Lipset's distinction paves the way towards the idea of a status struggle (Gusfield 1986, 17). In status politics, the defining social issues are expressive, rather than instrumental, in the sense that the benefits acquired through it are not translatable into other benefits (Chong 2000, 22). More precisely, if "class politics is political conflict over the allocation of material resources," then status politics is "political conflict over the allocation of prestige" (Gusfield 1986, 18). When transported into the realm of ethnic politics, status politics translates into the fact that "[t]he advancement of a fellow ethnic is not instrumental to some material end but is taken as a gratification in itself, evidence of the group's worth, its identity and its very existence in America" (Parenti 1962, 295).

In this sense, the real question that must be answered becomes whether ethnic groups seek through their political participation and voting behavior "tangible rewards" or "symbolic rewards," to use the terminology developed by Wolfinger (1966, 46). If an ethnic group decides to vote for a representative of their same group due to symbolic rewards, then the only link between the group and its representative should be a common ethnic background. Clearly, if each individual constituency and each individual representative is analyzed separately, several common traits linking one to the other will emerge. Consequently, the only way to empirically test this hypothesis, the "symbolic rewards hypothesis," is to utilize a statistical sample that is large enough and diverse enough in order to rule out any ulterior similarity between constituents and representatives and find the real nexus between these two groups. More formally, the main hypothesis of this work becomes, therefore, that if members of an ethnic group seek symbolic rewards from their elected representatives, then the best and only predictor in the country at large of electoral victory of a member of a particular ethnic group will be membership in the same group of a considerable number of constituents.

SOME DESCRIPTIVE STATISTICAL EVIDENCE

A very simple and quick glance at some descriptive statistical data stresses the importance of Italian Americans as an ethnic group in the United States. Figure 1 shows that, considering all congressional districts between 1972 and 2008, Italian Americans are the fifth ethnic group most present overall. Only African Americans, German Americans, Hispanic Americans and Irish Americans enjoy a mean presence across the country that is larger than the mean presence of Italian Americans. It means that, excluding Anglo-Saxon groups, Italian Americans are the second most present ancestry group in the country, since African Americans and Hispanic Americans are ethnic groups that comprehend a great number of subdivisions based on ancestry.

Interestingly, as figure 2 graphically represents, once the focus of the descriptive analysis shifts from the mean presence across all congressional districts to the analysis of the individual district containing the largest percentage of the total population belonging to each ethnic group, the Italian-American group becomes the non-Anglo-Saxon ancestry group with the highest percentage in a district in the entire country for the time period analyzed. This piece of information alone shows that Italian Americans as an ethnic group cannot be overlooked while analyzing American politics, for their geographical concentration may have numerous political consequences at different levels of government.

Figure 1. Mean Percentage of the Total Population of Congressional Districts by Ethnic Groups, 1972–2008

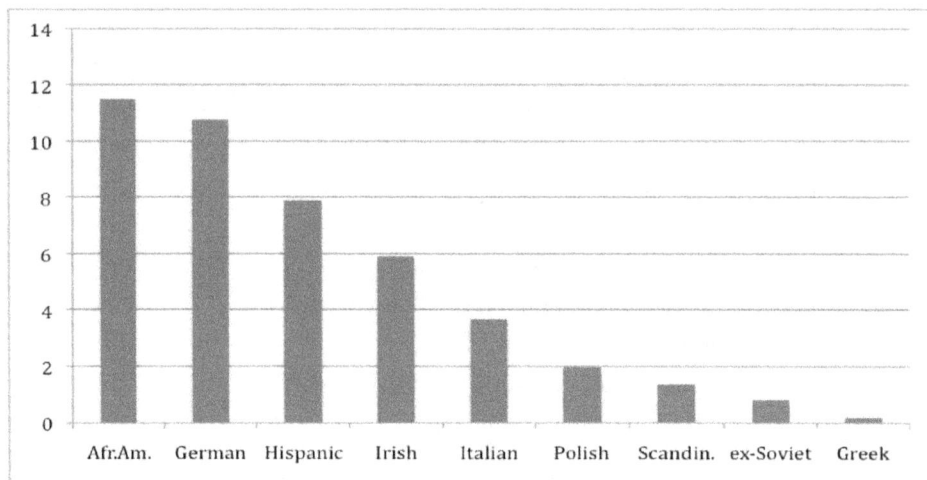

Source: compiled by author

Figure 2. Maximum Percentage of the Total Population of Members of an Ethnic Group
within Congressional Districts, 1972–2008

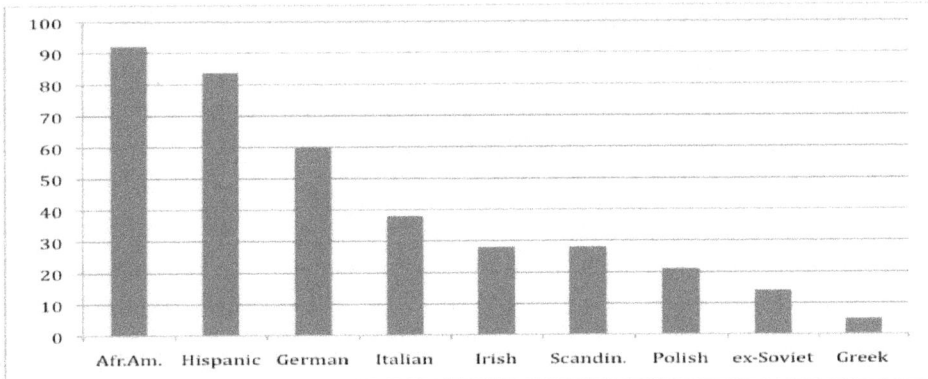

Source: compiled by author

Figure 3. Percentage of U.S. House of Representatives Elections with an Italian-American Winner by
State and Region, 1972–2008.

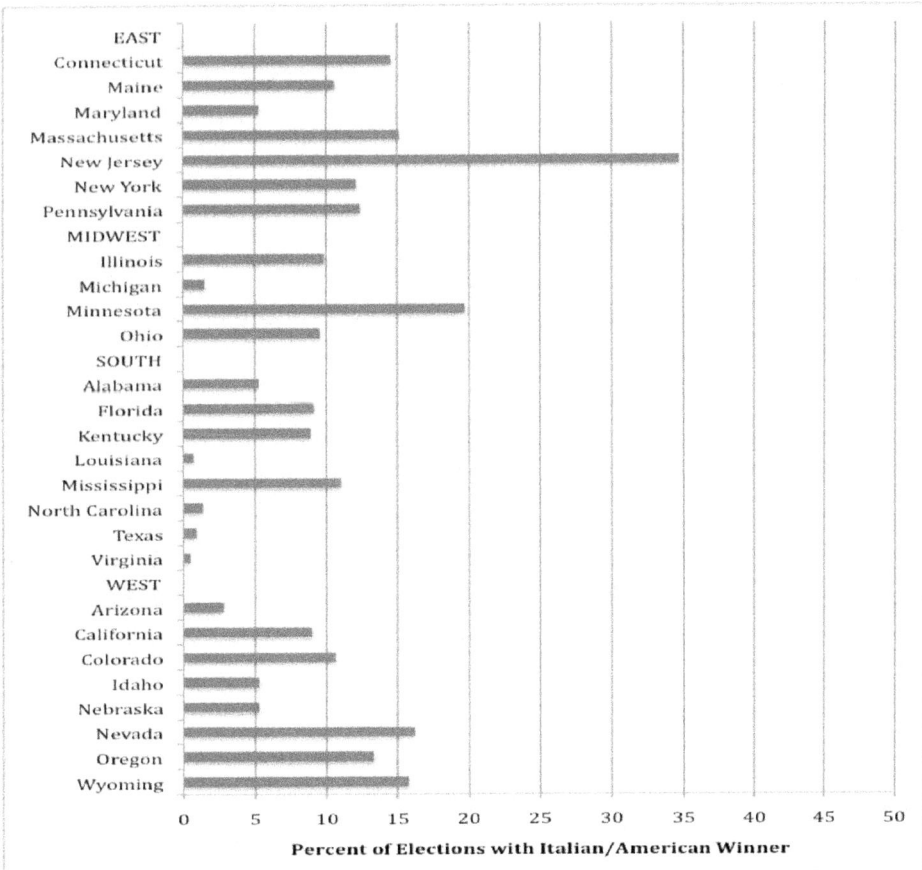

Source: compiled by author

Even more importantly, the combination of the two facts described above is probably enough to justify a detailed political analysis of the voting behavior of Italian Americans as an ethnic group. In fact, if the group is fairly present across the entire country and yet presents high levels of geographical concentration in individual districts, then it is only fair to hypothesize that the group may have an important political influence in the country as a whole.

Figure 3 provides further detail on the geographical concentration and distribution of successful Italian-American candidates for the U.S. House of Representatives between 1972 and 2008. Even though the states in the East tend to elect more Italian Americans than the states in the other regions of the country, Italian-American House candidates are quite successful in all regions, with several states in the Midwest and West, and even one Southern state, electing an Italian American in over 10 percent of all their House elections held between 1972 and 2008. This particular piece of information shows that any quantitative analysis of the Italian-American political influence as an ethnic group should not be concentrated in a specific area of the country, but should take into consideration, at least at the beginning, the entire nation. In fact, any analysis centered in states such as New Jersey, Connecticut, Pennsylvania, New York, Massachusetts, or Rhode Island may incur estimation bias and provide a partial and skewed picture of the entire Italian-American experience in the United States. Once an overall picture is established, specific analyses concentrated in the most interesting geographical areas may be extremely useful, providing insightful, detailed information, but such activity must take into account the overall status of the ethnic group within the entire country.

Further analyzing some descriptive data, it appears that there is some possible connection between the presence in congressional districts of a large Italian-American community and the electoral success of Italian-American candidates. Figure 4 shows the percentage of U.S. House of Representatives elections held between 1972 and 2008 with an Italian-American and a non-Italian-American winner divided by the Italian-American percentage of the total district population. In districts with less than 10 percent of the total population being of Italian origin, the overwhelming majority of electoral contests produce a non-Italian-American winner. When the Italian-American population increases to 11 to 25 percent of the total population the number of successful Italian-American candidates increases considerably. In districts where over 25 percent of the total population are Italian Americans, over 90 percent of electoral contests produce an Italian- American winner.

In brief, while it is hardly enough to establish causal relationships, the descriptive data seems to encourage the elaboration of a hypothesis linking the presence of Italian-American voters to the election of an Italian-American politician.

Figure 4. Percent of U.S. House of Representatives Elections with Italian-American Winners by Italian-American Percentage of Total District Population, 1972–2008

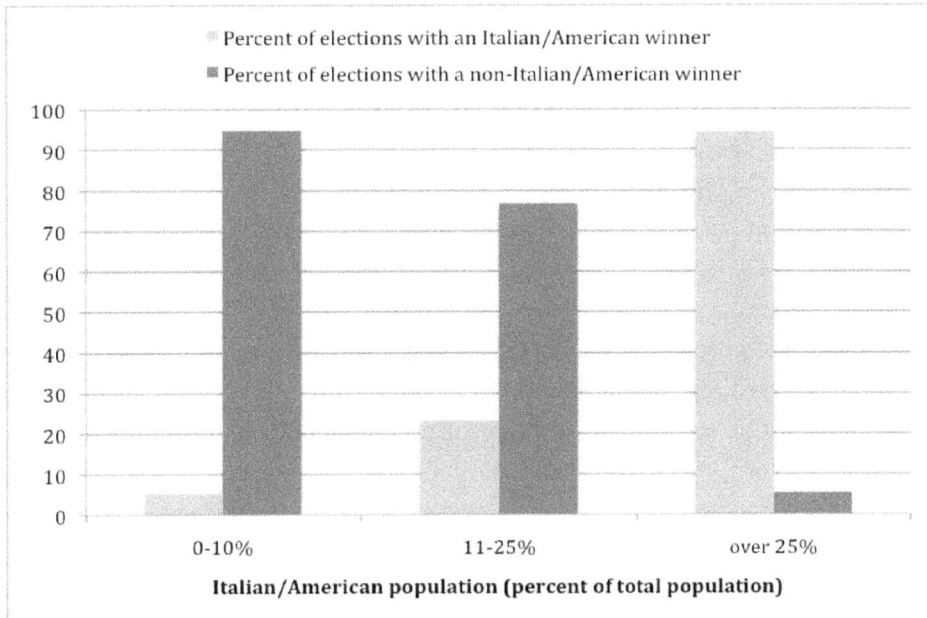

Source: compiled by author

METHODOLOGY AND DATA

In order to test my hypothesis, I compiled a comprehensive dataset gathering data obtained from a variety of sources. The dataset comprehends all relevant electoral information for every U.S. House of Representatives electoral contest held between 1972 and 2008, as compiled by the Office of the Clerk of the U.S. House of Representatives. It was coded in order to allow the tracking of specific congressional districts, but also in order to track individual congressional careers. To the electoral and personal data, I added some data of interest gathered by the U.S. Census Bureau for each congressional district between 1972 and 2008.

Particularly important for this analysis was the information about the total number of people belonging to specific ethnic and racial groups. In fact, I included in the dataset for each year and every congressional district not only the total number of Italian Americans, but also the total number of African Americans, Hispanic Americans, German Americans, Greek Americans, Irish Americans,

Polish Americans, Scandinavian Americans, and ex-Soviet Americans. The American census did not have a question pertaining to the ancestry of respondents until 1980. Therefore, the data gathered before this date reflects the total number of people that decided to classify themselves as "foreign stock" in the 1970 census. This particular information was included in the dataset for the years 1972 and 1974 as a proxy for the total population within the districts of the different ethnic groups. Even though "foreign stock" and "ancestry" are not the same concept by any possible definition, once the numbers gathered by the census are analyzed, it appears that respondents in 1970 confused the two concepts. For the years 1976, 1978, and 1980 I used the data gathered by the 1980 census transformed through the use of mapping techniques to reflect the geographical design of congressional districts associated with the 1972–1980 redistricting period.

To the ethnic-affiliation data, I added other potentially relevant socioeconomic indicators. To account for the level of education of the population analyzed, I added the total number of people who completed their high school education and the total number of people who completed a college degree for each congressional district. I also added the total number of people employed in white collar and blue collar occupations and the log of the median yearly family income in all districts. Finally, I included in the dataset the percentage of the total population in the district that can be defined as "urban population." All this information provides a quite interesting socioeconomic overview of each congressional district in the country between 1972 and 2008. Coupled with the electoral data and the data concerning affiliation with ethnic groups, this data should ~~be able to~~ reasonably prove whether the Glazer and Moynihan (1963; 1975) idea that some sort of class-like interest drives the political behavior of ethnic groups, or the Hofstadter-Lipset (1963) "status politics" approach can be successfully applied to Italian-American ethnic politics through the symbolic rewards hypothesis (Wolfinger 1966).

After gathering all the data described above, I proceeded to identify the ethnicity of every elected member of the House of Representatives in the time period of interest. This step, crucial for the analysis, was extremely challenging and had to be divided in two different stages. First, I proceeded to individually code the over eight thousand names of elected officials included in the dataset, identifying all those with an Italian surname. It is, however, impossible to limit the analysis to the congressmen with Italian surnames, given the fact that along history many Italian surnames were Anglicized (LaGumina 2000, 670) and some elected officials may simply have non-Italian surnames due to inter-ethnic marriages. Consequently, I proceeded to analyze the biographical notes of candidates and gather all ethnic-related information available through newspapers, magazines, and online.

SPECIFICATION OF THE MODEL AND RESULTS

The dependent variable of interest, *Italian Representative*, was coded as a dichotomous variable, which assumes value one in case of the election of a member of the U.S. House of Representatives of Italian origin and value zero for all other cases. Given the nature of this variable, it was necessary to estimate a logistic model. Since the dataset presents repeated observations in different points in time, I estimated a binary time-series-cross-sectional model with maximum likelihood estimation.

On the right side of the equation, I included a number of independent variables of interest. First, I included the ethnic variables *Italians, African Americans, Hispanics, Germans, Greeks, Irish, Polish, Scandinavians* and *ex-Soviets*. All these variables were coded as continuous variables that express the percentage of the total population of every individual congressional district belonging to each one of these ethnic groups. Even though among these independent variables the variable of interest is *Italians*, the other variables were included in the equation as controls to add certainty to an eventual causal relationship between the independent variable of interest and the dependent variable. Moreover, their presence in the model will show whether the considerable presence of any other ethnic group in the district makes the election of an Italian-American member of the House any less likely. Given my hypothesis, I expect, therefore, to find statistical significance and a positive coefficient only for the variable *Italians*.

I then included in the model a number of socioeconomic control variables, coded as continuous variables that represent the percentage of the total population of each congressional district that may be classified within a specific category. To control for the level of education within the district I included the variables *College Educated* and *High School Educated*. These variables were calculated as the total percentage of constituents over 25 years of age. In order to account for the urban and rural populations, I included the variable *Urban Population*, which is the percentage of the total population of the district living in urban areas. I also added the variables *White Collar* and *Blue Collar*, in an attempt to control for social class based on occupation. These two variables represent the percentage of the workforce of the district that is employed in one of these two maxi-categories. *White Collar* was defined as any management, professional, sales, or administrative occupation, while *Blue Collar* was defined as any construction, production, or transportation occupation. In conclusion, I added the variable *Median Family Income (Ln)*, which is a continuous variable reflecting the log transformation of the median family income within the congressional district for each of the years included in the dataset. All these control variables provide a quite complete socioeconomic picture of each congressional district, accounting in different ways for the social class of constituents. In order to confirm the symbolic rewards hypothesis (Wolfinger 1966), I expect all these variables to be statistically insignificant in the model. On the contrary, should the Glazer and Moynihan (1963; 1975) class-related approach to ethnic politics be correct, some or all of these variables should turn out to be significant in the model and determine in various degrees the election of Italian-American members of the House.

Finally, in order to control for possible political influence in the results, I included the dichotomous variable *Democrat*, coded one for all cases where a member of the Democratic Party won the electoral contest, zero otherwise. In conclusion, I included in the model three regional dichotomous variables, *South*, *Midwest*, and *West*, coded one for all cases that belong to a particular region of the country and zero otherwise, leaving, therefore, the region *East* as baseline.

Table 1 gathers the results of the binary time-series-cross-sectional model with maximum likelihood estimation. Of all the variables included in the model, only two present statistical significance. In fact, it appears that only the presence of Italian Americans in the district and, to a smaller degree, the presence of Irish Americans, can determine the election of an Italian American to the U.S. House of Representatives.

The fact that none of the socioeconomic control variables included on the right side of the equation presents statistical significance is of great importance. It means that no causal relationship can be inferred in the country at large between certain socioeconomic conditions and the election of an Italian American to the House of Representatives. Consequently, the Glazer and Moynihan (1963; 1975) approach to ethnic politics appears to be falsified through the analysis of empirical evidence. In fact, should Italian Americans present in the United States some sort of concealed class-like interest as an ethnic group, most Italian Americans throughout the country would also share some other socioeconomic connotation, and this further characteristic should determine—or contribute in the determination of—the electoral success of Italian-American candidates. The model estimated accounts for this possibility and rules out such variables as a factor determining the election of an Italian American to the U.S. House of Representatives. Therefore, it is reasonable to entirely reject the Glazer-Moynihan theoretical approach and explanation, in favor of a different theoretical framework, at least for what concerns the Italian-American experience in the United States.

Table 1. Election of Italian-American Members of the U.S. House of Representatives, 1972-2008

	β	Standard Error
Constant	-24.268**	(11.705)
Ethnic Groups		
Italians	0.790***	(0.096)
African Americans	0.009	(0.028)
Hispanics	-0.042	(0.042)
Germans	0.004	(0.051)
Greeks	-0.049	(0.687)
Irish	-0.223*	(0.116)
Polish	-0.074	(0.159)
Scandinavians	0.149	(0.130)
ex-Soviets	-0.205	(0.372)
Socioeconomic Controls		
College Educated	-0.068	(0.061)
High School Educated	0.014	(0.066)
Urban Population	0.028	(0.024)
White Collar	-0.095	(0.078)
Blue Collar	-0.059	(0.084)
Median Family Income (Ln)	0.949	(1.404)
Political/Regional Controls		
Democrat	0.556	(0.732)
South	-1.491	(1.147)
Midwest	-1.684	(1.175)
West	1.159	(1.292)
N	8,260	
* $p < 0.1$, ** $p < 0.05$, *** $p < 0.001$ (two-tailed)		

A slightly different but equally important set of concerns was expressed in the model by the political and regional control variables. The fact that the dummy variable *Democrat* presents no statistical significance shows that the Italian-American ethnic group is politically diverse. In essence, it means that Italian Americans cannot be classified as a "captured group," a group which supports one and only one political party consistently across time and space, such as African Americans with their allegiance to the Democratic Party (cf. Frymer 1999; Philpot 2004). In other words, it could be stated that Italian-American voters tend to support Italian-American candidates regardless of political party or, alternatively, that Italian Americans in different points in time and space support different political parties. In addition, the results obtained by including in the equation the regional dummy variables show that there is no statistically significant difference in the support of

Italian-American candidates across the macro regions of the country. Notoriously, the Italian immigration in the United States was concentrated in the East, with states such as New York, New Jersey, Connecticut, Rhode Island and, in part, Pennsylvania, attracting most immigrants and, consequently, presenting larger numbers of Americans of Italian origin in comparison to the other states of the country (cf. Alba 1985). Therefore, the fact that the model shows no difference between geographical areas of the country adds confidence to the results obtained, in the sense that, according to the model, no matter where in the country there is a large concentration of Italian Americans, an Italian-American candidate is more likely to be elected.

Among the ethnic group variables, the model establishes a not particularly strong, but still statistically relevant, causal relationship between the presence in the district of Irish Americans and the electoral success of an Italian American in the same district. The analysis of the coefficient of the variable *Irish* shows that this relationship has a negative sign. In other words, the higher the number of people of Irish origin in the district, the lower the chances of an Italian American winning an election to the U.S. House of Representatives will be. These results are more than consistent with an intricate and long history of political rivalry between these two ethnic groups in the United States (cf. Nelli 1970; McFarland 2001). This fact means that while no socioeconomic group is more or less likely to support an Italian-American candidate in the entire country, the Irish appear to still be reluctant to support a member belonging to the group of its historical ethnic rivalry.

When it comes to the main variable of interest of this study, *Italians*, a quick glance at the model presented in table 1 shows that it is by far the best predictor of electoral success for an Italian-American candidate. Not only the variable has unquestionable statistical significance, but also the sign of the coefficient obtained is in the correct and expected direction. In brief, the model shows that the more Italian Americans are present in a congressional district, the more likely is the election of an Italian-American member of the U.S. House of Representatives. Given the fact that none of the control variables included in the model contribute to the election of an Italian American, it is possible, as briefly indicated above, to rule out the theoretical explanation provided by Glazer and Moynihan (1963; 1975) and, simultaneously, to accept the symbolic rewards hypothesis developed by Wolfinger (1966). More in detail, if the presence in large numbers of members of an ethnic group in a given congressional district make the election of an Italian American more likely and no socioeconomic indicator contributes to this event, then the empirical evidence provides no reason to believe that Italian Americans are voting for Italian Americans in order to obtain material benefits of various sorts that are needed by the entire ethnic group. In other words, the idea introduced by Hof-stadter (1963) and Lipset (1963) of status politics provides a better theoretical and explanatory framework to the Italian-American experience in the United States. According to this view, voters tend to give their political support to a member of their own ethnic group in order to obtain and intangible, symbolic reward. As Wolfinger (1966, 47) put it:

> "Recognition" is the prize in ethnic politics. When the first Irishman was nomi-nated for alderman in the mid-nineteenth century, this implied recognition of the statesmanlike qualities of all Irishmen. The same process works in the mid-twentieth century. It is an economical strategy, for the benefits given to a few eth-nics are appreciated by many others.

To Wolfinger's remarks, it is now possible to add that this process appears to work even through the twenty-first century in the case of the Italian Americans.

Further analyzing the results of the model presented in table 1, it is now neces-sary to interpret the coefficient obtained for the variable of interest. It is impossi-ble to interpret the coefficients of a binary time-series-cross-sectional model beyond its statistical significance and its sign. Therefore, I proceeded to calculate the prob-ability transformations of the coefficient obtained. Figure 5 graphically represents the probabilities of electoral victory of an Italian-American candidate in a congres-sional district, based on the percentage of Italian Americans present in the district. As it is clear from the figure, the probability of election of an Italian American to the U.S. House of Representatives rises dramatically when between 25 and 35 per-cent of the entire population of the district is of Italian origin. According to the model, districts where more than 35 percent of the total population is of Italian origin virtually present chances of election of an Italian American of 100 percent.

The results of the probability transformation of the coefficient obtained by the model leave room for a number of considerations and speculations. In fact, it ap-pears that in order to obtain a strong causal relationship between the presence of Italian Americans in a given district and the election of an Italian-American repre-sentative, the total number of the members of this ethnic group in the district must be large enough to guarantee the election of their favorite candidate. Further research is necessary to obtain a better understanding of this phenomenon, but the fact that the probability of election of an Italian American is extremely low even when there is a considerable presence of Italian Americans in the district—10, or even 20 percent of the total population—seems to indicate that in those places where there are other ethnic groups, or where the vast majority of the population is non-Italian, the presence of Italian Americans does not translate into the election of an Italian-American representative.

Figure 5. Probabilities of Election of an Italian-American Representative

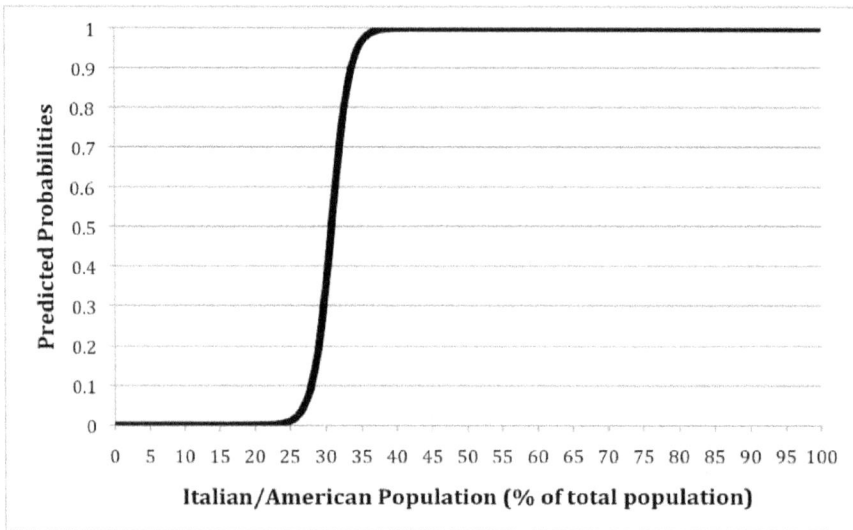

CONCLUSION

It is often assumed throughout the literature that "when an ethnic group is regionally concentrated, the representative is more likely to be a member of an ethnic group" (Banducci and Karp 2008, 78). This analysis provided empirical evidence supporting this assertion for what concerns Italian Americans in the United States. More specifically, by testing and confirming the symbolic rewards hypothesis (Wolfinger 1966), this work also provided a reason to take some distance from the class-centered theoretical argument developed by Glazer and Moynihan (1963; 1975), in favor of a theoretical framework of analysis which takes into account Hanna Pitkin's (1967) idea of descriptive or symbolic representation and proposes to interpret ethnic politics as status politics (cf. Hofstadter 1963; Lipset 1963).

The consequences of the analysis developed above are multifaceted. First, accepting the existence of ethnic politics as status politics requires a broader conceptualization of voting as more than the traditional "one instrument to reach two goals: to select better policies and politicians, and to induce them to behave well while in office" (Manin, Przeworski and Stokes 1999, 45). In fact, the policy dimension was deliberately left out of this analysis, for voting for an ethnic group may be a way to achieve intangible objectives that cannot be expressed through traditional policy-oriented approaches. Second, the approach adopted here potentially paves the way to a slightly different approach to the idea of "race-conscious," or "ethnic-conscious" districting. In fact, even though further analysis and research is required on this topic, such process could be viewed as a process that would enable effective group representation (cf. Guinier 1995, 156), at least at the symbolic/descriptive level, instead of a practice that simply fails to advance minority representation (cf. Lublin 1997, 10; Lublin 1999), since majority-minority districts ultimately leave fewer representatives with incentives to be open to the requests and interests of minorities (cf. Overby and Cosgrove 1996). In conclusion, the results presented above undoubtedly open a new dimension to the representative-constituents relationship, since a representative who belongs to an ethnic group may "be the object of heightened interest because a good performance by him would be especially gratifying and a poor performance especially dismaying" (Parenti 1962, 294) for the ethnic group as a whole.

WORKS CITED

Alba, Richard M. *Italian Americans: Into the Twilight of Ethnicity*. Englewood Cliffs, NJ: Prentice-Hall, 1985.

Banducci, Susan A. and Jeffrey A. Karp. "Mobilizing Political Engagement and Participation in Diverse Societies: The Impact of Institutional Arrangements." *Designing Democratic Government: Making Institutions Work*, edited by Margaret Levi, James Johnson, Jack Knight and Susan Stokes. New York: Russell Sage Foundation, 2008.

Berelson, Bernard, Paul F. Lazarsfeld and William N. McPhee. *Voting: A Study of Opinion Formation in a Presidential Campaign*. Chicago: The University of Chicago Press, 1954.

Bratton, Kathleen A. and Kerry L. Haynie. "Agenda Setting and Legislative Success in State Legislatures: The Effects of Gender and Race." *Journal of Politics* 61.3 (1999): 658-679.

Cameron, Charles, David Epstein and Sharyn O'Halloran. "Do Majority-Minority Districts Maximize Substantive Black Representation in Congress?" *American Political Science Review* 90.4 (1996): 794-812.

Chong, Dennis. *Rational Lives: Norms and Values in Politics and Society*. Chicago: University of Chicago Press, 2000.

Dawson, Michael C. *Behind the Mule: Race and Class in African-American Politics*. Princeton: Princeton University Press, 1994.

Dovi, Suzanne. "Preferable Descriptive Representatives: Will Just Any Woman, Black, or Latino Do?" *American Political Science Review* 96.4 (2002): 729-743.

Frymer, Paul. *Uneasy Alliances: Race and Party Competition in America*. Princeton: Princeton University Press, 1999.

Glazer, Nathan and Daniel P. Moynihan. *Beyond the Melting Pot: Negroes, Puerto Ricans, Jews, Italians and Irish of New York City*. Cambridge: MIT Press and Harvard University Press, 1963.

⸺. "Introduction." *Ethnicity: Theory and Experience*, edited by Nathan Glazer and Daniel P. Moynihan. Cambridge: Harvard University Press, 1975.

Guinier, Lani. *The Tyranny of the Majority: Fundamental Fairness in Representative Democracy*. New York: Free Press, 1995.

Gusfield, Joseph R. *Symbolic Crusade: Status Politics and the American Temperance Movement*. Urbana: University of Illinois Press, 1986.

Haynie, Kerry L. *African American Legislators in the American States*. New York: Columbia University Press, 2001.

⸺⸺⸺⸺. "The Color of Their Skin or the Content of Their Behavior? Race and Perceptions of African American Legislators." *Legislative Studies Quarterly* 27.2 (2002): 295-314.

Hibbing, John R. and Elizabeth Theiss-Morse. *Stealth Democracy: Americans' Beliefs about How Government Should Work*. New York: Cambridge University Press, 2005.

Hofstadter, Richard. "The Pseudo-Conservative Revolt." *The Radical Right*, edited by Daniel Bell. Garden City, NJ: Doubleday, 1963.

LaGumina, Sal J. *The Italian American Experience: An Encyclopedia*. New York: Garland Publishing, 2000.

Lipset, Seymour M. "The Sources of the 'Radical Right.'" *The Radical Right*, edited by Daniel Bell. Garden City, NJ: Doubleday, 1963.

Lublin, David. *The Paradox of Representation: Racial Gerrymandering and Minority Interests in Congress*. Princeton: Princeton University Press, 1997.

_____. "Racial Redistricting and African-American Representation: A Critique of 'Do Majority-Minority Districts Maximize Substantive Black Representation in Congress?'" *American Political Science Review* 93.1 (1999): 183-186.

Manin, Bernard, Adam Przeworski and Susan C. Stokes. "Elections and Representation." *Democracy, Accountability and Representation*, edited by Adam Przeworski, Susan C. Stokes and Bernard Manin. Cambridge: Cambridge University Press, 1999.

Mansbridge, Jane. "Should Blacks Represent Blacks and Women Represent Women? A Contingent 'Yes.'" *The Journal of Politics* 61.3 (1999): 628-657.

McFarland, Gerald W. *Inside Greenwich Village: A New York City Neighborhood, 1898-1918*. Boston: University of Massachusetts Press, 2001.

Nelli, Humbert S. "John Powers and the Italians: Politics n a Chicago Ward, 1896-1921." *Journal of American History* 57.1 (1970): 67-84.

Nelson, Albert J. *Emerging Influentials in State Legislatures*. New York: Praeger, 1991.

Overby, L. Marvin and Kenneth M. Cosgrove. "Unintended Consequences? Racial Redistricting and the Representation of Minority Interests." *The Journal of Politics* 58.2 (1996): 540-550.

Pantoja, Adrian D. and Gary M. Segura. "Does Ethnicity Matter? Descriptive Representation in Legislatures and Political Alienation Among Latinos." *Social Science Quarterly* 84.2 (2003): 441-460.

Parenti, Michael J. *Ethnic and Political Attitudes: A Depth Study of Italian Americans*. New York: Arno Press, 1962.

_____. "Ethnic Politics and the Persistence of Ethnic Identification." *American Political Science Review* 61.3 (1967): 717-726.

Parsons, Talcott. "Some Theoretical Considerations on the Nature and Trends of Change of Ethnicity." *Ethnicity: Theory and Experience*, edited by Nathan Glazer and Daniel P. Moynihan. Cambridge: Harvard University Press, 1975.

Phillips, Anne. "The Politics of Presence." *Democracy: A Reader*, edited by Ricardo Blaug and John J. Schwarzmantel. New York: Columbia University Press, 2000.

Philpot, Tasha S. "A Party of a Different Color? Race, Campaign Communication, and Party Politics." *Political Behavior* 26.3 (2004): 249-270.

Pitkin, Hanna. *The Concept of Representation*. Berkley: University of California Press, 1967.

Preuhs, Robert R. "Representation is Not Enough: The Limits and Possibilities of Minority Inclusion and Influence in Representative Policy-Making Bodies in the American States." Paper presented at the American Political Science Association's Annual Meeting, San Francisco, CA, August 29-September 2, 2001.

_____. "The Conditional Effect of Minority Descriptive Representation: Black Legislators and Policy Influence in the American States." *The Journal of Politics* 68.3 (2006): 585-599.

Swain, Carol M. *Black Faces, Black Interests*. Cambridge: Harvard University Press, 1993.

Tate, Katherine. "The Political Representation of Blacks in Congress: Does Race Matter?" *Legislative Studies Quarterly* 26.4 (2001): 623-638.

Wolfinger, Raymond E. "Some Consequences of Ethnic Politics." *The Electoral Process*, edited by M. Kent Jennings and Luther H. Zeigler, Englewood Cliffs: Prentice-Hall, 1966.

TALES OF AN ITALIAN-AMERICAN POLITICAL CLASS
Monopolistic Elections and Hegemonic Districts in New York

Ottorino Cappelli[*]
UNIVERSITÀ DI NAPOLI L'ORIENTALE
JOHN D. CALANDRA ITALIAN AMERICAN INSTITUTE, QUEENS COLLEGE, CUNY

INTRODUCTION

Italian-American intra-ethnic races are not at all uncommon in the State of New York, where Italians are the largest ancestry group. In the fall 2010, while Andrew Cuomo confronted Carl Paladino for the governorship, there were 14 such races at the Assembly and Senate levels—actually 17 if one adds the cases where an Italian-American incumbent ran unopposed and thus the "ethnic outcome" of the election was pre-determined. Table 1 (see appendix) lists all such races over a twelve-year period (1998–2010) during which seven consecutive elections were held: there are 137 cases, affecting 51 Assembly and Senate districts combined. I refer to these elections as Italian-American *monopolistic elections*—i.e., elections where, whatever the individual result, the ethnicity of the winner is pre-determined. Here Italian-American politicians indeed run the show alone.

Monopolistic elections are not distributed evenly throughout the districts. In some cases, they take place only once or twice in the period considered; in others, they take place in each and every election year. I call the districts where monopolistic elections take place most of the time (four times or more between 1998 and 2010) Italian-American *hegemonic districts*—i.e., districts where Italian-American politicians apparently exercise continued, consolidated leadership on the nomination and election process in both parties. They form a dominant local *political class* that controls the representation of all major interests, political divisions, and conflicts, whether in government or the opposition. Politics, in other words, is an Italian-American matter here. There were 16 hegemonic districts in the State of New York between 1998 and 2000.

Not surprisingly, the majority of our cases are located in areas characterized by a comparatively high presence of Italian Americans among the population. Well over half of the monopolistic elections *and* of the hegemonic districts are found

---

[*] With the assistance of Luca Delbello.

where Italian Americans are above 20 percent of the population, and the relative majority of cases (41 districts) is concentrated where Italian Americans make up at least one-fourth of the population—i.e., on or above the threshold of 30,000 people for an Assembly District (AD) and 78,000 people for a Senate District (SD). By contrast, only slightly more than one-fifth of the monopolistic elections and just one hegemonic district can be found where Italian Americans are less than 15 percent of the population (less than 20,000 people for an AD and less than 45,000 for a SD).

Table 2. Monopolistic Elections and Hegemonic Districts

Presence of Italian Americans in the district	Monopolistic Elections		Hegemonic Districts	
	number	percentage	number	percentage
25% +	41	30	6	37.5
20–24%	34	25	4	25.0
15–19%	32	23	5	31.3
0–14%	30	22	1	6.2
Totals	137	100	16	100

These data suggest that a strong—though not necessarily predominant—presence of Italian Americans in a district tends to create over time a social and political *milieu* in which an Italian-American person may find it comparatively easier to work his/her way up in the political arena. Such is the meaning of "hegemony" as used here, which refers to a cultural-social situation in which ordinary voters, party officials, and major interests accept as a matter of fact the monopoly of one group over community leadership and representation. In hegemonic districts, wherever one turns, there is no alternative to having an Italian American in office.

This is not to say that a numerous Italian-American electorate is a sufficient condition for the existence of hegemonic districts. As table 1 shows in some districts with an above-average presence of Italian Americans, monopolistic elections may be as rare as they are in districts with a much smaller presence of Italian Americans. For instance, Assemblymen Robert Barra and Thomas Alfano, who in the 2000s represented two heavily Italian districts on Long Island, have faced intra-ethnic races only once and twice respectively. The same occurred with Assemblyman Joseph Lentol (Williamsburg, Brooklyn) and Senator George Onorato (Astoria, Queens), who held their seats for decades, even though Italian Americans—once an important presence in their districts—by 2000 had sunk well below 10 percent of the population. They, too, were rarely challenged by fellow ethnics in the period considered.

What emerges in these cases is that, whatever the district's demographics, the local political class is ethnically differentiated and the political process escapes the monopoly of a single group. This is why these districts cannot be called "hegemonic," even if they are dominated for a long time by an Italian-American incumbent. In short, to make an Italian-American hegemonic district, the ethnic factor is a facilitating but not sufficient condition. Other factors also have an influence, including among others the local force and roots of political parties, and the personal resources of power and influence of individual politicians.

A comprehensive analysis of these situations would be outside the scope of the present chapter.[1] However, observing a little more closely the data from our hegemonic districts may shed some light on how different factors interact, which may merit further study.

To this end, hegemonic districts can be divided into three typologies:

1. *Power Districts*: the same Italian-American elected official *and* his/her party dominate over a long period of time.
2. *Swinging Ethnic Strongholds*: although elected office regularly goes to an Italian American, different officials *and* parties alternate in power over the years.
3. *Personal Fiefdoms*: the same Italian-American official monopolizes elected office over time, *but* the party-political coalition that supports him/her varies.

TYPE 1: POWER DISTRICTS

In "power districts," an individual politician of Italian-American origin stays in office over a long period of time, either running uncontested or prevailing regularly over challengers of the same ethnicity. The opposite party either gives in, or appears to believe that its only chance to unseat the incumbent is to nominate another Italian American—but, even so, it fails. Here party influence, ethnic appeal, and personal power reinforce each other in making the incumbent virtually invulnerable, so that it is difficult to discern which of these factors, if any, is predominant. However, since the electorate is firmly aligned with one party, and attempts

---

[1] Electoral data presented in the following tables are drawn from *OurCampaigns.com*'s online database <http://www.ourcampaigns.com>. Ancestry data are based on Census 2000 and have been obtained via *American Factfinder Online* <http://factfinder.census.gov>.

to unseat the incumbent take the form of fierce party competition, the party element is comparatively more visible than it is elsewhere. Indeed, we can speak here of (Italian-American) Democratic and Republican power districts.

Table 1 shows several cases of this type between 1998 and 2010. The Assembly presents more cases of downstate (Italian-American) Democratic power districts characterized by a high rate of intra-ethnic races—for instance in Brooklyn with Peter Abbate and William Colton, and in the Bronx with Michael Benedetto, although Long Island should also be added with James Conte, in this case a Republican. The Senate, instead, presents cases of upstate (Italian-American) Republican power districts characterized by a higher incidence of uncontested elections. Michael Nozzolio for instance, who served 10 years in the Assembly before conquering SD 54 in 1992, twice defeated a fellow Italian American and twice ran unopposed. Joseph Bruno (SD 43), on the other hand, the powerful Republican Majority Leader in the Senate since 1994, always ran unopposed until he was forced to resign over a corruption scandal in 2008.

The paradigmatic example of an (Italian-American) Democratic power district can be found in AD 49 in Kings County, which includes part of Bensonhurst—a neighborhood also known as Brooklyn's Little Italy, an area that in 2000 still had a 20,000-strong Italian-speaking immigrant population. Since 1986 this district has been the reign of Democratic Assemblyman Peter Abbate, Jr., a lifelong Democratic leader born and raised in Bensonhurst. A locally known community activist for civil rights since his early years, he later served as district leader for Congressman Stephen J. Solarz in the 1970s, and then became the executive director of the Kings County Democratic Committee in the 1980s prior to being elected to the Assembly. Republicans have challenged him in each and every election over the past 25 years, always by nominating an Italian American but never winning.

What is particularly interesting about this district is that before realigning to the Democrats with Peter Abbate in the mid-1980s, it had long been an Italian-American Republican power district. From 1957 to 1964 the incumbent assemblyman was Republican Luigi Marano, later a State Supreme Court Justice, followed for 15 years by fellow party member Dominick J. DiCarlo, who later became a U.S. federal judge in the Court of International Trade. From 1964 to 1980, DiCarlo won eight elections in a row, most of them against an Italian-American challenger. When, in 1981, he left the State Assembly for Washington, he tried to engineer a dynastic succession, but his son Robert lost to Louis Freda and the Democrats took control for the first time (see table 3).

Table 3. The Electoral History of an Italian-American "Power District"

	Year	Winner	Party	Votes	Loser	Party	Votes
District: 49 County: Kings Italian Ancestry: 36,299 (30.2%)	2010	Peter J. Abbate	D, I, W	7,416	Peter Cipriano	R, C	4,659
	2008	Peter J. Abbate	D	14,034	Lucretia Regina-Potter	R	5,487
	2006	Peter J. Abbate	D	7,884	Lucretia Regina-Potter	R	2,737
	2004	Peter J. Abbate	D	14,553	Fred Martorell	R	5,417
	2002	Peter J. Abbate	D	7,603	Cynthia Gallo	C	541
	2000	Peter J. Abbate	D	15,705	Josephine N. Frediani	R	5,212
	1998	Peter J. Abbate	D	10,249	Luigi R. Marano	R	5,059
	1996	Peter J. Abbate	D	12,148	Vincenzo DiGiacomo	R	4,131
	1994	Peter J. Abbate	D	13,041	Vito J. Settineri	R	5,603
	1992	Peter J. Abbate	D	17,279	Antonio DiPasquale	R	7,147
	1990	Peter J. Abbate	D	9,350	Arnaldo Ferraro	R	3,935
	1988	Peter J. Abbate	D	14,954	Arnaldo Ferraro	R	9,570
	1986	Peter J. Abbate	D	9,923	Arnaldo Ferraro	R	7,299
	1984	Arnaldo Ferraro	R	13,953	Louis Freda	D	13,455
	1982	Louis Freda	D	13,877	Aldo G. Frustaci	R	5,373
	1981	Louis Freda	D	11,818	Robert DiCarlo	R	10,284
	1980	Dominick DiCarlo	R	21,205	Edmond Harrison	D	7,480
	1978	Dominick DiCarlo	R	15,168	Edmond Harrison	D	8,350
	1976	Dominick DiCarlo	R	20,369	Joseph Bova	D	13,075
	1974	Dominick DiCarlo	R	17,388	Arnaldo Ferraro	D	11,192
	1972	Dominick DiCarlo	R	30,019	Arnaldo Ferraro	D	12,152
	1970	Dominick DiCarlo	R	20,404	Ronald Aiello	D	10,425
	1968	Dominick DiCarlo	R	22,334	Anthony Mennella	D	13,395
	1966	Dominick DiCarlo	R	16,390	Joseph Rinaldi	D	13,486

Power in the district briefly switched to the Republicans again in 1984, when the winner was Arnaldo A. Ferraro—an Italian-born self-made politician who immigrated to the U.S. in 1961. Ferraro, a very active if controversial local figure who had twice challenged DiCarlo in the 1970s, is the founder of the Fiorello LaGuardia Republican Club and the National Federation of Italian-American Societies, the first Italian-American Federation in New York State—both of which were instrumental in his winning the Assembly seat in 1984.[2] By that time, however, the GOP electoral base had shrunk dramatically in a district where voters were now two to one Democratic.

It was at that junction that Peter Abbate won the seat and turned AD 49 into a stable and (Italian-American) Democratic power district. Politically, 1986 marked a "critical election" that firmly realigned the voters on the democratic side. Ethnically, it consolidated a long tradition of Italian-American near-total hegemony on the local political class of all parties. Abbate, as we have seen, has confronted Italian-American candidates at every election since his first inauguration. As a consequence the Italian electorate, though sizable, is permanently split, although such division of course has no impact on the ethnic outcome of the elections.

Peter Abbate is very actively involved in several Italian-American organizations at the local and state levels. However, faced with repeated intra-ethnic contests in which his Italian ancestry is a harmless political weapon, he has developed a pragmatic approach based on a mix of party politics, local interest representation, and ethnic politics. And in all these matters he tends to act in a carefully balanced way—which makes him look less like a moderate or a centrist than as a shrewd politician focused on enlarging his personal base of power as broadly as possible.

Although his opponents often accuse him of being a liberal, for instance, his political record is mixed: on the one hand, he is pro-choice, supports abortion and gay rights, and opposes vouchers for elementary and secondary schools; on the other hand, he has advocated stiffer penalties for criminals, including the death penalty.[3] In the field of interest representation, although he enjoys strong support from the unions, Abbate is also known for his readiness to side with local businesses. His decade-long effort to enact legislation that would ease the statewide ban on smoking in bars and restaurants could be cited in this regard. While the press has often overstated Abbate's policy as a sign of subservience to the powerful to-

---

[2] See LaGuardia Republican Club's website <http://www.laguardiarepublicanclub.org/about/ about-dr-arnaldo-a-ferraro>.
[3] Jonathan P. Hicks, "A Veteran Candidate Runs Once More, With Feeling," *The New York Times*, October 29, 1998.

bacco industry, it can be better understood as a capacity to lobby for locally influential constituents such as the restaurateurs, who make up an important part of his
district's business structure (and are mostly Italian American).[4] Finally, part of the
secret of Abbate's success also rests on his capacity of cross-ethnic representation,
i.e., a capacity to enlarge his personal base by courting not only the Italians, but
also other sizable ethnic constituencies. As his official biography in the State Assembly website candidly states: "Since Brooklyn's 49th Assembly District is comprised of a large number of people of Italian and Jewish heritage, Mr. Abbate has
made trips to both Italy and Israel to gain a greater understanding of his own heritage as well as that of the people he represents."[5] This is indeed what we would
expect from the leader of a hegemonic district of this type: the capacity to combine
his ethnic base with a broader cross-ethnic appeal, and an inclination to use his
personal influence to craft a consensus that goes beyond his party's base.

As stated above, in a "power district" long dominated by the same individual
and party, the incumbent and his party may eventually be defeated, but the district
itself may remain in Italian-American hands—that is, a stable party realignment
takes place and an Italian-American political class continues to dominate in both
government and opposition parties. Interestingly enough, this may hold true even
in the face of a declining proportion of Italian Americans in the electorate.

This can be observed by looking at two Queens Senate Districts long held by
Republican powerhouses Serph Maltese and Frank Padavan, who stayed in power
for 20 and 38 years respectively, before losing in 2008 and 2010 to Italian-
American challengers.

Serph Maltese, the founder and chairman of the New York Conservative Party, was first elected to the Senate in 1988 when, in a rather unusual move, the majority of the Republican committee of SD 15 endorsed him as their candidate. The
district had been held by (German-American) Republican Martin Knorr for almost
15 years, during which period most of the democratic challengers were Italian
Americans. When the seat became available and Maltese ran and won for the first
time, he defeated Democrat Frank Sansivieri, Jr. This was the only intra-ethnic race
afforded by Maltese until his defeat by Italian-American Democrat Joseph P. Ad-

---

[4] The endorsement Abbate received from the *New York Times* in 1998 is rather telling in this regard:
"Although Mr. Abbate has nuzzled too close to the tobacco interests in recent years, we endorse him
for his efforts on behalf of senior citizens, his work pushing for improvement of legislative operations
and for tax abatements in historic districts. See "For the Legislature From New York City," *The New
York Times*, October 23, 1998.
[5] See Senator Abbate's official profile at the NYS Assembly website <http://assembly.state.ny.us
/mem/Peter-J-Abbate-Jr/bio>.

dabbo, Jr. in 2008. He did, however, monopolize the election process running un-opposed six times in a row between 1994 and 2004. Maltese, who also became the powerful chair of the Queens County Republican Committee, stayed in power for twenty years by enlisting the crucial help of his own personal machine, centered in areas with a high presence of Italian-speaking immigrants.

Table 4. Elite Circulation in an Italian-American "Power District" /1

	Year	Winner	Party	Votes	Loser	Party	Votes
District: 15 County: Queens Italian Ancestry: 61,983 (19.5%)	2010	Joseph Addabbo	D	23,272	Anthony Como	R	17,594
	2008	Joseph Addabbo	D	39,978	Serphin Maltese	R	29,544
	2006	Serphin Maltese	R	17,940	Albert Baldeo	D	17,046
	2004	Serphin Maltese	R	34,331	-	-	-
	2002*	Serphin Maltese	R	23,588	-	-	-
	2000*	Serphin Maltese	R	33,135	-	-	-
	1998	Serphin Maltese	R	23,823	-	-	-
	1996	Serphin Maltese	R	34,045	-	-	-
	1994	Serphin Maltese	R	32,572	-	-	-
	1992	Serphin Maltese	R	46,347	Arthur M. Laske	D	20,008
	1990	Serphin Maltese	R	25,680	Joan C. DeCamp	D	11,771
	1988	Serphin Maltese	C, R	39,192	Frank Sansivieri	D	32,513
	1986	Martin J. Knorr	R	32,727	Frank Sansivieri	D	17,001
	1984	Martin J. Knorr	R	43,487	Thomas Santucci	D	40,779
	1982	Martin J. Knorr	R	33,746	Thomas Santucci	D	31,204
	1980	Martin J. Knorr	R	45,098	Patricia M. Reilly	D	21,672
	1978	Martin J. Knorr	R	35,826	Thomas W. Connolly	D	21,995
	1976	Martin J. Knorr	R	53,264	Albert Alloro	D	23,939
	1974	Martin J. Knorr	R	43,746	Marco Giovanelli	D	23,858
	1972	Martin J. Knorr	R	57,294	Frederick D. Schmidt	D	46,807

* Unopposed by major parties.

In 2006, Maltese experienced the first serious Democratic challenge by Albert Baldeo, a Guyanese who came a few hundred votes short of defeating him; he later charged that the reason Baldeo performed so well was that his name ended in a vowel, which made many of his constituents believe he was an Italian. Be that as it may, in the next election in 2008 the Democrats challenged him by nominating Addabbo, a much younger Italian American who had built a strong power base in the district as a City councilman for 10 years. Addabbo also had strong name-recognition, being the son of popular Queens Congressmen Joseph P. Addabbo, Sr., who had served in Washington for 25 years (1961–86). When Addabbo, Sr. died, a number of public projects were named after him, including a park, a bridge, a senior center, an elementary school, a social security building, and a family health center. Italian-American name recognition, however, explains only part of Addabbo, Jr.'s success.

In an interview for the Calandra Institute's Oral History Archive[6], he explained to me how he had learned from his father that, in order to maintain power, a politician should be able to adapt to the changing ethnic composition of his district:

> Back in the early 1960s my father's district was probably 70 percent Italian, German, Irish . . . white Caucasian. Somewhere in the 1980s, around 1982 or so, it changed to roughly 68 percent African-American or minority in general. And my father was faced with a very difficult decision to make – either you stay running or you retire. He loved what he did, he loved his work, helping people, so he stayed in . . . and a lot of people thought, "How could he, a white person, represent a district that is now 70 percent minority?" But then he won two subsequent elections and was running for a third one when he passed. . . . You have to adapt! In Queens our ethnic shifts happen so frequently and so drastically that if you don't adapt to change as an elected official you suffer.

For Addabbo, Jr. that was a life lesson: an Italian-American politician may well need a sizable Italian-American voter base to access power, but he does not necessarily need it to keep his power. By adapting his ethno-political strategy he may succeed even in the face of an "unfavorable" ethnic composition of his constituency. Serph Maltese, in Addabbo's words, did not adapt well:

---

[6] The following quotes are drawn from an interview conducted for the Oral History Archive—an extensive interview project dedicated to New York State legislators of Italian origin that I direct at the John D. Calandra Italian American Institute, Queens College, CUNY. The projects' materials, all televised, can be consulted at the Calandra Institute's library.

I think he unfortunately stayed in a very close circuit, a very small circle, without taking advantage of the position he was in, in helping other parts of the district. We have a growing Latino population, we have a growing Polish population, certainly we have a growing South Asian population, and I think these growing ethnic segments of the district had not been attended to. And certainly I would not have gone so far in office without attending to all parts of the district. I think you have to. You have to adapt. Each community is different, each has its own distinct needs, each family has its own distinct needs. And you have got to address them all; you cannot just address some and not the others.

Interestingly enough, notwithstanding these ethnic changes in the district, Italian Americans still dominate the local political class of both parties: in 2010 the GOP tried to regain power by nominating yet another Italian American against Addabbo, Councilman Anthony Como, though to no avail.

A somewhat similar situation can be found in SD 11, where Republican senator Frank Padavan dominated for almost four decades. Padavan was first elected to the Legislature in 1972, favored by both a large Italian-American presence and the coattails of Nixon's huge re-election victory. Prior to his election, the district had been briefly represented by Italian-American democrat John Santucci, who the Republicans tried to unseat in 1970 by running another Italian-American against him. Since Padavan's first inauguration in 1972, instead, only once was he challenged by a fellow ethnic. During much of his long reign the district's political class was divided into an Italian-dominated Republican party and an Anglo-Saxon-dominated Democratic party.

The ethnic-power configuration of the district gradually begun to change after 1980, when Padavan won re-election by a remarkable showing of 96 percent of votes; he consolidated his power in the following decades by never falling below 60 percent. By the early 1990s, notwithstanding a steady decline of Italians voters, the district had acquired the form of an Italian-American hegemonic power district, with Padavan running unopposed most of the time from 1990 until 2006—when the Democrats began targeting him again, this time by enlisting Italian-American candidates. An Italian-American political class had, in fact, grown stronger within the local Democratic Party and they were entrusted with the task of unseating the longtime Italian-American incumbent who was now in his 70s and had spent over 30 years in power.

Three times an Italian-American challenger was nominated before Padavan could be unseated. These were bitterly contested elections, especially in 2008, when the incumbent senator was challenged by political science professor and City

Councilman James Gennaro and the race was so close that the recounting of ballots lasted three months; in the end Padavan was declared the winner by a mere 480 vote margin.

Table 5. Elite Circulation in an Italian-American "Power District" /2

	Year	Winner	Party	Votes	Loser	Party	Votes
District: 11 County: Queens Italian Ancestry: 48,857 (15.4%)	2010	Anthony Avella	D	31,573	Frank Padavan	R	26,571
	2008	Frank Padavan	R	45,294	James Gennaro	D	44,811
	2006	Frank Padavan	R	31,019	Nora C. Marino	D	21,283
	2004	Frank Padavan	R	45,832	'	'	'
	2002	Frank Padavan	R	33,305	'	'	'
	2000	Frank Padavan	R	53,190	Rory I. Lancman	D	32,635
	1998	Frank Padavan	R	33,887	Morshed Alam	D	23,637
	1996	Frank Padavan	R	41,780	'	'	'
	1994	Frank Padavan	R	41,122	'	'	'
	1992	Frank Padavan	R	52,398	Jeremy S. Weinstein	D	35,660
	1990	Frank Padavan	R	29,334	'	'	'
	1988	Frank Padavan	R	57,560	Edward Nicastro	D	31,194
	1986	Frank Padavan	R	38,074	Robert H. Schwartz	D	21,974
	1984	Frank Padavan	R	65,256	Ann J. Jawin	D	35,721
	1982	Frank Padavan	R	50,627	Nicholas Garafis	D	30,612
	1980	Frank Padavan	R	84,193	Charles Greenspan	L	3,908
	1978	Frank Padavan	R	47,350	Alvin Frankenberg	D	24,067
	1976	Frank Padavan	R	58,166	William H. Caulfield	D	40,006
	1974	Frank Padavan	R	44,513	Donald J. Evans	D	34,901
	1972	Frank Padavan	R	60,109	Murray Schwartz	D	51,190

The man who was eventually able to beat Padavan in 2010 was former City Councilman Tony Avella, a lifelong resident of the same district who Queens Democratic Party officials had long tried to enlist for the job. A prominent Italian-American activist, and the founder and chair of the first Italian-American Caucus of the Council, Avella had served for two decades as an aid to several city- and state-level politicians, including the Italian-American Speaker of the City Council Peter Vallone, Sr. In 2009 he left the City Council to run in the Democratic primary for mayor of New York City, but was defeated. The 2010 victory against Padavan thus signaled Avella's successful return to politics.

In the two cases just analyzed, Italian Americans remain a hegemonic force—if no longer among the electorate, then surely among the local political class. True, formerly unbeatable Republican organizations, reinforced by a sizable Italian-American electorate and the personal power of incumbents Serph Maltese and Frank Padavan, gradually disaggregated over time. Moreover, while the ethnic composition of the districts changed and the Italian-American electorate shrunk, power swung to the opposite party. And yet, both districts remained firmly in the hands of Italian-American politicians whose chances of persistence paradoxically rest on their capacity to sever their dependence on their own declining ethnic base. If in the future new incumbents Joe Addabbo and Tony Avella will prove to be capable of continually defeating their Italian-American challengers and consolidate power, like Abbate did in Brooklyn after decades of Republican dominance, these districts may remain "power districts"—demographic changes notwithstanding. If instead a permanent party realignment does not take place, they might fall into the hybrid category of "swinging ethnic strongholds," a transitional power configuration to which we now turn.

TYPE 2: SWINGING ETHNIC STRONGHOLDS

I refer to "swinging ethnic strongholds" as those districts where, although elected office regularly goes to an Italian American, different officials and parties alternate in power over the years. In these cases the ethnic factor prevails over party and personality as the main, stable characteristic of the district's power structure. In other words, parties and politicians come and go, but ethnicity endures: the local political class remains Italian American, regardless of whatever party, personality, or clan is in power.

We have already observed such a situation in AD 49 (table 3), when Republican DiCarlo's 15 year rule was followed by a short period of electoral uncertainty and then permanently fell to Democrat Peter Abbate for another 25 years. If one focuses on the data from the early 1980s, when no one could tell whether Abbate would guarantee a stable party realignment, we see the swing: a power district indeed turning into a swinging ethnic district with five elections—four of which were intra-ethnic races—and four different winners in six years, with the Republicans losing, regaining, and then losing power again in political contests almost totally dominated by Italian Americans.

In more recent years an example of a swinging ethnic district is AD 1, in Long Island's Suffolk County, an area populated by over 36,000 Italian Americans, almost 28 percent of the population.

Table 6. A "Swinging Ethnic Stronghold"

	Year	Winner	Party	Votes	Loser	Party	Votes
District: 1 County: Suffolk Italian Ancestry: 36,199 (27.6%)	2010	Daniel P. Losquadro	R, C, STR	23,860	Marc S. Alessi	D, I, W	22,943
	2008	Mark S. Alessi	D	36,680	James M. Staudenraus	D	24,095
	2006	Mark S. Alessi	D	24,366	Daniel J. Panico	R	15,446
	2005	Mark S. Alessi	D	6,239	Michael J. Caracciolo	R	5,705
	2004	Patricia Acampora	R	42,997	James McManmon	D	19,630
	2002	Patricia Acampora	R	28,895	Darren Johnson	D	9,453
	2000	Patricia Acampora	R	37,347	Joseph A. Turdik	D	14,705
	1998	Patricia Acampora	R	26,100	Michael A. D'Arrigo	D	10,665
	1996	Patricia Acampora	R	31,484	Therese Scofield	D	14,115
	1994	Patricia Acampora	R	24,223	James McManmon	D	12,641
	1993	Patricia Acampora	R	15,669	James McManmon	D	11,937

A traditional Republican district, in the 1960s and 1970s the political class of both parties was of British-Irish extraction. In the 1980s, the Polish took over in the Republican Party and Joseph Sawicki, Jr. was elected to the Assembly for over 10 years. In the following years, while the old ethnic stock remained entrenched in the Democratic Party, a Polish-Italian succession took place in the GOP and in 1993 Patricia Acampora was elected the first assemblyperson of Italian origin. In more than a decade until 2004, only once did the Democrats run an Italian candidate against Acampora. Yet by the mid-2000s Italians had taken over in both parties and power begun to swing. When Acampora left the Assembly in 2005 to be appointed to the New York State Public Service Commission, the district experienced its first Italian-American intra-ethnic race ever, with Marc Alessi defeating Michael Caracciolo and bringing the Democrats to power for the first time in 40 years. Alessi then beat an Italian-American challenger in 2006 and a non-Italian one in 2008, and eventually lost to fellow ethnic Daniel Losquadro, a Republican and a former Suffolk County legislator.

Thus in the past 12 years (1998–2010), while AD 1 switched parties twice and three people rotated in office, the winner was invariably an Italian American. Democrats and Republicans have tried to unseat each other by running both Italian and non-Italian candidates, but only the former have proved able to deliver. In order to win an election, being Italian American seems to have become what matters most in heavily Italian Suffolk. Indeed, in "swinging ethnic strongholds," party and personality apparently count less than ethnicity as a constant of power.

As we noted earlier, "swinging ethnic strongholds" is a residual—or, better, a *transitional*—typology. Swinging, in fact, is not likely to continue indefinitely and experience shows that sooner or later power will consolidate around an incumbent. Chances are that in AD 1 this will be an Italian American. From our point of view, however, the interesting development to watch is whether Italian Americans will continue to dominate the political class of both parties, producing a series of monopolistic elections and, in this case, whether the district will take the form of a power district, as occurred in Abbate's Brooklyn, or will instead become a "personal fiefdom"—the last typology we are analyze here.

Type 3: Personal Fiefdoms

Bluntly stated, what we call "personal fiefdoms" are districts in which the party in power may change, but the *person* in power remains the same. Or, in a less extreme version, the elected official remains the same for a long period of time during which he comes to be endorsed by different, even opposite parties and coalitions. Obviously in these cases the party factor is secondary and the official's personality, popularity, and organizational and patronage machine (in short, his personal power) is the predominant factor underlying his success. The relative unimportance of party politics here depends on the fact that these politicians (supported by their "clans") possess the resources and connections to go about the electorate on their own terms; it is they, actually, who "own the votes," not their party. So a politician may be able to switch parties and still remain in power; he can even become such an indisputable power in his district that all of the major parties endorse him (this is different than just running unopposed, for in this case the candidate actually runs on several party lines at once). Ethnicity in this context may be part of the candidate's strategy or it may not, depending mainly on the size (and thus the electoral salience) of the Italian-American population. It is reasonable to expect that the powerful politician who runs a "personal fiefdom" would want his fellow ethnics on his side—but his personal success rests less on ethnic appeals than on family connections, patronage distribution, and individual popularity.

We can observe this situation in Yonkers, Westchester County, the fourth most populous city in the State of New York, and one where Italian Americans are the largest ethnic group, comprising 20 percent of the population in 2000. Here we turn to Assemblyman Michael J. Spano, the child of one of the most influential dynastic political families of Westchester. All were Republicans—until Mike.

Son of a former Republican County Clerk, and brother of a former State senator, Mike Spano began his career at 18 as a Republican district leader. In 1992, at 28, he won a special election to the Assembly to succeed Terence Zaleski, a Democrat, who had left to become the mayor of Yonkers. The district Mike conquered that year was AD 83, the "Yonkers only" district that his brother Nicholas had represented in the 1980s. Just after his election, however, the district was eliminated by the state's reapportionment plan. A new hybrid district was created in its place which, with less than 2 percent of Italian Americans among the population, was peculiarly inhospitable to the Spanos. Refusing to run again there, Mike focused instead on a seat in the Westchester County Legislature, which had been his father Leonard's for the past 20 years. In 1993, Leonard left the post to be elected County Clerk and his seat easily went to Mike. The year after, Mike went back to the Assembly winning in nearby AD 87, on the periphery of Yonkers—a moderately Italian district in ethnic terms (Italian Americans made up close to 9 percent of the population), and an old family stronghold, which had been represented by his brother Nick in the late 1970s. Mike remained there until 2002, when he finally targeted AD 93, which includes the city of Yonkers and fully hits the threshold of Italian-American hegemonic districts (25 percent of the population was of Italian ancestry). Indeed Mike had to defeat an Italian-American opponent, Pasquale Fiorelli. But another year passed and he left the Assembly again, this time to run for mayor of Yonkers. He won the Conservative Party primary against Italian-American Vincent Natrella, but lost the Republican nomination to Deputy Mayor and fellow ethnic Philip Amicone, who then went on to beat him in the general election. So in 2006 Mike returned to the assembly seat he had vacated in 2003—which in the meanwhile had been occupied by fellow Italian-American Republican Louis A. Mosiello, who then left to take an appointed state job from Governor George Pataki, leaving room for Mike's comeback.

Finally, in 2007, Mike did the unthinkable as the child of such a Republican family: he switched his party affiliation from Republican to Democrat. And as a Democrat he was re-elected twice to the Assembly, demonstrating that he had a base of his own that would remain loyal even in the face of harsh accusations of being a cynical "turncoat." "This is where I belong," Mike told the press to explain his party switch, adding that he believed the *national* Republican Party "has basically lost its ability to communicate with the average American."[7] However, as it was widely rumored at the time, the real reason could be that, in a district where Democrats outnumbered Republicans two to one, as a Democrat Mike would be in a better position to run for mayor of Yonkers, his ultimate goal. And indeed, after being re-elected to his Assembly seat one more time in 2010, again beating an Italian-American challenger, Spano left Albany to fight his "Make Mike Mayor" battle and get his long-sought victory in the 2011 mayoral race. The party switch notwithstanding, the newborn Democrat had all of his powerful Republican family on his side.

Table 7. Michael Spano's "Personal Fiefdom"

	Year	Winner	Party	Votes	Loser	Party	Votes
AD 93 County: Westchester Italian Ancestry: 32,366 (24.5%)	2010	Michael Spano	D	17,900	Michael Ramondelli	R	12,536
	2008	Michael Spano	D	33,650	Jim Faulkner	R	12,043
	2006	Michael Spano	R	17,472	Shelley B. Mayer	D	16,088
	2004	Louis Mosiello	R	21,291	Steve Ploski	D	18,877
	2002	Michael Spano	R	19,059	Pasquale Fiorelli	D	9,534
AD 87 County: Westchester Italian Ancestry: 11,287 (8.6%)	2000	Michael Spano	R	26,669	Thomas Byrne	RTL	2,343
	1998	Michael Spano	R	20,743	John Guarneri	D	12,673
	1996	Michael Spano	R	25,395	Steve Ploski	D	14,413
	1994	Michael Spano	R	25,073	Edward Stanton	RTL	2,392
AD 83 County: Westchester Italian Ancestry: 2,480 (2%)*	1992	Michael Spano	R	3,401	Frank McGovern	D	2,077

* *After reapportionment.*

---

[7] "White Plains: Assemblyman Switches Parties," *The Associated Press*, July 12, 2007.

The root of Mike Spano's power lies without doubt in his family clan, a "party" in its own right. Local critics and the press often accuse the Spanos of nepotism due to a host of "children, in-laws and cousins [who] are sprinkled through the county bureaucracy." But the most important aspect, perhaps, is that, as the *New York Times* reported, "There are well over 400 Spanos in Westchester, many available to serve as campaign foot soldiers."[8]

Besides foot soldiers, however, it is the generals we are most interested in here. And there was no shortage of these among the Spanos either. Grandfather Nicola, from Italy's Apulia region, came to the U.S. in the early 1900s with his brothers and formed an ice and coal business. As Mike told me in an interview for the Calandra Institute's Oral History Archive project, that door-to-door business was "the perfect kind of business" to pave the way for the rest of the family's political career "because grandpa knew everyone." When in 1967 his son Leonard, who also worked in the family business, first ran for office, Grandpa Nicola lent all possible support. He went to an influential Italian-American family in Yonkers, the Martinellis, who owned a printing business, and "traded oil for printing" so that Leonard could have materials printed for his campaign. Mike also recalled that Leonard had his 14-year-old son Nick ringing doorbells, while Mike himself, then in third grade, plastered campaign posters on his school's windows. That time things did not work out well and Leonard lost—but that was, in Mike's words, the origin of "well over 40 campaigns" that the Spanos have fought and won in Yonkers since then. Leonard finally became a county legislator shortly thereafter, in 1971, and held the post until 1993, when he let Mike run for his seat. That same year Leonard got elected as County Clerk, a position he kept until his retirement in 2005.

Meanwhile Mike's older brother Nick, now an influential lobbyist in Albany and formerly the influential chairman of the County Republican organization, had started his career at 18, like Mike, as a Republican district leader. He won his first bid for the Assembly at 25 and was first an assemblyman (1979–1986), then a senator (1987–2006), and served as the senior assistant (and heir apparent) to Senate Majority Leader Joseph Bruno, also an Italian American. Nick was also very helpful to his brother Mike, who twice in his early career ran and won in districts that Nick had previously represented. As an article in the *New York Times* colorfully observed: "There are moments when government in Westchester County seems like a family business, the Spano family business [...]. The Spanos have absorbed

---

[8] Joseph Berger, "When County Politics Is a Family Business; Westchester Feels the Spanos' Presence," *New York Times*, April 26, 1996.

politics by the same osmosis that children raised in real estate families pick up the intricacies of balloon mortgages."[9]

Mike Spano is thus the ideal example of personal power, where party affiliation may be secondary or even irrelevant to the ultimate goal of gaining, increasing, and consolidating family or clan influence. We may then accurately characterize today's Yonkers as the "personal fiefdom" of Mayor Spano and his powerful Italian-American dynasty.

But the paradigmatic and somehow less folkloric example of this political typology is certainly found in Staten Island, the most Italian and Republican-leaning borough of New York City—and especially in SD 24, a district with an Italian-American population of over 140,000 people, nearly 50 percent of the total population according to the 2000 census. For decades, this area has been the indisputable personal fiefdom of a legendary senator, the late John Marchi, who retired in 2006 after holding his seat for 50 years—the longest-serving lawmaker in New York and one of the longest-serving state legislators in the U.S.

Over his five-decade political career Senator Marchi—who was challenged by an Italian American in the vast majority of his races—ran at least 30 times including ordinary Senatorial elections, the 1961 race for borough president, two unsuccessful races for mayor in 1969 and 1973, and a few primaries. Most noticeably, he ran on all party lines, sometimes several at once, including Republican, Conservative, Liberal, and, most notably, Democratic. In fact in 1980, with the help of then New York City mayor Ed Koch, Marchi was first endorsed by the Democrats, an anomalous situation that lasted 22 years and made him practically invulnerable until 2002 (see table 8).

Marchi's electoral history, therefore, is a textbook example of the prevalence of personality over party. His ability to move across the political spectrum—or, better, to have the political spectrum rotate around him—clearly indicates that he could count on a personal base of his own, independent of party or ideology. He was a Republican of conservative orientation, strongly pro-life, but he also harbored some liberal values: his opposition to capital punishment, for instance, nearly cost him the election in 1977 in what was his closest race. Indeed what, in common parlance, was seen as Marchi's political ambiguity was in fact due to a misunderstanding of his Roman Catholic faith, where "pro-life" simultaneously means both anti-abortion and anti-death penalty.

---

[9] Ibid.

Be that as it may, Marchi's popularity did not rest on issues of conscience, but on what he had accomplished for his district and the whole of Staten Island over the years. This goes from an unrivaled ability to bring home the bacon, to his crucial backing of broader local interests—from the 1993 referendum for the secession of Staten Island from New York City, which he advocated and which overwhelmingly passed, to the law he drafted to close the Fresh Kills Landfill on Staten Island.

Given the demographics of the Island, there is no question that John Marchi's base was overwhelmingly Italian American—although he himself was an "atypical" Italian American whose family came from Tuscany and "who loved the classics and could converse about Marcus Aurelius, Ovid, and Aristotle."[10] At the same time, the Italian-American community—both the electorate and the political class—was certainly not all on his side, as one can easily gather from the plethora of fellow ethnics who opposed him in nearly every election. Yet, Marchi always came out as the winner—as long as the battles were fought on the Island. What really counted in his district and county was Marchi's own popularity, influence, and personal power rather than party or even ethnicity. Although being Italian and Republican certainly helped, what Marchi really needed to be elected was to just be...Marchi.

Proof that his power was predominantly personal in nature came in 2006 when, upon retiring, Marchi tried to influence his own succession. As may happen in succession crises after long monarchical rule, factional divisions among the local elite emerged in clear light. Interestingly, the "atypical" Italian-American monarch of Staten Island had not endorsed an Italian American as his heir, but had picked instead Robert J. Helbock—his longtime counsel and the chairman of County Republican Committee. Having relinquished his power, however, Marchi was now unable to impose his choice on the party. True, important party leaders supported Helbock, including former U.S. Congressman and powerful Staten Island Borough President Guy Molinari. But the winner of this bitterly fought primary turned out to be City Councilman Andrew J. Lanza, who was endorsed by prominent elected officials from the Island, including U.S. Representative Vito J. Fossella, Jr., City Council Republican leader James S. Oddo, and Assemblyman Vincent Ignizio, who had replaced Helbock as the County Republican Party chairman.[11]

---

[10] Robert D. McFadden, "John J. Marchi, Who Fought for Staten Island in Senate, Dies at 87," *The New York Times*, April 26, 2009.

[11] See Jonathan P. Hicks, "Split G.O.P. May See a Rare State Senate Primary on Staten Island," *The New York Times*, July 6, 2006; Jonathan P. Hicks, "Staten Island Candidate Drops Out of Senate Race," *The New York Times*, September 26, 2006. On this and other episodes of Staten Island politics see the eassay by Jerome Krase in this book.

Helbock considered staying in the race as an Independent running on Marchi's legacy, but was persuaded to step aside by Senate Majority Leader Joseph Bruno, worried that a division within the Staten Island party could cost the Republicans the thin majority they still held in the upper chamber. After much negotiation, Helbock complied, effectively putting an end to Marchi's era. Lanza went on to beat the Democratic candidate Matthew J. Titone, a lawyer and the son of the late Vito J. Titone, a justice on the New York State Court of Appeals who had challenged Marchi in two consecutive elections in the 1960s.

CONCLUSION

As Rodrigo Praino has shown conclusively in chapter five of this book, a high presence of Italian Americans among the electorate has a significant statistical association with a high probability that an Italian American be elected to Congress. The present chapter, while implying that this is valid at the State level as well, also points to a broader socio-political phenomenon: the presence of a sizable Italian-American community in a legislative district not only facilitates the election of Italian-American politicians, but makes it more likely for Italian-American incumbents to either run unopposed or be challenged by fellow Italian Americans. In districts with an above-average Italian-American population, in fact, it is comparatively easier for Italian Americans to be *elected* to office, to *remain* in office once first elected, and—preceding all of this—to be *selected* as viable candidates for office by the major parties. This is why we find in these districts a higher number of intra-Italian races. When such *monopolistic elections* take place over a long period of time, the district emerges as an Italian-American *hegemonic district*—where an Italian-American political class dominates the local political process.

It is a well-known "sociological law" that any political class tends to reproduce itself in power, and Italian Americans are no exception. But how do they go about this? Here an interesting paradox emerges: the same ethnic factor that facilitates the political career of Italian-American politicians also makes it more difficult for them to campaign on ethnic grounds, especially within the Italian-American community itself. Indeed, in intra-ethnic races the argument of the candidate's *Italianness*—which might help to unite the Italian vote and defeat a candidate of different ethnicity—cannot be used. On the contrary, the Italian vote is split by definition and the Italian base of both candidates is actually thinner than it might be if one of them were not Italian. In other words, a heavily Italian district may make it easier for Italian Americans to be *selected* and *elected*, but once the district becomes a hegemonic district and Italian candidates must challenge one another, their lives become comparatively harder. Rhetorically, their ethnic appeal is neutralized; numerically, their chances of uniting the ethnic vote are—for all intents and purposes—nil. In theory this may mean that, at the same time, hegemonic districts represent the highest level of socio-cultural influence and political power an ethnic group may reach, and the most difficult situation for ethnic politicians to handle.

Unless—and here the paradox continues—they are able to downplay their own ancestry in favor of a broader, multi-ethnic political strategy, and to consolidate their power through consensus-building strategies of a different nature. These may include emphasizing party politics, both ideologically (party identification) and organizationally (party machine), developing particular skills in constituency service and the representation of influential local interests, or stressing one's personal power through popularity, charisma, family connections, and direct control over local patronage networks. I hope to have provided useful insight into how all these different factors interact in the different types of hegemonic districts that I have defined as *power districts*, *swinging ethnic strongholds*, and *personal fiefdoms*. Of course much deeper study should now be conducted to gain a comprehensive picture of how the Italian-American section of New York's political class has risen to (and sometimes fallen from) power.

Table 8. John Marchi's Electoral History

1956	Marchi is first elected to the State Senate (total votes 81,001)			
	Marchi	R	44,159	54.5%
	Edward V. Curry	D	36,842	45.5%
1958	Re-elected to the Senate (total votes 66,375)			
	Marchi	R, UT	36,423	54.9%
	Edmund J. Murphy	D	28,298	42.7%
	George Maki	L	1,645	2.5%
1960	Re-elected to the Senate (total votes 87,186)			
	Marchi	R	49,716	57%
	Ralph DiIorio	D	34,604	39.7%
	George Maki	L	2,866	2.5%
1961	Staten Island Borough President Election			
	Marchi challenges incumbent borough president (total votes 73,161)			
	Marchi	R	35,632	48.7%
	Albert V. Maniscalco	D, L, Br	37,529	51.3%
1962	Re-elected to the Senate (total votes 72,987)			
	Marchi	R	42,659	58.4%
	Aldo R. Benedetto	D, L	30,328	41.3%
1964	Re-elected to the Senate, receiving for the first time the endorsement of the recently funded (1962) Conservative Party (total votes 88,952)			
	Marchi	R, C	48,898	55%
	Joseph J. Holzka	D, L	40,054	45,00%
1964	After implementation of a court-ordered reapportionment plan, legislators must run again. Marchi is re-elected to the Senate (total vote 84,567)			
	Marchi	R, C	55,250	65.3%
	Vito T. Titone	D, L	25,933	30,7%
	Ferdinand Cubas	Lib.	3,384	4%
1966	Elected to the Senate (total votes 75,780)			
	Marchi	R	50,905	67.2%
	Vito T. Titone	D	21,296	28%
	Pearse O'Callaghan	L	3,579	4.8%
1968	Re-elected to the Senate (total votes 98,050)			
	Marchi	R,C	56,675	57.8%
	Daniel D. Leddy	D	38,696	39.4%
	Herman Zukowsky	L	2,679	2.7%
1969	Republican Mayoral Primary			
	With help from the Conservative Party, Marchi defeats incumbent Mayor of New York City John Lindsay and wins the Republican nomination.			
	Marchi		113,698	51.4%
	Lindsay		107,366	48.6%
1969	New York City Mayoral Election			
	Running on the Republican and Conservative lines, Marchi confronts Democratic nominee Mario Procaccino and incumbent John Lindsay, who stays in the race on the Liberal line–and wins.			
	Marchi	R, C	542,411	22%
	Procaccino	D	831,772	36%
	John V. Lindsay	L, I	1,012,633	42%

1972	Re-elected to State Senate (total votes 107,057; highest turnout for any of his re-elections)			
	Marchi	R	56,960	53.2%
	Pasquale Bifulco	D	28,544	26.7%
	Daniel Master	C	18,573	17.3%
	Norma Cossey	L	2,980	2.8%
1973	New York City Mayoral Election			
	Marchi again obtains the Republican nomination for mayor. Conservatives deny him their endorsement and nominate Mario Biaggi. Democrat Abe Beame wins.			
	Marchi	R	276,575	16 %
	Abe Beame	D	961,130	56 %
	Mario Biaggi	C	189,986	11 %
	Al Blumenthal	L	265,297	15 %
1974	Re-elected to the Senate (total votes 78,564).			
	Marchi	R	44,486	56.6 %
	Pasquale P. Caiazza	D	34,078	43.3%
1976	Re-elected to the Senate (total votes 101,231).			
	Marchi	R	53,583	52.9 %
	Ralph J. Lamberti	D	45,679	45.1%
	Ernest A. Kaarsberg	L	1,969	2,00%
1977	Re-elected to the Senate (total votes 74,777; Marchi's closest senatorial election).			
	Marchi	R, C	38,578	51.6 %
	Robert J. Gigante	D	34,675	46.4%
	Carl F. Grillo	L	1,524	2,00%
1980	Re-elected to the Senate (total votes 99,296) with the endorsement of the Democratic Party. Marchi will run on both the Republican and the Democratic lines for 22 years.			
	Marchi	R, D	93,426	94.1 %
	Carl F. Grillo	L	5,870	5.9%
1982	Re-elected to the Senate (total votes 63,095).			
	Marchi	R, D, C	58,338	92.5 %
	Joseph F. Sully	L	1,515	2.4%
	Barbara Bollaert	RTL	3,242	5.1%
1984	Re-elected to the Senate (total votes 100,756).			
	Marchi	R, D, C	95,546	94.8%
	Joseph F. Sully	L	2,259	2.2%
	Barbara Bollaert	RTL	2,951	3,00%
1986	Re-elected to the Senate on the Republican, Democratic, and Liberal lines (total votes 56,607; lowest turnout until 2002).			
	Marchi	R/D/L	49,233	87 %
	Michael V. Ajello	C	5,545	9.8%
	Barbara Bollaert	RTL	1,829	3.2%
1988	Re-elected to the Senate (total votes 92,038).			
	Marchi	R, D, L	81,539	89.5 %
	Albert P. DeLillo	C	7,471	8.2%
	Barbara Bollaert	RTL	2,108	2.3%

1990	Re-elected to the Senate (total votes 57,749).			
	Marchi	R, D, L	47,250	81.8 %
	George Boncoraglio	C	7,471	12.9%
	Barbara Bollaert	RTL	3,028	5.2%
1992	Re-elected to the Senate (total votes 91,029).			
	Marchi	R, D, L	85,098	93.5 %
	Barbara Bollaert	RTL	5,931	6.5%
1994	Democratic Senatorial Primary.			
	Marchi is challenged in a Democratic primary for the first time since 1980.			
	Marchi		7,687	77%
	Eugene Prisco		2,338	23%
1994	Re-elected to the Senate (total votes 75,550)			
	Marchi	R, D, L	67,284	89.1 %
	Ralph J. Rubinek	C	5,713	7.6 %
	Barbara Bollaert	RTL	2,553	3.4 %
1996	Re-elected to the Senate (total votes 79,199)			
	Marchi	R, D, L	70,870	89.5 %
	Ralph J. Rubinek	C, RTL	6,547	8.3%
	Janet Rispoli	I	1,782	2.2%
1998	Re-elected to the Senate (total votes 63,090)			
	Marchi	R, D, L	60,842	96.4 %
	Maria D. Colon	I	1,321	2%
	Jody Magnasco	L	927	1.6%
2000	Re-elected to the Senate (total votes 94,352)			
	Marchi	R, D, C	91,110	96.2%
	Henry Bardel	G, I, W	3,242	3.8%
2002	Re-elected to the Senate (total votes 53,060).			
	For the first time since 1980, Marchi fails to receive the Democratic nomination and runs on the Republican and Conservative lines only.			
	Marchi	R, C	39,488	74%
	Michael J. Cocozza	D	13,752	26%
2004	Last Senate election (total votes 121,479).			
	Marchi runs unopposed for the first time.			
	Marchi	R, D, I, C	99,006	81.5%
2006	Marchi retires from the New York State Senate before the elections.			

UT=United Taxpayers
Br=Brotherhood
RTL=Right to Life

Source: Adapted from A Guide to the Senator John J. Marchi Papers, 1956-1998, Archives & Special Collections. College of Staten Island Library, CUNY, 2003. Finding Aid by Mary Hedge, Catherine Carson, and Jeffrey Kroessler (www.library.csi.cuny.edu/archives/FindingAids/fa0006.htm)

APPENDIX

(1) ITALIAN-AMERICAN INTRA-ETHNIC RACES AND NON-CONTESTED SEATS IN THE NYS ASSEMBLY (1998-2010)

	YEAR	WINNING CANDIDATE	PARTY	VOTES	SECOND CANDIDATE	PARTY	VOTES
District: 62 County: Richmond Italian Ancestry: 64,225 (53.1%)	2004	Vincent Ignizio	R	26,649	Emanuele innamorato	D	7,538
	2006	Vincent Ignizio	R	16,131	-	-	-
	2008	Lou Tobacco	R	30,410	Albert J Albanese	D	11,816
	2010	Lou Tobacco	R, I, C	22,856	Albert J. Albanese	D	6,179
District: 12 County: Nassau Italian Ancestry: 50,265 (38.4%)	2000	Steven L.Labriola	R	32,148	John A. Tartaglia	D	14,544
	2008	Joseph S. Saladino	R	38,800	Keith A Scalia	D	18,307
District: 49 County: Kings Italian Ancestry: 36,299 (30.2%)	1998	Peter J. Abbate Jr	D	10,249	Luigi R.Marano	R	5,059
	2000	Peter J. Abbate Jr	D	15,705	Josephine N. Frediani	R	5,212
	2002	Peter J. Abbate Jr	D	7,603	Cinthia Gallo	C	541
	2006	Peter J. Abbate Jr	D	7,884	Lucretia Regina-Potter	R	2,737
	2008	Peter J. Abbate Jr	D	14,034	Lucretia Regina-Potter	R	5,487
	2010	Peter J. Abbate, Jr.	D, I, W	7,416	Peter Cipriano	R, C	4,659
District: 3 County: Suffolk Italian Ancestry: 39,727 (30.3%)	1998	Debra J. Mazzarelli	D	16,358	Icilio W. Bianchi Jr.	R	12,570
District: 14 County: Nassau Italian Ancestry: 38,909 (29.7%)	2002	Robert D. Barra	R	21,744	Vincent M. Grasso	D	12,851
	2008	Robert D Barra	R	31,167	Joseph J Ferrara	D	23,178
District: 21 County: Nassau Italian Ancestry: 38,778 (29.5%)	2002	Thomas W. Alfano	R	23,110	Joseph F. DeFelice	D	9,303
District: 1 County: Suffolk Italian Ancestry: 36,199 (27.6%)	1998	Patricia L. Acampora	R	26,100	Michael A. D'arrigo	D	10,665
	2005	Mark Alessi	D	6,239	Michael J Caracciolo	R	5,705
	2006	Mark S. Alessi	D	24,366	Daniel J. Panico	R	??
	2010	Daniel P. Losquadro	R, C, STR	23,860	Marc S. Alessi	D, I, W	22,943

Assembly Districts, Continued /2

	YEAR	WINNING CANDIDATE	PARTY	VOTES	SECOND CANDIDATE	PARTY	VOTES
District: 10 County: Nassau/Suffolk Italian Ancestry: 35,506 (27.0%)	1998	James D.Conte	R	18,318	Roberta Grasso-Tarlen	D	10,010
	2000	James D.Conte	R	24,933	Raymond J. Sansiviero	D	15,400
	2006	James D.Conte	R	18,881	Barbara A Lo Moriello	D	16,381
	2010	James D. Conte	R, I, C, W	23,766	John Capobianco	D	13,571
District: 47 County: Kings Italian Ancestry: 31,891 (26.3%)	1998	William Colton	D	9,564	Anthony A Laucella	R	5,278
	2000	William Colton	D	15,034	Nora DeAngelo	R	4,973
	2002	William Colton	D	7,681	Rose Delgiudice	C	561
	2006	William Colton	D, W	9,168	Phyllis Carbo	R,C	2,509
	2008	William Colton	D	14,949	Russel C Gallo	R	5,627
	2010	William Colton	D, W	8,605	Phyllis Carbo	R, C	4,457
District: 116 County: Oneida Italian Ancestry: 30,444 (23.9%)	1998	Ro Ann Destito	D	19,727	Malcom R. Didio	R	7,146
	2000	Ro Ann Destito	D	20,232	John Arena	RTL	2,502
	2004	Ro Ann Destito	D	27,267	John E Dote	I	8,011
	2006	Ro Ann Destito	D	21,319			
District: 82 County: Bronx Italian Ancestry: 28,543 (23.5%)	2004	Michael R. Benedetto	D	22,953	Raymond Capone	R	7,166
	2006	Michael R. Benedetto	D	16,632	Raymond Capone	R	3,795
	2008	Michael R. Benedetto	D	29,619	Raymond Capone	R	6,092
	2010	Michael R. Benedetto	D, W	17,035	Michael A. Rendino	R, I, C	4,901
District: 90 County: Putnam/Westchester Italian Ancestry: 29,811 (22.7%)	2004	Sandra R. Galef	D I W	32,970			
	2006	Sandra R. Galef	D I W	26,028			
District: 91 County: Westchester Italian Ancestry: 28,094 (22.6%)	2004	George S Latimer	D	28,913	Vincent J Malfetano	R	13,050
	2006	George S Latimer	D	21,830			
	2008	George S Latimer	D	31,886	Rob Biagi	R	12,816
District: 93 County: Westchester Italian Ancestry: 32,366 (24.5%)	2002	Mike Spano	R	19,059	Pasquale R.A. Fiorelli	D	9,534
	2010	Mike Spano	D, C, W	17,900	Mike Ramondelli	R, I, CMT	12,536

Assembly Districts, Continued /3

	YEAR	WINNING CANDIDATE	PARTY	VOTES	SECOND CANDIDATE	PARTY	VOTES
District: 105 County: Montgomery/Schenectady Italian Ancestry: 27,703 (21.0%)	2010	George A. Amedore, Jr.	R, I, C	21,438	Angelo L. Santabarbara	D, W, CAN	15,089
District: 103 County: Saratoga/Schenectady Italian Ancestry: 26,980 (21.0%)	1998	James N. Tedisco	R	31,306	Michele A. Paludi	D	10,765
District: 138 County: Niagara Italian Ancestry: 26,877 (21.0%)	2006	Francine DelMonte	D	19,788	Daniel J Bazzani	R	12,835
	2010	John D. Ceretto	R, I	16,722	John G. Accardo	D, C	11,985
District: 26 County: Queens Italian Ancestry: 26,007 (21.0%)	2000	Ann Margaret Carrozza	D	25,486	-	-	-
	2006	Ann Margaret Carrozza	D	17,332	-	-	-
	2008	Ann Margaret Carrozza	D	25,124	Robert J Speranza	R	12,258
District: 132 County: Monroe Italian Ancestry: 26,367 (20.9%)	1998	Joseph D. Morelle	D	29,345	Dean J. Fero	R	11,835
	2002	Joseph D. Morelle	D	26,933	Dean J. Fero	R	12,975
	2004	Joseph D. Morelle	D	34,831	-	-	-
	2006	Joseph D. Morelle	D	29,036	Samuel R Trapani	R	13,344
	2008	Joseph D. Morelle	D	41,721	-	-	-
	2010	Joseph D. Morelle	D, I	24,640	Mark S. Scuderi	R	15,722
District: 61 County: Richmond Italian Ancestry: 24,656 (20.4%)	2006	John W Lavelle	D	13,963	Rose Margarella	R	5,249
	2007	Matthew Titone	D	3,088	Rose Margarella	R	1,934
District: 120 County: Onondaga Italian Ancestry: 25,014 (19.4%)	2006	William B. Magnarelli	D	22,953	-	-	-
District: 144 County: Erie Italian Ancestry: 25,113 (19.0%)	2000	Sam Hoyt	D	25,727	Antoinette Guercio	R,I	8,290
	2002	Sam Hoyt	D	22,694	David L Penna	R	8,666
	2004	Sam Hoyt	D	32,404	David L Penna	R	12,222
	2008	Sam Hoyt	D	30,228	Sheila A Ferrentino	R	12,418

Assembly Districts, Continued / 4

	Year	Winning Candidate	Party	Votes	Second Candidate	Party	Votes
District: 110 County: Saratoga/Schenectady Italian Ancestry: 24,371 (18.5%)	2002	James N. Tedisco	R	33,638	Barbara Mauro	D	11,583
	2008	James N. Tedisco	R	41,889	-	-	-
District: 59 County: Kings Italian Ancestry: 21,717 (18.0%)	2002	Frank R. Seddio	D	12,314	Peter C. Evangelista	R	4,221
District: 145 County: Erie Italian Ancestry: 22,663 (17.2%)	2010	Mark J. F. Schroeder	D, I, C, W	34,894	-	-	-
District: 16 County: Nassau Italian Ancestry: 20,161 (15.4%)	1998	Thomas P. DiNapoli	D	26,256	Thomas Zampino	R	13,027
	2000	Thomas P. DiNapoli	D	35,621	Jerome J.Galluscio	R	15,053
	2006	Thomas P. DiNapoli	D	27,296	Louis F Chisari	R	9,516
District: 106 County: Albany/Rensselaer Italian Ancestry: 19,234 (14.9%)	1998	Ronald J. Canestrari	D	24,414	John J. Ferrannini	R	8,090
	2004	Ronald J. Canestrari	D, I, W	35,085	-	-	-
	2008	Ronald J. Canestrari	D	37,952	-	-	-
	2010	Ronald J. Canestrari	D, I, W	26,583	-	-	-
	1998	Ronald J. Canestrari	D	24,414	John J. Ferrannini	R	8,090
District: 126 County: Broome Italian Ancestry: 19,163 (14.7%)	2006	Donna A Lupardo	D, W	25,714	Jay J. Dinga	R, I, C	13,626
	2008	Donna A Lupardo	D	33,877	-	-	-
District: 130 County: Livingston/Monroe/Ontario Italian Ancestry: 18,163 (14.4%)	2008	Joe Errigo	R	37,790	-	-	-
District: 38 County: Queens Italian Ancestry: 15,956 (12.9%)	1998	Anthony S. Seminerio	D, C, I	13,025	-	-	-
	2004	Anthony S. Seminerio	D, R, I, C	20351	-	-	-
	2006	Anthony S. Seminerio	D	10,849	-	-	-
	2008	Anthony S. Seminerio	D	19,857	-	-	-

Assembly Districts, Continued /5

	Year	Winning Candidate	Party	Votes	Second Candidate	Party	Votes
District: 112 County: Lewis/St. Lawrence Italian Ancestry: 15,586 (12.0%)	1998	Dierdre K. Scozzafava	R	17,498	Frank A. Pastizzo	D	9,941
District: 52 County: Kings Italian Ancestry: 14,075 (11.6%)	2004	Joan L Millman	D	43,311	Scot J Santandrea	R	4,053
	2010	Joan L Millman	D, W	31,441	John A. Jasilli, Jr.	R, C	3,292
District: 87 County: Westchester Italian Ancestry: 11,287 (8.6%)	1998	Mike Spano	R	20,743	John Guarneri	D	12,673
District: 149 County: Allegany/Cattaraugus/Chattauaqua Italian Ancestry: 9,509 (7.5%)	2005	Joseph M. Giglio	R	5,637	Carmen A. Vecchiarella	D	3,722
	2010	Joseph M. Giglio	R, I, C	23,916	Travis C. Lecceadone	D	8,247
District: 37 County: Queens Italian Ancestry: 8,417 (6.8%)	2004	Catherine T. Nolan	D, W	18,537		-	-
	2006	Catherine T. Nolan	D	10,102		-	-
	2008	Catherine T. Nolan	D	20,601		-	-
District: 50 County: Kings Italian Ancestry: 6,382 (5.3%)	2008	Joseph R. Lentol	D	24,538	Teresa Puccio	R	2,742
District: 122 County: Jefferson-Lewis-Oswego-St. Lawrence Italian Ancestry: 6,403 (5.0%)	2004	Dede K. Scozzafava	R, I, C, W	32,777		-	-
	2008	Dede K. Scozzafava	R	29,384		-	-
District: 53 County: Kings Italian Ancestry: 4,700 (3.9%)	2004	Vito J. Lopez (Lopesino)	D	21,515	Theresa Prevete	R	1,618
	2006	Vito J. Lopez (Lopesino)	D	12,194	Ameriar Feliciano	R	785
	2008	Vito J. Lopez (Lopesino)	D	25,733	Frances J Cutrone	R	1,531

(2) Intra-Ethnic Races and Non-contested Seats in the NYS Senate (1998-2010)

	Year	Winning Candidate	Party	Votes	Second Candidate	Party	Votes
District: 24 County: Richmond Italian Ancestry: 142,412 (45.7%)**	1998	John J. Marchi	D, R	62,838	Maria D Colon	I	1,402
	2002	John J. Marchi	R	39,488	Michael J Cocozza	D	13,752
	2004	John J. Marchi	R, D	99,006	-	-	-
	2006	Andrew J. Lanza	R	34,160	Matrew J Titone	D	23,074
	2008	Andrew J. Lanza	R, I	75,471	Joseph J. Pancila	D	32,013
	2010	Andrew J. Lanza	R, I, C	54,602	-	-	-
District: 3 County: Suffolk Italian Ancestry: 87,013 (28.5%)**	2002	Caesar Trunzo	R, I, C	37,928	Bryan Galgano	D	19,673
District: 34 County: Bronx/Westchester Italian Ancestry: 79,802 (27.7%)**	1998	Guy J. Velella	R	29,577	Henry Spallone	D	21,135
District: 1 County: Suffolk Italian Ancestry: 78,341 (25.6%)**	2000	Kenneth P. LaValle	R	81,441	Linda E Minardi	D	38,245
	2006	Kenneth P. LaValle	R	54,971	Michael Comando	D	31,503
	2008	Kenneth P. LaValle	R	81,062	-	-	-
District: 15 County: Queens Italian Ancestry: 61,983 (19.5%)**	1998	Serphin R. Maltese	R	23,823	-	-	-
	2004	Serphin R. Maltese	R	34,331	-	-	-
	2008	Joseph P. Addabbo Jr	D	42,302	Serphin R Maltese	R	31,028
	2010	Joseph P. Addabbo Jr	D, I	23,272	Anthony Como	R, C	4,979
District: 35 County: Westchester Italian Ancestry: 60,269 (19.3%)**	2000	Nick Spano	R	55,104	Thomas J Abinanti	D	48,451

Senate Districts, Continued / 2

YEAR	WINNING CANDIDATE	PARTY	VOTES	SECOND CANDIDATE	PARTY	VOTES
District: 43 County: Rensselaer/Saratoga Italian Ancestry: 49,386 (16.3%)						
1998	Joseph L. Bruno	R	72,499	-	-	-
2000	Joseph L. Bruno	R	96,368	-	-	-
2002	Joseph L. Bruno	R	76,036	-	-	-
2004	Joseph L Bruno	R	95,877	-	-	-
2006	Joseph L Bruno	R	70,156	-	-	-
District: 11 County: Queens Italian Ancestry: 48,857 (15.4%)						
2002	Frank Padavan	R	33,305	-	-	-
2004	Frank Padavan	R	45,832	-	-	-
2006	Frank Padavan	R	31,019	Nora C Marino	D	21,283
2008	Frank Padavan	R	45,294	James F Gennaro	D	44,811
2010	Tony Avella	D	31,573	Frank Padavan	R/I/C	26,571
District: 53 County: Cayuga-Seneca-Wayne-Monroe-Ontario Italian Ancestry: 26,117 (8.90%)						
2000	Michael F Nozzolio	R	89,872	-	-	-
District: 54 County: Cayuga/Seneca/Wayne/Monroe/ Ontario/Tompkins/Wayne Italian Ancestry: 44,566 (15.3%)						
2002	Michael F Nozzolio	R	70,330	Joanne M Vacca	RTL	2,985
2004	Michael F Nozzolio	R	92,101	-	-	-
2006	Michael F Nozzolio	R	62,495	-	-	-
2008	Michael F Nozzolio	R	87,433	Paloma A Capanna	D	34,991
District: 23 County: Kings/Richmond Italian Ancestry: 38,490 (12.4%)						
2000	Vincent J Gentile	D	45,077	Robert J DiCarlo	R	27,721
2006	Diane J Savino	D	23,497	-	-	-
2010	Diane J Savino	D, I	29,908	-	-	-
District: 12 County: Queens Italian Ancestry: 27,835 (8.7%)						
2004	George Onorato	D	48215	Daniel Maio	R	11,330
2006	George Onorato	D	27,836	-	-	-
District: 13 County: Queens Italian Ancestry: 8,457 (2.7%)						
2004	John D Sabini	D	37,238	-	-	-
2006	John D Sabini	D	22,336	-	-	-

INDEX OF NAMES